DEEP COVER

The Inside Story of How DEA
Infighting, Incompetence, and Subterfuge
Lost Us the Biggest Battle of the Drug War

MICHAEL LEVINE

**Delacorte
Press**

Published by
Delacorte Press
Bantam Doubleday Dell Publishing Group, Inc.
666 Fifth Avenue
New York, New York 10103

ISBN: 0-385-30128-6

Manufactured in the United States of America
Published simultaneously in Canada

March 1990

10   9   8   7   6   5   4   3   2   1

BVG

DEEP COVER is an undercover assignment in which the operative completely abandons the protection of his official identity and adopts a new one as a criminal, isolating himself in the dominion and complete control of his target. This type of assignment is rare in law enforcement and even rarer in overseas operations, where exposure will almost always be fatal.

—Drug Enforcement Administration lecture on undercover

One deceit needs many others, and so the whole house is built in the air and must soon come to the ground
—*The Art of Worldly Wisdom,* Baltasar Gracián y Morales (1647)

DEDICATION

On February 7, 1985, **Enrique "Kiki" Camarena,** an American DEA
agent on assignment in Guadalajara, Mexico, was kidnapped in
broad daylight, almost in front of the American consulate, by Mexican police officers working for narcotics traffickers. Kiki, a thirty-
seven-year-old husband and father of three boys, was tortured to
death over a twenty-four-hour period while his murderers tape-recorded his "confession." His crime: carrying out his mission in our
government's war on drugs—a mission he believed in.

After Kiki's murder it was revealed that he and his supervisor
had complained to the "suits" (the DEA bureaucrats) of the "extremely dangerous and anarchic conditions" they were working under; that drug dealers had virtually taken over all governmental and
law-enforcement functions of Mexico's second-largest city. The
complaints had been ignored.

Just before Kiki's death he had complained to his supervisor,
"Does somebody have to get killed before something is done?" Well,
Kiki *was* killed and not only has nothing been done, but the same
politicians and bureaucrats who ignored his complaints are about to
waste more young lives than ever before—unless they are stopped.

On February 26, 1988, Edward Byrne, a twenty-two-year-old
rookie New York City patrolman, was executed by crack dealers as
he sat guarding the house of a witness in a drug trial. The man on
trial and the men who carried out the murder had long arrest and
conviction records that should have had them safely in cages long
before the murder. During the young man's funeral, while the politicians and bureaucrats wailed that the only answer is a campaign to
reduce the demand for drugs, a New York radio "personality"
bragged to over a million listeners of having supplied performers

with cocaine to appear on his show. An investigation was begun and top DEA officials, frightened of the media, secretly quashed it.

On October 19, 1988, New York City police officer Chris Hoban was murdered by a drug dealer as he tried to make an undercover drug buy of one gram of cocaine. Chris, surrounded by armed, suspicious drug dealers, was asked to take some of the drug to prove he wasn't an undercover officer. Suits who hadn't the slightest idea what it takes to enter a drug den, undercover, with your life depending on your acting ability, had created a regulation prohibiting an undercover agent from "ingesting" a drug. So Chris refused. The dealer panicked and shot him. Had the murder not been committed and the drug dealer arrested, in all likelihood he would have been on the street selling drugs again, long before the officer had finished the paperwork.

On February 28, 1989, DEA Special Agent Everett Hatcher, another one of my New York street brothers, was murdered during an undercover cocaine deal involving mere ounces of the drug. His killer has still not been caught. Shortly after Hatcher's murder the head suit in New York was quoted making an off-the-cuff remark after one of his many public appearances: "The drug war will never be won by a man with a badge." A copy of the news article was hung on the New York office bulletin board with an anonymous street agent's comment scrawled across it: *Why didn't you tell that to Everett Hatcher!*

On February 5, 1988, DEA special agents Paul Seema and George Montoya were murdered during an undercover drug deal in Los Angeles, California. Paul, who was born and spent most of his life in Thailand, was fifty-two when it happened. Twelve years earlier, when he worked for me in New York, his first U.S. street enforcement assignment, I used to tell him, "Paul, we're too old for this . . . too old."

This book is dedicated to the memories of Enrique Camarena, Edward Byrne, Chris Hoban, Paul Seema, George Montoya, Everett

Hatcher, and all the others whose lives have been, and are being, sacrificed for this war of lies, hypocrisy, and self-interest, which, like the Vietnam War, is being fought with no intention of winning. May they never be forgotten.

AUTHOR'S NOTE

It is both sobering and painful to realize, after twenty-five years of undercover work, having personally accounted for at least three thousand criminals serving fifteen thousand years in jail, and having seized several tons of various illegal substances, that my career was meaningless and had had absolutely no effect whatsoever in the so-called war on drugs. The war itself is a fraud.

If there is any deed I've accomplished in my career that *might* make a difference, it is the spreading of the message in these pages.

Twenty-five years of undercover work, and thousands of hours spent preparing for and testifying in criminal cases, have made me a trained observer and a meticulous documenter of facts—and *fact* is what this book is all about.

Some names have been changed to protect the innocent, or to avoid violation of secrecy laws, or because the individual involved was no more than the hapless fool I have been for the past twenty-five years.

This book will disturb many people in high places; which is exactly what it is intended to do.

INTRODUCTION

This book is about the biggest, costliest, most dangerous failure of American policy since Vietnam—the war on drugs. As the availability of drugs in the U.S. increases to unprecedented levels, at the lowest prices in history, we are being bombarded with hype—from ex-President Reagan's "We've turned the corner in the war on drugs" and Attorney General Edwin Meese's promise that Operation Snowcap (our government's latest two-hundred-million-dollar-a-year main thrust in South America) would "cut the availability of cocaine in the U.S. by fifty percent," to the supposed Colombian murder contracts on our bureaucrats and politicians, to the endless seizures and arrests called "drug-war victories."

As I write this, President Bush and—the latest rabbit out of the political hat—the "drug czar" are playing the media for all it's worth to convince us of the effectiveness of the drug war. It would have been laughable—had people not been dying—that when the Colombian government defied the cocaine cartels and our government rushed them a sixty-five-million-dollar "emergency package" of military equipment, it turned out to be all the wrong stuff. "The total package is more suitable for conventional warfare than the kind of struggle we are waging," said Major General Miguel Gómez-Padilla, the chief of the seventy-thousand-member Colombian national police force. Another Colombian official said that the aid will serve as a "symbolic show" of American support.

Can it really be the case that, after two decades of so-called drug war, our government did not know what equipment and aid Colombia really needed? Or was the sixty-five million in useless equipment nothing more than another public-relations hype aimed at American voters and taxpayers? *See! We are really fighting a war, America. We've got them on the run! Vote for us! Fund our programs!*

Or is the truth that our leaders cannot, and do not really want to, win a *real* drug war? Is it that the secret agencies and interests that *really* pull the strings of foreign policy believe that our two-hundred-billion-dollar-a-year drug habit is a *necessary* subsidy to keep the millions of poor in Third World countries from turning to communism? Has the choice of drugs over communism led our government to the halfhearted war on drugs and to the resulting cold sacrifice of the lives of those fighting that war?

Colonel Oliver North, for example, was given access to classified DEA information involving the first undercover penetration of the infamous Medellín, Colombia, cocaine cartel by an informant, Barry Seal, because it was believed that the Colombians were bribing high-level members of the Sandinista government of Nicaragua. It would have been a great propaganda coup for North in his "divine" struggle against communism. Seal was clearly one of the most significant informants in DEA's history and the drug investigation one of the most important and far-reaching. When it turned out that the bribery information was not accurate, North decided that he wanted to use Seal to ferry money to the Contras. *Finally,* one of the DEA "suits" (law enforcement bureaucrats and administrative types) objected. "But that'll blow the [drug] case," he whined. When an angered North didn't get his way, he leaked the story to the press. Seal's cover was blown and he was murdered by the Colombians.

The drug case was over, a life was lost, and North—while his secretary and shredding-machine partner, Fawn Hall, snorted a couple of lines of coke herself—continued blissfully on his anticommunist mission from God.* The war on drugs had been seriously damaged on the whim of a loose cannon in the basement of the Pentagon, yet not a word of complaint was heard from the suits, the other bureaucrats, or the politicians—the leaders of the drug war. In fact, the whole incident might have gone undiscovered were it not for the Iranscam Senate hearings.

If the war on drugs is our number-one priority, as our leaders never tire of telling us, why the hell was that boob given a key investigation to play with in the first place?

---

* Michael Isikoff, "Fawn Hall Told DEA of Using Cocaine in '85–'87," *Washington Post* (June 4, 1988).

One of the favorite inside jokes of John Lawn (DEA administrator and chief narcotics enforcement officer in the U.S.) is to quote ex-President Reagan: "We've turned the corner in the war on drugs." It's a line that always gets a laugh among the suits. Well, the time has come for the American public to be let in on the joke.

In these pages I will offer evidence that the North incident was no fluke; that the drug war is sacrificed regularly in favor not only of the war against communism but of a multitude of other interests; and that alongside these interests, human life and the ravaging of our society have become an inside joke.

I compiled the evidence by turning my skill at undercover against those in control of our drug war—the suits. I documented every one of their misdeeds until I had enough evidence to make an accusation that would stand up in court. In fact, I would like the reader to think of himself or herself as a grand juror reading a criminal indictment.

Chief among the accused are the suits—the leaders of this war. They are the ones you see on television, a badge hanging from their breast pockets, standing alongside the local bureaucrats and politicians, in front of tables piled with drugs, guns, and money, taking credit for another victory, another record drug bust, despite the fact that there are more drugs available at cheaper prices than ever before. They are the ones you saw looking appropriately somber at the funeral of an undercover officer killed trying to arrest a drug dealer for the sale of one gram of cocaine, while the traffickers smuggling tons are protected by our own government. *"His life was not given in vain," says the suit to the television camera, ignoring the reality of the failure of the drug war.* They are the experts seen on the news programs and panel shows, who, despite the unchecked torrent of drugs into this country, self-righteously tell us, *"Law enforcement is doing its part."*

The co-conspirators of the suits are the politicians and bureaucrats who support the drug war. *"What is needed is more funding for law enforcement, education, and rehabilitation,"* they bleat at anyone who will listen, knowing that even the most medically educated in our society—physicians—are among the biggest drug abusers, and that rehabilitation programs are about as effective as aspirin against syphilis in stopping our drug epidemic.

The suits, politicians, and bureaucrats are more the Enemy, in a real war on drugs, than any drug dealer who ever lived. It is their mistakes, false promises, and ineptitude that keep us on a path to more useless death and destruction. They—like the generals and the politicians of Vietnam—don't gamble with their own lives; they risk those of others. Their primary concerns are public image, their individual careers, and the funding of their election campaigns and bureaucracies. They are the ones who most fear the words of the frontline soldier.

To my family and friends, I'm sorry. I just can't stand the drugs anymore. . . . wrote my brother David sometime during the early morning hours of February 27, 1977. According to his landlady he had been pacing the floor, playing his radio loud all night. She thought she had heard voices but could not be sure if it was the radio or David talking to himself. He must have suffered terribly during that long, lonely night. Not long before dawn he put a gun to his head and pulled the trigger, ending his life and his nineteen-year battle with heroin.

Our father had to wade across a floor covered with blood and brain matter that clung to his shoes to find the suicide note; my brother had left it in a bureau drawer. He must have changed his mind back and forth all night, sticking the letter in a drawer and taking it out, and finally when things seemed blackest and another delay more painful and frightening than the idea of death, he forgot the note and quickly pulled the trigger.

"Fuck life! Fuck the note! Fuck the world!" might have been the words of any of the thousands of druggies who have managed to touch my life. My brother's final act spoke them with great eloquence.

Until the note was found the Miami police had listed the death as a possible homicide. "You never can tell with these druggies," said a detective, thinking he was talking to a DEA agent with nothing more than a professional interest in the case.

No, you never can tell with these druggies.

By the time my brother had killed himself our family had suffered with his addiction for nineteen years, twelve of which I had spent as an undercover federal agent. It was easy for me to believe the rhetoric of the suits and politicians, blaming our nightmare on some dark, money-hungry foreigners. I can now understand why we continue to vote for and fund the drug war. It is much easier to hate than to seek truth.

In 1978, the year that DEA transferred me to Buenos Aires, Argentina, I was full of hatred for the "foreign devils" responsible for my brother's death, and a one-hundred-percent believer in the war on drugs and my role in it. I was totally unprepared for the education in the real world of international politics and drug trafficking that I was about to receive.

By late 1979, after a series of successful undercover adventures in Argentina, Uruguay, and Bolivia, I managed to penetrate the Roberto Suárez organization—the biggest cocaine-producing cartel in history.* From the very beginning I found myself battling forces within my own agency who, for reasons I could not understand at the time, were opposed to the investigation. With the aid of a small group of dedicated undercover agents, I defied the DEA hierarchy and overcame a series of roadblocks to the investigation that put all our lives on the line, and succeeded in making the biggest drug case of that decade. Eight hundred fifty-four pounds of cocaine base were seized and two of the most powerful drug dealers in our history arrested after I paid them nine million dollars in a Miami bank vault.† It was the first time that we had proof that drug traffickers were in control of a government. The case also resulted in astonishing indications that drug traffickers had already infiltrated the highest levels of other South American governments. It was called "the biggest sting operation in history" by the media; the only problem was that it was the American people who wound up getting stung.

Instead of our government pursuing the investigation and its implications with all its resources, strange things began to happen.

---

* Believed to be the primary source of cocaine base for the majority of Colombian cocaine manufacturers, including the Medellín cartel.
† The biggest seizure on record, at that point, was two hundred kilos of cocaine seized by Border Patrol agents at a Florida checkpoint.

All charges were dropped against one of the two defendants and the bail of the other was mysteriously lowered, after which he was allowed to leave the United States without the slightest hindrance by our government. The biggest sting operation in law-enforcement history was suddenly without any defendants, and no one in our government seemed to care. My belief in the drug war was, for the first time, shaken to its foundation. What happened next blasted it to kingdom come.

The Roberto Suárez organization began a revolution in Bolivia to oust the element in that government that had dared to cooperate with DEA in allowing my sting operation to happen—a revolution supported by our CIA. When the smoke cleared, thousands had been tortured and killed and the cocaine traffickers were in control of Bolivia.

At the time this was all incomprehensible to me. It just didn't make sense that the CIA would be aiding drug traffickers in the takeover of a government. I began to complain, first through government channels, and finally, when that got no results, with a letter to the media. Within months I was mysteriously put under a long and intensive internal-affairs investigation that touched every corner of my professional and personal life. At the same time, Roberto Suárez issued contracts for my murder throughout the Americas.

In January 1982 I was removed from my post in Argentina and transferred to DEA headquarters, where I found myself more threatened by the so-called good guys in this drug war than I'd ever been by the enemy. One of the suits at headquarters who had taken a liking to me had counseled, "A bureaucracy has a short memory. Keep your mouth shut and show them that you're not a threat, and you'll come out okay."

I learned the lesson quickly. This was not a battle to be fought alone, and America of the late seventies and early eighties was just not threatened enough by drugs to really give a damn. The ruthless internal-affairs investigation and veiled threats had frightened the hell out of me. If I was to survive, I had to keep my mouth shut. Yet, being an undercover agent is far too murderous a life-style to live if you don't believe in what you are doing. It did not take much for me to convince myself that the Suárez case was a fluke. I would not allow myself to believe that the suits and politicians, as a matter of policy, would let Americans lose their lives in a war they did not want to win.

Just the same, being the professional investigator that I was, I had carefully documented everything that had happened, and dreamed wistfully of one day writing a book entitled *The Case That Might Have Won the Cocaine War.*

As it turned out, the suit was right. Before long, when it became apparent that the internal-affairs investigation would leave me unscathed, and that I no longer posed a threat, to the suits, of complaining outside DEA, my undercover talents were once again called upon. I was again deeply submerged in undercover work and too involved in my own survival to think of anything else. I managed to brainwash myself into again being a "believer" in the drug war, and above all, my role in it.

During the next five years—when I wasn't working undercover on some of the most sensitive and far-reaching cases in the agency—I was assigned duties as special operations officer, South American division; desk coordinator, cocaine desk; supervisor, Vice President's South Florida Task Force; group supervisor, New York Drug Enforcement Task Force, and group supervisor, New York Field Division; inspector in place (inspecting and evaluating DEA's worldwide field operations); and finally, as an instructor in "Narcotics Undercover Tactics" and "Informant Handling."

It was a period of time during which I turned a blind eye to the mounting evidence of the truth about our war on drugs, when more narcotics cops and agents—street men, not suits, *never* suits—were killed and injured than ever before and I felt the hurt of all their losses as if they were mine. It was a time when my son, Keith, became a New York City patrolman and began regularly risking his life in one bizarre drug-related incident after another, and I began hating myself for my cowardice. I knew the truth—the war on drugs was a fraud and we were all being sacrificed for nothing—and I had kept silent.

But then, in September 1987, I found myself working undercover in the biggest, most fraudulent operation in drug-war history
—Operation Trifecta.

My silence was over.

PROLOGUE

Oklahoma City, Oklahoma, August 25, 1986—Jerry Harris, undercover narcotics agent for the state of Oklahoma, helped his informer, Terry Judas,* on with his shirt. He took a step back and checked him out. Everything seemed fine; there was no way anyone could tell he was wearing a transmitter. But there was always the chance—and that's the risk the guy would have to take. If you live by the sword, you've got to be prepared to . . . Harris had been around long enough to know that you never take an informant's word for anything. People involved in crime (the narcotics business in particular), who trade their friendship, loyalty, and morality for money or to save their asses, are not known for their honesty. Most police departments call them "criminal informants," cops refer to them as "stool pigeons," "snitches," "rats," and even "dirt bags." Never trust a snitch is one of the maxims taught in just about every academy training course and drummed into the head of every cop or agent who works narcotics. It is one of the most important proverbs in the unwritten bible of a narc, and one of the important basics that help you survive a career full of more hidden traps and pitfalls than an Indiana Jones movie. But Harris also knew that you don't make drug cases without them. You had to listen to everything they said with smiling patience and believe nothing until you checked it out thoroughly. And there was no better way to do that than make the informant wear a bug.

Judas had claimed to know a local cocaine dealer hooked into some heavy California suppliers. Under Harris's direction he had set up a meeting with the dealer, David Kwilos, for later that evening. Harris would be able to hear and record every word of the conversation himself. If Judas's claims were on the money, Harris had a good case and the tape recording would speak for itself in court. Another rule of good police work is that you never want your case resting on a snitch's testimony. In the drug world they share the bottom of the barrel with the druggie. In most instances if you can't back up an informer's story in court with some corroborating evidence your case goes out the window. Jerry Harris was too good a cop to let that happen.

At about ten-thirty P.M. Harris, accompanied by Oklahoma agent Russ Higbie, followed Judas to his first meeting with David Kwilos at a Sav-A-Stop convenience-store parking lot on Northwest Fiftieth Street in Oklahoma City. The biggest fiasco of the drug war —by any measure—had begun.

Over the next twenty-four hours Harris followed Judas to several meetings with Kwilos, monitoring and tape-recording some interesting conversations. Judas, who had won Kwilos's confidence and trust, convinced the drug dealer that he knew some "big-money people" who were interested in buying two kilos of cocaine. Kwilos said the price for two kilos was sixty-five thousand dollars and that his connection would have to bring the stuff from Los Angeles. While a two-kilo coke case was not that big a deal in some parts of the United States—like Miami, where seizures of thousand-pound shipments seemed to be a weekly event and you could not get a United States attorney to prosecute a case involving less than five kilos—for Oklahoma City it was a hell of a lot of drugs. Judges there were sentencing dealers to ten years in prison for selling grams; two "keys" would buy these guys some heavy jail time. Under Harris's instructions Judas ordered the two kilos. Kwilos said that the connection would want to come to Oklahoma first to see the money. Judas told him to come ahead.

As intriguing to Harris as the drug case were some of the things Kwilos was saying about his suppliers. He said that they "shuffled a lot of things into Nicaragua" for the American government, including running guns for the CIA; and that even if the main man was arrested, the U.S. government would get him out of jail. According to Kwilos he had been running drugs in Cuba before Castro took over.

Pretty fascinating stuff for an Oklahoma City narcotics agent.

On August twenty-seventh Eric "Junior" Batista got off a plane in Oklahoma City, where he was met by David Kwilos. He was a long way from the place he listed as home—Mexico City—and an even longer way from the grandeur and fearsome image of his ancestors. Junior Batista was as treacherous and unreliable as all heavy cocaine users. His own father, Nilo Batista, known to deal cocaine in multi–hundred-kilo quantities, neither trusted nor would have anything to do with him. The idea of his son selling a miserable two kilos of cocaine in Oklahoma City would have been as disgraceful to the elder Batista as going on welfare. But Junior did not have much of a choice. He was broke, up to his ass in debt, and had a habit to support. If the customer was in Oklahoma City or in Oshkosh, that's where he'd have to go.

At ten P.M. Junior was brought to a parking lot in front of the Ramada Inn on NW Thirty-ninth Expressway by Kwilos's girlfriend, Debbie Hammons. Undercover agent Lonnie Wright peeked out at them from behind the drapes of room 168. When the headlights hit him he ducked back into the room. On the bed behind him was a paper bag full of hundreds and fifties—sixty-five thousand dollars' worth. Wright began to mentally prepare himself to play the role as one of the money men.

The Oklahoma narcotics bureau did not have that kind of cash on hand for a flash roll, so they had turned to DEA for help. On hearing Agent Harris's story the local DEA office not only furnished the money but also assigned federal agents to the case. Oklahoma state and DEA agents were scattered around the lot and the surrounding streets checking for countersurveillance, and in the adjoining room with shotguns and bulletproof vests in case the bad guys had any ideas of ripping them off.

Debbie Hammons was no fool; she had been dealing drugs with Kwilos for the past several years and knew how to recognize a police surveillance. Something was wrong. There were just too many people sitting around in cars. She started to say something but kept quiet. Batista was supposed to be big time, he could mean a steady flow of big business for her and Kwilos. Maybe it was just her imagination. This was the biggest deal she'd ever had anything to do with and she was nervous. Besides, they had no dope with them; nothing to get busted for. Batista didn't seem nervous, so why should she be? Hell, there was nothing to be nervous about. He was there to see money, and there was no law against that.

A car pulled up alongside of theirs. She recognized Judas immediately, but the big clean-cut-looking guy with him was a stranger. It had to be the money man. Once again she had a feeling of foreboding but kept quiet. She watched Batista shake hands with Judas and then the stranger. They seemed relaxed, like they knew each other. Finally Batista and the stranger, undercover narc Jerry Harris, went to room 168 just a few feet from her. The door opened and they disappeared inside.

From the moment Lonnie Wright opened the door, Batista was all business; there was no small talk; he wanted to see the money. His eyes lit up hungrily as three thick stacks of hundreds and one stack of fifties were dumped onto the table before him. His fingers trembled as he counted the bills. Harris watched him closely, recognizing the signs like a good hunter or fisherman. Junior was hooked. The look, smell, and feel of money would blind him, numb his senses, and draw him like a rat to the cheese until the cage clanged shut around him. It was time to reel the sucker in; the case was made.

Batista was satisfied. The only thing left was to call his partner, Dave Wheeler, in L.A., and get him on the next plane with the merchandise. That son of a bitch had better not be lying this time. He had sworn he could get the stuff fronted to him. He hated dealing with the tall, goofy-looking nonstop talker who claimed to be a famous screenwriter. The man lied and conned so much that he couldn't keep track of his own stories, but Junior had no choice. He had worn out all his own credit. Even his father had turned against him. Either Wheeler got the coke, or there was no deal. Batista barely listened as Harris told him that for the next transaction he would like to buy five kilos; he just prayed that Wheeler would show up with the two. He promised the two undercover agents that the stuff would arrive the next day.

Jerry Harris suddenly decided to play it cute. Sometimes it paid to put the bad guys on the defensive: it took their minds off the little discrepancies and slipups that undercovers can't avoid. He peeked out between the curtains at Debbie Hammons sitting nervously in her car. "Who's the girl?" he asked suspiciously. Batista opened the door a crack. Debbie saw him and leapt out of her car. The parking lot just seemed too busy to her. She could not shake the feeling that she was being watched. "I thought you were just going to count the money," she said, coming to the door.

She was making Batista nervous, so he let her in. "This is my friend Mike," he said, introducing her to Agent Harris as though they'd been through high school together. "We know each other for three years. Mike works for the House of Representatives."

Debbie smiled and relaxed. If the guy worked for the House of Representatives, one thing for sure: He couldn't be a cop.

On the morning of August twenty-ninth, two months short of his forty-fifth birthday, David Laird Wheeler, alias David Adam Milhaus, Wesley David Wylan, John Baylor Lands, David Raymond Laker, David Wilson, Ray D. Bloch, and other assorted names, boarded a plane at Los Angeles International Airport bound for Will Rogers World Airport, Oklahoma City. He had spent most of his money for the one-way ticket and used up whatever credit he had to scrape together the eight hundred grams of cocaine he was carrying. He was still twelve hundred grams short of the promised two kilos, but what the hell; when he got to Oklahoma maybe he and Junior could whack it with a little sugar. Those hicks might never know the difference. But then again maybe it wasn't such a good idea. Country boys could play pretty rough, and if there was anything in this world that David Laird Wheeler was decidedly *not,* it was a fighter. On the other hand, if there was anything that he *was,* it was a fraud.

He had spent most of his adult life listing his occupation as "screenwriter," claiming to have been the "protégé" of Otto Preminger, yet he had not a single screen credit to his name. His attempts at making the big time in other fields of endeavor, from the promotion of music concerts to the oil business, had been total failures. He was a voracious reader with a superficial knowledge of an incredibly wide variety of subjects, but had mastered none. He was possessed of a glib tongue, a quick intellect, and enough charm and wit to cause many opportunities to open for him, but not enough substance as a person to consummate them. He would impress at first, but he never failed to get caught eventually in self-glorifying exaggerations and outright lies. As fast as the doors had opened they would slam shut in his face. And now, entering middle age, there were no more doors on the horizon. In fact, he couldn't even see the horizon. David Wheeler, in the lexicon of the world he lusted to join but was never quite accepted in—Hollywood—was that most hideous and ill-favored of species: a loser.

Though unable to achieve a reputation as a screenwriter or in business, he had managed to get a name for himself in the only field that seemed to offer him a sporadic income—selling drugs. However, even on that ignoble career path success had somehow always eluded him. In the drug-dealing world, as in Hollywood, David Wheeler was always somewhere on the fringe. The famous and the infamous knew of him and even tolerated his presence, but none took him seriously, or trusted him enough to rescue him from the netherworld of nobodies. Even his arrests had all been small-time busts for peyote and marijuana in Los Angeles, San Diego, Santa Monica, Long Beach, and Riverside, California.

Who could trust a man such as he?

As his plane arced lazily over Los Angeles, David Wheeler faced the cold realization that as his life and list of aliases grew longer, his resume was growing shorter and seedier; this might be his last chance. He had to make it work.

■

On the evening of August 29, 1986, in Oklahoma City, Oklahoma, Eric "Junior" Batista, David Kwilos, Debbie Hammons, and David Laird Wheeler were arrested for possession and sale of eight hundred grams of cocaine. The charges carried a potential of forty-five years in a federal prison.

It did not take Wheeler long to recognize that unless he turned informant (something he already had some experience at), the odds were that he would be spending many years turning big Oklahoma rocks into little ones. Unhampered by notions of morality, and not one to stand on scruples or principles, Wheeler immediately offered to turn in everyone he had ever snorted a line of coke with, if he could save his own butt. The Oklahoma City narcs made avid, if not sympathetic, listeners.

Wheeler babbled on and on about having spent years in Mexico making deals with the heads of the military and the police and the top drug dealers in that country. He bragged of his role in the running of huge quantities of drugs across all our nation's borders, of the bribing of DEA agents, of being the first to bring *sinsemilla* (a highly potent, seedless brand of marijuana) to Mexico and of being so deeply involved with the Mexican federal police that he was furnished official credentials to travel unmolested across that country, dealing in drugs. This was all fascinating stuff for Jerry Harris, who decided to call in the local DEA chief to see what he thought. After all, DEA was the lead agency in the drug war, with offices all over the world; who better to judge whether there might be anything to this guy's story?

Wheeler's reception by DEA was not an enthusiastic one. While some of the names he had mentioned checked out in the computer, his own criminal history showed nothing but small-time busts for grass and peyote. What the hell was such a "big-time" drug dealer doing selling eight hundred grams of coke in Oklahoma City? He was broke and on his ass and could not even make bail for his arrest. None of his alleged big-time drug associates or Hollywood mogul friends had even volunteered to get him a lawyer, much less front his bail. And where was all the money he should have made if a hundredth of what he was bragging about was true?

It was finally decided that Wheeler would be put on the lie box. The big question would be whether or not Wheeler, if taken out of jail to work as informer, intended to deceive DEA. Wheeler did not pass the test. DEA was not interested.

To be rejected as a stool pigeon was truly the bottom of life's barrel.

Who could trust a man such as he?

This was to be the luckiest day in David Laird Wheeler's life.

ONE

OPERATION TRIFECTA

An Interesting Assignment

On September 17, 1987, at three P.M., I was in the middle of planning a drug raid when a telephone call came that would send me on the biggest and most bizarre undercover case in the history of law enforcement. I was just two years short of retirement and was supervising a street enforcement group out of DEA's New York City field division. The raid I had been planning was going to be a buy-bust operation for a kilo of cocaine. The bad guys were holed up in a heavily fortified apartment in the South Bronx, guarded by attack dogs. The twelve members of my group—ten men and two women—were sitting around trying to figure out a way to con the bad guys out onto the street to take them down without any of us getting hurt. We had been averaging two raids a week for the past year, with more or less the same setup, and no one had been hurt yet. I guess we were all feeling that our luck should be running out pretty soon.

During my twenty-three years of frontline combat in the so-called war on drugs, I had seen too much hypocrisy, lies, and corruption to keep kidding myself; I was OD'ing on it; it was as much bullshit as Vietnam. Most of the politicians and suits had their private little agendas and I didn't think there was a thing in this world that one man could do to stop them. I had tried once and the suits and the people behind the scenes had come after me and almost destroyed me. I knew I couldn't survive it again. They had frightened me into silence. Maybe, after I retired and felt safe, I'd go live in some secret place where no one could find me and try to tell the truth in a book or something . . . *maybe.* At least the thought helped to keep me from feeling too much like a coward.

But the truth was that I was afraid. I had decided that *my* agenda, for my final two years at least, would be to do the job they paid me for—locking up as many dope dealers as I could—and, most important, keeping the guys who worked for me alive.

My other great fear was the thought that some screwup of mine might give the publicity-hungry suits another opportunity to make media hay over the funeral bier of one of *my* men. Those bastards secretly loved the attention. They just ate it up. I don't think I could have endured that.

"Call for you, Mike," said Louise, the group secretary, forgetting that I had told her no calls. I hesitated a moment. I needed a break. I had been getting this ominous feeling in the pit of my stomach. There had been a lot of action lately—too much—too many close calls. My life seemed to be reaching some sort of crazy crescendo and I was just too close to the end of my career. It was almost as though I were part of some bad movie script and being set up for a big fall. I stepped into my little office cubicle, just off the squad room, picked up the receiver, and jabbed my finger down on the red flashing button.

"Hiya doin', Mike?" I immediately recognized the hard, clipped New York tones of Richard "Dick" Slattery, in spite of the many years we had not seen each other. The last news I'd had of him was that he was second-in-command in DEA's San Diego office and was close to retirement himself. He was one of the very few guys who had managed to go from being a street man to a suit-level manager. I had always felt a kind of kinship with him in that we had shared experiences that put us solidly in the category of "very lucky to be alive."

I had once had a gun shoved in my stomach, the trigger pulled, and it misfired. Later, when tested, it had fired every single time.

Years earlier, when Slattery was a New York street narc, he had tried to make an arrest by reaching into a drug dealer's car to grab his ignition keys. The guy had rolled his electric windows up and gunned the engine, dragging Slattery with him. With the car careening through New York streets, Slattery had emptied his revolver into the guy's head and neck. The car crashed and Slattery was thrown free, ending up with minor injuries. Incredibly, the doper also survived. The bullets had smashed through his neck, face, and jaw without hitting anything vital. Months later they faced each other in a courtroom.

"Suits," as the street men say, "have neither balls nor senses of humor." Slattery was not a suit; you cannot survive what he did and be one. If anyone but he had called, the incredible story you are about to read would probably never have happened.

"Are you real busy?"

"Why?" I asked, already feeling the pit of my stomach churning. I remembered his starting off a phone call, some ten years earlier, with the same question. Then, he had been assigned to the Internal Security Division and had asked if I would do an undercover job on some "bad DEA agents." I had accepted and traveled to Boston and Connecticut, where I posed as a Mafia don, convincing the agents to sell me the identities of informants from DEA's secret computer system.

I was shocked silly and depressed at how easy it had been to convince men carrying the same badge I did, to sell a human life so cheaply. I was good at what I did—sometimes too good. To placate my conscience I had to make sure I wasn't conning the two agents into doing something they wouldn't do for anybody. When I met one of them in a Connecticut hotel room to make the deal, I told him, *in a loud, clear voice for the hidden microphones,* that I was going to kill the guys they were naming.

It didn't bother them a bit; they just wanted their pay—five hundred dollars a name and some cocaine. It was a great case, one of the first, if not the first, computer theft cases in history.* Two years

* U.S. *v* George Girard and Paul Lambert, prosecuted by Connecticut U.S. Attorney Richard Blumenthal, 1977.

later I was transferred to Argentina and Slattery to California. Then ten years flashed by during which, in typical DEA life-style, we had no contact.

"I know you're a short-timer, but I got something that might interest you," said Slattery as if we'd spent the last ten years in the same car pool. "You ever been to San Diego?"

"No," I said as I peered out the door of my little cubicle at my group lounging restlessly around the squad room in their flak jackets, their eyes signaling me that they were waiting for me to get off the phone. "I hear it's really nice," I heard myself say.

"It's fantastic. You'll love it."

"Why? Am I coming there for some reason?"

Slattery laughed. "I got a real interesting case—it's perfect for you. You got a few minutes to listen?"

"Only for you," I said, meaning it. The man knew I could never resist an interesting case.

Slattery quickly launched himself into the story of the arrest of a guy named David Laird Wheeler in Oklahoma for eight hundred grams of cocaine. "The guy flips right away and is ready to give up his mother to get out of jail. But he sounds like he's so full of shit that DEA tells him to take a fucking walk. So what do you think he does then? He calls Customs."

Wheeler, a voracious reader, had read of U.S. Commissioner of Customs William von Raab's having been harshly criticized by Congress for accusing the entire Mexican government of being corrupt, without having any hard evidence. He immediately contacted Customs from his jail cell in Oklahoma, with his claims of having a close association with Mexican corruption at the highest levels and offering his services as an informant. It was the aging con man/drug dealer's last hope.

Even Wheeler was astonished at how quickly Customs had gulped down his bait. Unbeknownst to the aspiring informer, Commissioner von Raab—not to make Congress eat its words—had already made personal visits to all his Mexican border offices to "inspire" his agents into making extra effort in their investigations of Mexican corruption. An official probe dubbed Operation Saber was begun. Quicker than you could say, "I'm gonna teach those Mex bastards a lesson," David Wheeler was out of the rough prison denims of the Oklahoma City jail and into a new wardrobe, provided by our taxpayers, including a twelve-hundred-dollar pair of alligator boots and a twelve-thousand-dollar Rolex watch, and living in a luxury beachfront home in La Jolla, California, from where he began attempting to contact all his alleged corrupt Mexican police friends. Wheeler had never had it so good. He suddenly found himself living in more luxury than he had ever had in his life. Not only was Customs paying his expenses, they were also footing the bill for two of his teenaged children. Once again the story took a strange and (for me) fateful twist.

The only undercover contact that Wheeler had made that seemed to be going anywhere was a telephone call to a Mexican named Pablo Girón, who claimed to be a member of the MFJP (Mexican federal police). Wheeler claimed that years before he and Girón, who at that time was a member of the DFS (the Mexican CIA), had trafficked in drugs together. Girón told Wheeler that he had "the biggest cocaine connection in the world" and wanted him to find a customer. Wheeler tried like hell to con the Mexican into violating any of the scores of laws coming under Customs's direct authority—and away from the jurisdiction of DEA, now hated by both Customs and Wheeler—like smuggling gold or laundering money, but the only laws Girón was ready, willing, and happily able to violate were our drug laws. Ironically, Customs was now mandated—by federal law—to turn the investigation back over to DEA.

"Where do I come in?" I asked.

"I need a guy that can play Mr. Big, with real experience working in South America," said Slattery. "I thought of you and the Roberto Suárez case. The word I got is that the coke connection is in Bolivia, so you fit the bill to a T. The other thing is, I need someone who can come in and kind of take the thing over. We don't want to get Customs pissed off or anything, but we *are* the lead agency."

"You mean take over the case, but don't let them know I'm doing it."

"You got it! Drugs is DEA turf, and they know it. The boss out here is getting along pretty good with the head Customs guy and he doesn't want to hurt his feelings. According to this guy Wheeler, it's a one-shot deal anyway. He claims that the Mexicans and Bolivians have already agreed to deliver a thousand kilos of coke off the Baja, California, coast, ship to ship. They just want to meet Mr. Big before the deal goes down. Customs got an undercover yacht ready for the deal, a whole crew. . . . You're perfect, Mike. What do you say?"

It did not sound right to me. I had made undercover drug deals with the top Bolivian cocaine traffickers and never heard of one of them delivering that kind of quantity outside their country. If you wanted Bolivian merchandise they could get you as many tons of the best-quality cocaine as you could handle, but you had to go there to get it. The mild-mannered, gentle people were not looking for the hassles, rip-offs, and all the problems and dangers that lay outside their borders. That was one of the reasons the Colombians had dominated the market for the past decade. They did not mind going to Bolivia, where the most potent coca leaf in the world is grown, to buy ninety percent of their cocaine base, converting it to cocaine in Colombia and then smuggling it into the U.S. But then again, the drug business was like any other—changes could be quick and drastic.

"Well, who's your case agent?" I asked, deciding not to voice my suspicions. A case agent with a strong personality would take a lot of the turf battle off my shoulders. I was as much intrigued by the constant interagency territory wars as I was by the phony-sounding drug case. I had been on both sides of the battle lines in the "secret war." I had been a Customs agent prior to becoming a DEA agent in 1973, during a time when arresting or embarrassing an agent from the opposing agency would win you more praise, rewards, and promotions than locking up the biggest drug dealer alive. I had sort of half-consciously planned on writing a book called *The War No One Knew About,* and had already gathered a pile of material. Maybe this case would give me some more. But as the Suárez case had taught me, being alone in the spotlight was not worth it. I needed a good case agent to face some of the heat with me.

"That's part of the problem," said Slattery. You know how laid-back some of these California guys are. I need someone who can run with the ball. Mike, I'm telling you, this case can be a monster. Hey,

I got nothing to gain by it. I'm retiring in two months. I'd just like to see the thing go."

I had had no experience working in California. I just could not imagine *any* street narc being *that* laid-back. I had to see for myself. It was also quite flattering that he would—with an agency full of narcs—reach across the country for me. My curiosity was working overtime.

"What about headquarters, did they say it was okay to use me?" I asked doubtfully. Since the Suárez case the suits were very sensitive about using me for anything. The case sounded like pure bullshit, but something was piquing my curiosity.

"I already checked. I won't lie, I got a lot of static; but they finally said okay. I also checked with Kevin [Kevin Gallagher, associate special agent in charge, New York DEA]. It's all cleared. It's up to you. Like I said, Mike, I got nothing to gain. I got a funny feeling about this case; it could be real big."

He had no idea how much of an understatement that was.

"Okay, I'll do it," said a voice sounding suspiciously like my own. *I couldn't resist. I never could resist.*

"There's one more thing, Mike. You know Lydia Soto?"

"Yes," I said, recalling an attractive young Customs agent who had been assigned to then Vice President Bush's Miami Task Force at the same time I was. I had never known her well, but she had seemed nice enough.

"Well, she's a Customs supervisor out here now. She asked if we could bring this DEA agent from Miami out here to do a little UC work with you on the case. Tommy Sharp, it's her boyfriend. I told her I'd ask you if you had any objections."

I remembered Sharp from Miami too. He was supposed to be ex-CIA, an expert boat handler and fluent in Spanish. I didn't think it would hurt. "Sure. If it's, like you say, a one-shot deal, why not? The more the merrier."

■

On September 19, 1987, I arrived in San Diego, where I was met by the case agent, Hubert Hoopel. He was, as Dick had described, a very laid-back, quiet, almost lethargic young guy who drove his OGV very slowly and carefully. He smiled a lot at nothing and seemed barely to notice as California drivers angrily swerved around him cursing and waving their arms. One almost clipped his fender. For a moment I wondered if he was on Valium. He was the silent, unassuming type that in movies makes a great hero, but in the narc's world—for lack of aggression—is the most dangerous kind of partner to have. By the time we reached the San Diego DEA office I had decided that Slattery's "laid-back" description might have been one hell of an understatement.

At the office I said hello to Slattery and noticed that Hoopel's mailbox had the notation *Helmet Head* scrawled in crayon above his name.

I would try to reserve decision.

In the evening, after I had been furnished a black Mercedes 450SL sports coupe as my undercover car, checked into the Catamaran Hotel in La Jolla, showered, and changed, Hoopel drove me to the undercover house to meet the rest of the cast. The moment we parked the car I could hear the roar of the surf and smell the sea. I loved the smell of that air. I took a deep breath, smiled, and thought to myself: *Maybe I didn't make such a bad decision after all.* What the hell, a quick trip to San Diego for a one-shot deal; who had it luckier than me?

I would never have that thought again.

The house was an impressive California ranch house perched on the edge of a cliff overlooking the Pacific.

"They're really going all out," I said as Hoopel led me through the garage into the main house.

"They sure are," he said dully.

The living room, long, spacious, and plushly furnished, with an entire glass wall facing the ocean, was alive with activity. Technicians worked at perfecting the wiring of hidden cameras and electronic listening devices as the members of the undercover team and another half-dozen Customs agents assigned for surveillance lounged on plush, comfortable furniture. Hoopel introduced me around.

The first to rise and greet me was Jim Ross, the Customs agent charged with handling Wheeler. He was an intense, balding, and prematurely graying worrier who had little experience working narcotics investigations. (I was later told that this was his first such case). Alongside the almost lethargic Hoopel, Ross was a dynamo of energy fueled by ambition. He was handling the biggest case and most important informer of his career. Commissioner von Raab himself was being kept apprised of every development. In his agency he had center stage and the spotlight was on him. Success meant instant recognition, awards, and promotion—his career was on the line and you could see it in his eyes and in his every movement.

I shook hands with a half a dozen others. Lydia Soto was there seated comfortably with Tommy Sharp, who had arrived the day before from Miami. They seemed content enough. She had added quite a few worry lines in the four or five years since we had met in Miami. The olive-skinned Lydia had also begun using vivid blue contact lenses that made her eyes constantly blink and water. There was something unnatural and disconcerting about the effect. On the way to California I had toyed with the idea of using her undercover. Sometimes having a female undercover agent present during an undercover drug meet can have a disarming effect on the bad guys— depending on the woman. On seeing her I mentally ruled out the possibility.

This wasn't going to be as easy as I thought. She was Ross's supervisor and wanted a piece of the case—as big a piece as she could get. I didn't know it then, but everyone in Customs was fighting for a piece of it.

Finally, a tall, dark, broadly smiling Mexican-American introduced himself. Jorge "George" Urquijo shook hands with me. He was the Customs undercover agent, assigned to live and work with Wheeler as his partner for the duration of the case. He had an open, friendly smile that was at once infectious and disarming; he was likable—a strong plus for an undercover agent.

And finally I was introduced to David Laird Wheeler. I had noticed him studying me closely, from off to one side. He was a tall, balding beanpole of a man with a hawk nose and beady little eyes, who seemed a lot older than his forty-five years. As we all settled down to get acquainted, Wheeler took center stage. He was a man who loved to talk and talk . . . and talk. And that suited me fine. It would not take me long to get a good picture of what he was all about.

He was eager to impress me—too eager. He told stories, all of which involved him doing some outrageous, inventive, or ingenious feat, usually illegal and usually in the company of some famous trafficker, corrupt politician, or Hollywood star—stories, I noticed, that were difficult, if not impossible, to verify. At times he spoke of things any prudent man—even an informer—would be silent about, such as his father's alleged CIA work. He even hinted at his own CIA connections. He seemed unafraid to claim knowledge of everything—but was obviously expert at nothing.

When he claimed responsibility for the introduction of *sinsemilla* (seedless marijuana) to Mexico, I asked him a couple of questions about what wealth or property he had. Introducing *sinsemilla* to Mexico, in the drug world, was roughly equivalent to inventing the wheel. He should have earned hundreds of millions, if not billions, of dollars. He spoke openly of taking part in drug deals that sounded as big as a hostile buy-out of General Motors. When I learned that he was broke and that the government was now fully supporting him and two of his kids, I checked the faces of Hoopel and the Customs agents sitting around the room listening with rapt attention, and saw not a glimmer of suspicion. He had them one-hundred-percent conned. But then I had to admit that while his claims were wild, he hadn't really said anything that could be *proven* a lie.

Then he made his first mistake. *Men who live by the tongue eventually die by it.* He bragged of being co-owner of a restaurant in the Cayman Islands and having "heavy banking and business connections" there. Not only did I have my own sources of information there, but his alleged partner in the restaurant was a friend of mine. I could not jeopardize the security of the investigation by calling my friend, but it *was* something that could be verified.

The second mistake was a bit more subtle. The subject of the Miami DEA office came up; both Soto and I had worked there. Wheeler chimed in, "I wouldn't trust DEA Miami for anything." When he was on a roll there was no way you could keep him quiet.

"Why not?" I asked.

"They're as dirty as hell. If we do anything there, they'll sell us out. I used to buy information from them myself. They are the dirtiest."

"You're kidding," I said innocently. I glanced at Hoopel. He was listening with his face fixed in the unreadable little grin that was usually there. It was his duty as case agent to report allegations of corruption—a very, very big deal in DEA. I was going to be working undercover with Wheeler, so I decided to drop the subject.

What I did not realize at that moment was that Wheeler had supplied me with the only real weapon—a bomb—that I would have in the war that was about to begin.

I was beginning to understand why DEA in Oklahoma had been unable believe him. He had the look and sound of a Times Square pervert trying to con a fifteen-year-old boy up to his room to watch wrestling matches on television. I had spent half my career working undercover and deep-cover investigations with the top cocaine dealers in South America. I doubted that any one of them would have had anything to do with a man like Wheeler, much less trust him enough to deal drugs with him. The jerk had been arrested in Oklahoma for dealing eight hundred grams of cocaine—an amount the top dealers in South America would give away as a sample. Who was he kidding? The whole setup seemed as phony as hell, yet I had not traveled three thousand miles to walk out on an undercover assignment. Besides, it was so weird that I was beginning to enjoy it. It was one of the most bizarre undercover setups I had ever been in. I was hooked. I had to see how it would turn out.

Another problem I soon recognized was that since Customs had lost its jurisdiction over narcotics investigations in 1973, they had very few agents with any experience working them—none were assigned to this case. Wheeler had not only won their confidence and trust, he had manipulated himself into a position where he was being treated with the deference reserved for a senior agent—as phony as he seemed, he knew more about the business than they did.

Wheeler settled himself into an easy chair and ordered a young Customs agent to make him coffee. Another held his chair and—*I couldn't believe my eyes*—Hoopel lit his cigarette. Wheeler looked at me and winked. *Remember!—this was a man out on bail, facing a possible forty-five years in jail.*

"Why doesn't somebody fill me in on where we are with this case?" I said, purposely excluding Wheeler from my gaze, looking from Ross to Hoopel. "We can start working on a game plan."

They both looked at Wheeler, who, still smiling, said, "There's really not much for you to do. I've set the whole thing up." He explained that his friend Pablo Girón, a Mexican federal cop, had made contact with a Bolivian connection who could deliver "tons of cocaine." Wheeler had told Girón that he had been working for a top organized-crime figure from New York who could buy as much as they could deliver. "The deal's already made," he said, his ferret eyes darting from face to face. "All you've got to do is play the godfather."

I listened quietly, taking in everything he said. As he spoke, around him and at his feet sat a group of silently adoring young milk-faced federal agents and, of course, Hoopel, whose Stan Laurel face never changed expression.

I thought I was dreaming.

"I've negotiated the whole deal," said Wheeler matter-of-factly. "They just want to meet you—Mr. Big"—big pause for effect—"to see who they are dealing with. But it's all been done." Wheeler claimed that the Mexicans were bringing a thousand kilos of cocaine that they had received from Bolivia, up the coast in a Mexican navy boat, and that we were supposed to meet them with a yacht off the coast of Baja. At that time everyone was to be arrested.

"The Coast Guard has already been alerted," said Ross. "These guys are coming in a regular war vessel. There's liable to be some shooting."

The whole thing sounded like bullshit. I had done a lot of undercover deals with Bolivians and never heard of them delivering a load of that size outside their country. It just never happened. They were too cautious, preferring to sell to Colombians who would come to their country to pick up the drugs. The Colombians, of course, paid cheaper prices, but there was a lot less risk. Bolivia is also a landlocked country. I had never even heard of a transaction involving an ocean delivery. Almost every kid old enough to ride a bike, in a Bolivian doper family, could fly a plane, but no one knew a thing about boats. As doubtful as it sounded, I decided to keep my mouth shut and see what developed. I had seen a lot of strange things in my career, and in the wonderful world of drugs you *never* say *never*.

Customs, taking Wheeler at his word, had already prepared an undercover yacht for me, complete with a heavily armed undercover crew. It was a huge Hatteras cruiser, equipped with an advanced radar system and high-powered engines that had been valued at more than a million dollars. It had been seized from drug dealers.

Pablo Girón was supposed to arrive within the next couple of days, bringing with him his cocaine connection, a Mexican living in Bolivia, to meet me and finalize the deal. "It's like I said; the whole thing is already set," said Wheeler for perhaps the sixth time. "Meeting you is just a formality. All you've got to do is convince them you're the big-time Mafia connection I told them you were, and they'll deliver. It's a piece of cake." The others stared from Wheeler to me, smiling and nodding. In their minds the case was fait accompli—Wheeler said so. The Customs agents were already counting their award and promotion money.

"What about price?" I asked. "Don't I talk price with them? Do they think I am buying the stuff without talking price?"

"I've even taken care of that," said Wheeler proudly. "We're getting it for twelve thousand dollars a kilo. You can't beat that price."

I was starting to feel an all-too-familiar tightness in my stomach —a feeling that I thought I had left behind in Argentina: maybe it was me being set up, and not the drug dealers. There was just too much wrong with the whole deal—there was no way it could be real. The only person involved that Wheeler knew, or had direct conversations with, was Pablo Girón, and Bolivians *never* made deals through third parties. They were very formal businessmen who always dealt face-to-face and *never* with a cop—Mexican or not.

There was something else about Wheeler that bothered me; he had a secret he wasn't telling anyone. I was sure of it. I could see it in his frightened little eyes and feel it in the waves of oily fear that wafted off his scrawny body. My instincts screamed, *Watch him! Never turn your back!* But he belonged to Customs, and DEA didn't want me to upset them. Whatever he was up to, I would have to catch him red-handed before I could risk saying anything.

The discussion was suddenly diverted by Lydia Soto. She wanted herself and Tommy Sharp to be at the undercover house for the first meeting and had a couple of different suggestions about what they would "pretend" to be doing.

"For the first meeting," I told her, "the less confusion the better. There's already George, Wheeler, myself, and at least two bad guys. If we have any more, it will just make them uneasy."

Lydia didn't like my answer and argued for a while, but it was soon obvious that she just wanted to get herself and Sharp on camera. All the Customs people knew that Commissioner von Raab himself would be reviewing the videotapes. It could mean instant stardom. *Awards, promotion, your name in the papers, your picture in the* Customs Newsletter.

"I think it's a great idea," chimed in Wheeler suddenly, his beady little eyes on Lydia. "They make a great couple." The slick bastard was going to exacerbate every moment of friction between DEA and Customs.

"*Agents* make game plans!" I said angrily. It was the first time I had lost my temper. "I'm here for a one-shot deal. If I'm calling the shots for the undercover deal, this is the way it's going to be!"

The first session ended on that note. Soto and Tommy Sharp weren't too happy, and I was looking forward to getting the thing over with—one way or the other—and heading back to New York. I looked at my fellow DEA agent, Hoopel. He smiled his Stan Laurel smile and didn't say a word.

That evening after a dinner at a local Chinese restaurant and another hour of nonstop Wheeler stories, we all (with the exception of Soto and Sharp) returned to the house, for some role-playing in our undercover roles. Before beginning I decided to have a look around. To play my role effectively I had to be familiar with the house. It had been wired with some sophisticated electronic surveillance equipment that I wanted to check out for myself so that I would know where to "pose" the defendants during the undercover meetings for the best possible recordings. The attic, reachable only with a ladder lowered through a trapdoor in the garage roof, had been converted to a control room from where all the action and conversation below could be viewed and recorded with hidden cameras and microphones. It was an impressive setup. It would be hard for anyone in the living room to *avoid* being recorded.

After checking out the rest of the house, with the drone of Wheeler's voice behind me, I stepped through the sliding glass doors and onto a short, well-kept lawn that ended abruptly in a vertical drop to the sea. There was no protective fence. I stood at the edge of the cliff and stole an anxious peek at the water crashing against jagged rocks about a hundred feet below, sending up huge sheets of white hissing spray. In the brightness of the moonlight I could see the other houses stretching up and down the beach on either side of us. None of them had protective fences. *Californians are some crazy bastards.* I turned and found George Urquijo watching me; he had hardly spoken all night and looked worried.

"I guess nobody's gonna escape out the rear," I said.

"No," he answered, smiling politely. "Hey, look," he said uncomfortably. "I just wanted to tell you something before this whole thing begins."

"What's that?"

"I've done a lot of undercover, but I never worked a dope case before."

I looked at his broad, pleasant face and said, "I'll bet you conned a lot of people out of their freedom, didn't you?"

He smiled slowly. George told me that he had done most of his work on corruption cases, working first for Internal Revenue, Inspection Division, and then the Bureau of Customs. He had already filled more than his share of cages with "victims" who would like nothing better than to read his obituary.

"Don't worry about it," I told him. "The trick is to just play your part like it's real. Keep thinking, *If I were* really *a doper, would I say what I'm about to say, do what I'm about to do?*—and you'll never go wrong."

"Thanks," said George, hesitating. There was something else bothering him, but he wasn't talking and I couldn't blame him. He didn't know me.

Later, I laid out a simple scenario for the undercover meetings, calling for the creation of a mythical organization of investors from the East Coast. I was to play Luis García-López, the organization's half-Italian, half–Puerto Rican front man. Wheeler and Urquijo were to be my employees. If at any point during the undercover meetings the Mexicans made requests that I could not agree to, I could say that I had to check with my investors. The pretext would give us time to work out counteroffers without curtailing negotiations. The plan was to end with us agreeing to accept delivery of the ton of cocaine off the coast of California, as Wheeler had arranged.

Everyone was happy with the plan except for Wheeler. "Why do you have to answer to an organization, if *you* are Mr. Big?"

"Well, supposing the Mexicans want a couple of million dollars out front," I said, trying to be patient. It was the first time in my career I'd had to get an informant's approval for a game plan. "This isn't *Miami Vice*. DEA doesn't front that kind of money. I can't tell them I'm a government agent and I'm not allowed to do that. Instead, I say, 'Let me talk to my investors.' Later, I will say, 'My investors don't know you, so they don't want to put any money out front.' I turn them down, but I do it in a way they will understand is logical and businesslike. *Capisce?*"

"I know the Mexicans a long time," he countered. "They've never known me to work for anyone. I've always been on my own."

Asshole, I thought. *On your own you got caught in Oklahoma with a couple of ounces of coke. On your own you've become a stool pigeon. We really ought to count on you operating on your own.* But I couldn't say anything. I wasn't supposed to offend Customs. I looked at Ross and Hoopel; neither said a word. "I thought you had already agreed to that. If you didn't, what the fuck am I doing here playing Mr. Big?"

The debate went on until the wee hours of the morning, with Wheeler's objections getting more frivolous and baseless as my suspicions grew. I fought the urge to tell him what I would tell any informant: *"You're a fucking 'stool' who's turning in his buddies. Just shut up and let agents plan the investigation."* Again I held my temper and my tongue, figuring that if I gave him enough time and rope he would show his hole card and hang himself.

By about three o'clock in the morning I finally wore Wheeler down and he agreed to my plan. As it turned out, it really hadn't mattered anyway.

On the morning of September 21, 1987, Wheeler and George parked their rented Mercedes sedan at the Tijuana border crossing and watched three grinning Mexicans cross into California on foot. They already knew the barrel-chested Pablo Girón but the other two were strangers.

The first, a tall, gaunt man with a thick shock of white hair, introduced himself as Efrén. He was later identified as Efrén Méndez-Dueñas, listed in the DEA computer as a "Mexican national," and an "enforcer for Bolivian cocaine traffickers." The machine called him "extremely dangerous." I later learned that the reason his body was so emaciated was from having had half his stomach shot away in a gunfight. The third man was introduced as "Hector." Hoopel later told me that he was Hector Alvarez, a member of the press corps for Salinas de Gotari, the then leading candidate for the presidency of Mexico.

By early evening everyone was in a panic. George and Wheeler had spent the afternoon treating the Mexicans to a long, very "wet" lunch and were now relaxing at the undercover house. The word from the attic control room was that the Mexicans had not come ready to ship us a ton of cocaine as Wheeler had said, but instead had come only to meet the East Coast mob figure and *perhaps* talk a deal. There was no indication that they knew anything about a boat deal. My apprehensions about Wheeler were confirmed.

"He lied," I told both Hoopel and Ross.

"Well, not really," said Ross, shrugging it off. "It was just a mistake. He didn't get Girón's message right."

"Mistake? How the hell do you explain away a one-ton load of cocaine supposedly being delivered by the Mexican navy as a mistake?" I looked at Hoopel, the only DEA agent there, for support. He shrugged his shoulders and grinned dumbly. It was a motion that he would repeat a thousand times over the next few months.

"Those things happen," insisted Ross.

"He's your 'stool,' " I said, mindful of not offending Customs. "If he were mine I would wanna know why he lied."

Ross grinned tightly. "Hell, if what I heard about you is true, a couple of Mexicans ought to be like duck soup, anyway."

At six-thirty P.M., with the cameras in the attic rolling, amid reports that the Mexicans were getting "edgy," I made my grand entrance as Luis García-López, dressed in solid white from head to foot, with diamonds and gold on my hands, wrist, and around my neck. The man I had to impress was Méndez. According to the DEA computer *he* had the Bolivian connection, and a Bolivian connection meant as much cocaine as you could get anywhere in the world. The other two guys were along for the ride, hoping to make some money off the introduction. If the drug deal turned out satisfactorily they would be in line for a finder's fee—usually a percentage of the total dollar amount of the transaction. Wheeler and Girón were already out of the picture. *If* there was a deal to be made, it was going to happen between myself and Méndez.

I love theater and that is exactly what undercover work is—live theater of the absurd. I played my role of Mafia don to the hilt. George backed my act up beautifully by fluttering around me as if I were the pope visiting a local parish. He brought me juice, then made me coffee, bowing slightly and calling me "señor" every time he addressed me. Even Wheeler got caught up in the act. The scene was going beautifully. The three Mexicans spoke to me with the kind of respect that can only be expressed in the Spanish language; but Méndez, I could see, was still not totally taken in. He was not a man to be fooled easily. He studied me very closely.

Hector Alvarez, seated several feet away on a couch, studied me even more intensely. Only, his look was different; it had—I feared—a hint of lust in it.

After several minutes of small talk I got down to business by politely putting the Mexicans on the defensive. "This man," I said, indicating Wheeler, "told me that everything was ready. I have made some very costly arrangements. I have a boat ready. The money is here and my investors are quite anxious." I described the arrangement Wheeler had claimed he had made.

Girón looked shocked. He could not understand how Wheeler could have made such a claim. Due to the current elections he could not even guarantee me safe passage across Mexico, much less the use of a naval boat. "David must have misunderstood me," he said, giving Wheeler a curious look. "Nothing like that was said."

I looked at Wheeler. He could not meet my gaze.

Why had he lied?

The old man, Méndez, evidently making a decision about me, joined the conversation before Wheeler could answer. He explained that he worked as a "collector" for the biggest cocaine manufacturers in Bolivia and that he could provide connections for as much powder as I wanted, but that they never did anything by ocean. "Hell," he said, laughing, "they don't even have an ocean." I watched Wheeler flush a bright crimson. "They have many, many landing fields and planes," continued Méndez. "Everyone in Bolivia flies. Everything is done by air." Méndez then proposed what I had predicted—the traditional Bolivian way of doing a cocaine deal. He wanted my mythical organization to get a plane and pilots and fly it into a clandestine airstrip in the jungles of Bolivia to pick up the cocaine. *I felt that queasy feeling in my stomach again. It was exactly what I* had *done eight years earlier, in the Roberto Suárez case.*

"That is something we have never done before, my friend," I said. "My investors own casinos but they don't gamble with their own money." Méndez impressed me as the real thing. But because of Wheeler's lies I had to hold back and find out for myself. A *real* drug dealer in my position would not suddenly switch from a washed-out boat-smuggling deal in California, to flying down to Bolivia, without some heavy coaxing. If I acted any other way, I was sure Méndez would smell a rat—or a DEA agent.

I listened politely as Méndez continued to describe the "Bolivian way" of doing business. When he had finished, feeling it was the right moment, I started to rise. "I'm really sorry that our business did not work out," I said, addressing Méndez, "but I'm glad we met. Perhaps another day."

"What do you consider a cheap price for cocaine?" said Méndez before I straightened.

"You tell me."

"What price did you come here prepared to pay?"

"Twelve thousand a kilo," I said, looking at Wheeler. He looked away again. I wondered if Ross could see his stool pigeon's crimson color on the TV monitor in the attic.

"Suppose I tell you I can sell you cocaine for five thousand dollars a kilo," said Méndez, watching my face closely for a reaction. I reacted with suitable shock and sat. Méndez smiled. "You're interested now, aren't you?"

"Yes, I am," I said. I was more than interested. It was the cheapest price I'd ever heard of. I could remember paying as much as $125 for a gram of cocaine on the streets of New York. A kilo was a thousand grams. If it was for real, the old man had to be representing people who had many tons of the stuff. It was the source of sources. The fever had me. I was going after this one.

By the end of the evening Efrén Méndez and I had agreed to agree. I was to try and get approval from my investors for aircraft and equipment to fly to Bolivia, where I would pick up a minimum of two thousand kilos of cocaine at five thousand dollars per kilo. Méndez expected a two-million-dollar one-time finder's fee, no matter how much cocaine I bought, or how many future dealings I had with the Bolivians. The problem was that the Bolivians did not deliver. If I wanted the deal I would have to go to Bolivia for it.

"My people may have a big problem with sending an expensive plane into Bolivia," I said. "We see in the newspapers that DEA is sending agents to work with the Bolivians," I said, referring to DEA's "main thrust" in the drug war—Operation Snowcap. I figured I might as well probe Méndez for some intelligence on the operation's effectiveness, and at the same time see how much authority the old man had.

Méndez laughed politely. "They pose no threat, Luis. The very people assigned to the gringos report to us. They give us three days' notice before they fly a mission. My organization controls all civil aeronautics in Bolivia. There is absolutely no interference from law enforcement."

I had been told exactly the same thing eight years earlier by Marcello Ibañez, Roberto Suárez's right-hand man and an ex–minis-

ter of agriculture of Bolivia, during an undercover meeting in a Buenos Aires restaurant. I guess nothing ever changes.

Méndez was definitely not the type to boast, but then again, he *was* trying to convince me to come to Bolivia. What else would he say? But just the idea that DEA's massive program—"the new direction," as it had been advertised throughout DEA by the suits to attract volunteers—*might* have no effect, was a chilling one to me. Snowcap had already been in operation for over a year, but no statistics had yet been released. If it was really as much of a bust as Méndez said it was, headquarters probably did not realize it yet. It would be important that we get his statements to Washington for evaluation. There was more than just money at stake. We were sending young DEA agents down to the jungles of South America to fly Ramboesque low-flying missions, to try and find jungle cocaine labs. If it was a wasted, compromised effort, someone should know about it right away, *before* people got killed.

I asked Pablo Girón about the possibility of bringing the cocaine into the United States by way of Mexico. "I will be of no use to you," he said, "until the election is over and the new government takes control." I wondered if Wheeler's friend was as much of a liar as he was. The two had joked about "old times," but the alleged Mexican *federal* looked more like something out of the old Humphrey Bogart movie *The Treasure of the Sierra Madre* than the graft-rich cop and drug dealer Wheeler had said he was. Well, why not? If Wheeler could con the U.S. government, Girón could certainly con the drug dealers. Maybe the whole deal was a con job. In any case, whether it was a phony deal or not no longer mattered. What the Mexicans did not realize was that the televised meeting was already enough to convict them for conspiracy. I just had to make sure they said the right things—things that would demonstrate that they had knowledge they were taking part in a meeting to arrange a cocaine deal and that each was going to profit by it. It was truly a time when talk was *not* cheap.

I promised Girón a finder's fee if Méndez and I did any business. "You deserve it," I said, insuring his complicity in the conspiracy and his eventual arrest. "If it were not for your introduction, there would be no business." I thought he was going to kiss my hand.

"There are three men I must speak with," I said mysteriously, "—my investors. We never speak on the phone. I must visit each one personally. I will need ten days to give you an answer."

"Take all the time you need, Luis," said Méndez. "There is no rush."

"I would also like to iron out all the details, face-to-face, with the owners of the merchandise," I said, setting him up to arrange a meeting between myself and the Bolivians—the *real* big players.

"Of course," said Méndez. "That is the way the business is done."

I told Méndez and Girón that they were truly the kind of people I wanted to do business with and hoped that everything worked out. They were in anxious agreement—exactly the condition I wanted them in. Before the meeting ended I instructed them to contact George and Wheeler at the undercover house with any messages they had for me.

My suspicions about Hector Alvarez were confirmed when, toward the end of the meeting, he asked permission to join us at the dining-room table. The conversation continued as he continued to stare at me. He wanted to know what sports I played. He was particularly interested in whether or not I was a bodybuilder. Finally, he asked permission to squeeze my bicep—I let him.

The only thing I will not do for my country is soul-kiss with a stranger.

At the end of the meeting Girón had followed me out to the Mercedes. "Don Luis," he said when we were alone in the darkness, "right now I cannot be of much use to you, but I am very close to the man who is going to be president of Mexico. After the election I have been promised the job of chief of police in Tijuana. *Then* we can really do something." The weasel was trying to cut Wheeler out of *his* action. He *was* a phony.

"Don't worry, my brother," I said, clasping his hand. "I have a feeling that you and I are going to do much business."

Later we reviewed the videotapes. There was a moment when we left the three of them alone. Méndez shook his head slowly in wonder and said the Spanish equivalent of "That guy is a cock." He meant that I was not an easy guy to do business with—a tough, hard bargainer. It was a great sign; it meant that the last thing in the world he was thinking was that I was an undercover agent.

"Even if I was an old lady," said Hector, "I would have fallen in love with him."

I left San Diego generally pleased with the meeting. Wheeler, with just a few momentary slips, had confined himself to playing his designated role. George was perfect. I flew back to New York, leaving the negotiations up to the San Diego Customs and DEA. I had left word that we should aim for a meeting with the Bolivians on some neutral ground, like the Cayman Islands, where Wheeler had boasted of "heavy connections," or Panama. My role in the investigation was at a temporary standstill, but not my role in the drug war.

Shortly after my return to New York I found myself sitting across a table from two Colombian cocaine traffickers in Victor's Café, on Columbus Avenue and Seventy-first Street. I had been asked by the New York Drug Enforcement Task Force to play "Mr. Big" in arranging a large purchase of cocaine from a group believed to be importing as much as fifteen hundred kilos per month into the New York area. During a three-hour dinner I tried to convince the Colombians to deliver more than the forty kilos they said they would deliver on the spot.

"Listen to me, Miguel," said Hector Vélez-Posso, a Colombian engineer who had found the cocaine business a lot more lucrative. "I like you, and trust you. But I am not authorized to sell any more than forty kilos for a first deal. And I cannot lower the price. Our organization brought in twelve hundred kilos last month. But there are many of us, and most do not even know all the members, only a few. We don't want to sell more than forty or fifty to any one customer. Why should we risk the whole organization if one customer should turn out to be bad?"

It was a logic I could not argue with. No matter how much I tried to con him, he would not budge. We eventually got seventy-two kilos and arrested Hector and two others. The best lawyers available were immediately hired. None of the Colombians would cooperate. Why should they? Their families were all in Colombia, where they were vulnerable to a certain and terrible retribution, and how much jail time did they expect to serve? Not much. While the penalties *are* steep and the politicians keep screaming for them to be even steeper, few judges will impose them. If Snowcap was a failure in the Bolivian jungles, so were our own efforts right here in the good old U.S.A. Hector's organization is still bringing in fifteen hundred kilos a month, only now they are a little wiser and harder to stop.

On September twenty-ninth I received a call from Slattery to keep me up-to-date on the negotiations. Dozens of phone calls had been made between Wheeler and the Mexicans, during which he could not resist playing the role of Mr. Big, even though it was inconsistent with the scenario we had presented them. He was "out of control," according to Slattery, and the Customs agents did not know enough to direct him. Hoopel, the DEA case agent, had virtually no say in what was going on and either could not or would not assert himself. It looked as if the case could be in danger of floundering before it got off the ground.

"If you can just get me a meeting with the Bolivians," I said, "I'll straighten the whole thing out. All I need is a face-to-face with the source." I started to worry—thinking back eight years, to Argentina and the Suárez case—but I stopped myself; it was a memory that brought too much pain with it.

October 2, 1987, I received a call from Hubert Hoopel, who put me on a speaker phone so that Jim Ross could join the conversation. They told me that Wheeler was still negotiating with Méndez in the name of "Luis," and that they had reached a tentative agreement to do the whole transaction in Panama.

"I'm ready to go," I said, remembering Wheeler's "boat deal" and feeling my stomach go queasy. "Just let me know when."

On October tenth I received a phone call from Jim Moody, a sharp old-time San Diego agent with a lot of South American experience. He had been called in to help Hoopel in planning strategy. Moody complained that he was being kept in the dark about what was going on. He said he trusted Wheeler about as far as he could throw him, but that the Customs people were protecting him "like gold."

There was nothing I could tell him.

As I hung up the phone, I again felt the sinking sensation of other nightmares of years ago. I decided I would try and get myself through this case as quickly as possible and finally retire from undercover work. I had done enough in my career. I had only two years left to retirement. I had beaten a lot of heavy odds in getting that far. *What the hell did I have to prove? Was I nuts?*

On October thirteenth Hoopel called me to say that Wheeler had "talked so much shit" that the Bolivians had doubted he was "for real." This was no surprise to me; there was no telling *what* he was saying, and I felt in no mood to know. "Evidently," said Hoopel, "they made some inquiries of their own and found out that he had some heavy backing in Mexico. They say they want to meet us in Panama and that they have an offer we can't refuse."

Heavy backing? Wheeler? I still couldn't believe it. The "heavy backing" had to be nothing more than a frantic Girón doing anything he could to make sure the deal was a success. And "an offer we can't refuse"? I wondered how many times in my career I had heard that before.

"Tell Wheeler to tell them, 'Luis is too busy to come to Panama just to listen to an offer.' Let them tell him the offer over the phone first."

On November third Hubert Hoopel called to tell me that Hector Alvarez, "the man who loves you," was part of the Secret Service detail for the leading presidential candidate of Mexico, Carlos Salinas de Gotari. "I still feel no temptation to come out of the closet," I heard myself say. The man called Helmet Head did not laugh.

"How did we find that information out?" I asked.

"Wheeler found it out."

I was silent.

"They want to offer you two tons of cocaine and five tons of marijuana," said Hoopel. "Girón does not understand what the delay is."

"Look, they haven't told us anything new. Only the Man"—that is, the police—"would run to Panama to meet them on vague bullshit. A real dope dealer would want to know what he was getting into. We've got to turn them down. I don't even know what Wheeler is *really* telling them, anyway. We've got to wait until they do the thing our way. If they give us an offer that makes sense, Luis will come to Panama to talk."

On November sixth I received a call from Albert Scuzzo, Hoopel's new group supervisor, just transferred in from Bangkok. In San Diego I had noticed his mailbox had the crayon-scrawled notation *Fast Albert.*

Albert Scuzzo—as Hoopel's superior—was now directly charged with overseeing the running of the investigation. As the undercover operative I was also under his supervision. "Fast Albert" Scuzzo was the slowest-talking man I had ever met in my life. DEA *had* promoted him as far as group supervisor, so I had to assume there was some movement in his "control tower."

Scuzzo clattered around with the phone system and finally got me on a three-way conference call with Jim Ross and Hubert Hoopel. Ross reported that Wheeler had been in contact with Méndez, and that the old man was "pushing for a meeting in Panama," which Wheeler had already agreed to.

Ross went on to describe how Wheeler had almost lost the whole deal by proposing that it be done through some complicated Panama bank transfers—more like a Hollywood version of a dope deal than reality. The Bolivians had immediately smelled a rat. Drug deals just weren't done that way in South America. They immediately rechecked his criminal references in Mexico. Apparently the one bona-fide thing about the man was the fact that he had moved *some* dope through Mexico. Either that, or Girón was working double time getting people to vouch for him. Or more likely: Girón was the only one vouching for him. In any event, the case was still alive.

"Méndez said they had sixteen tons of cocaine ready," said Ross. "If the first ton goes down they are ready to deliver the rest in five-ton increments; they only want to see if we are for real."

Sixteen tons. *Could it be for real?* That was almost sixteen times the amount of cocaine that Operation Snowcap had seized in Bolivia for the entire year. Even if he were exaggerating by half, we were still onto the biggest case anyone had ever heard of, by far.

We've come a long way since the seventy kilos seized in the French Connection.

Ross seemed to think that we could convince the Bolivians to deliver the cocaine in Panama. I did not. I had had too many dealings with them to believe they would ever deliver outside their country. It was just not their way. I was sure they had agreed to meeting us in Panama in order to check us out in person—a free look at our act before making up their minds whether to deal with us. They were pushing too hard for the meeting. In any case, it was a moot question; Wheeler had already committed us. The trouble was that he was a lying sonofabitch, and as far as Méndez and the Bolivians were concerned, he was talking in my name. I was going to have to overcome whatever lies he had told them. As it turned out, in Panama, Wheeler was to be the least of my problems.

"What kind of living quarters are we going to have in Panama?" I asked. "That's going to be very important."

"We talked to Duncan [Alfredo Duncan, DEA, country attaché to Panama] about that," said Hoopel. "He said he was going to take care of it for us. He's going to get us a real plush place and wire it up and everything. . . ." I listened silently as Hoopel and Ross rambled on excitedly about the "Hollywoodesque" arrangements that were being made for the assignment. They sounded like a couple of Boy Scouts planning a camping expedition. Their innocence frightened me. This was no longer a routine undercover assignment. We were now headed for the land of Manuel Noriega and a whole new, and a lot more dangerous, ball game—this was deep cover.

If Méndez was as real as I had judged him to be, we were about to take a giant step to the top of the drug world. We would be away from the protective arms of Mother America and in the hands of men who not only had far more resources than DEA and Customs combined, but who would not think twice about killing anyone they perceived as a threat. Game playing was over. Our act had to be flawless. It was no longer just the success of the case that hung in the balance—it was our lives. I decided to say nothing of my fears to the others because as risky as it was, I wanted them to feel confident. If they were afraid, the Bolivians would detect it.

On November eleventh, my son's birthday, I received my copy of a Teletype originating in San Diego that synopsized the whole investigation and requested permission from DEA headquarters for us to proceed to Panama to meet with Efrén Méndez and his Bolivian cocaine dealers. Paragraph nine reported some of what Méndez had said about Operation Snowcap:

> *Méndez-Dueñas stated that the Americans [Operation Snowcap] posed no threat to their cocaine manufacturing operations. . . .*

On Friday, November thirteenth, the day before I was to leave for Panama, I received word to call Albert Scuzzo in San Diego. The slow-talking Californian had also developed a penchant for talking in code.

"You know the thing that we're doing . . . with all the people down there . . . in South America?"

Give me a break, I thought, Operation Snowcap was no national secret. "Yeah, I know."

"Well, uh . . . headquarters is happy with, uh . . . the things we are doing. . . . They, uh . . . think that we can accommodate them with some intelligence . . . you know, about things down there. . . ."

His code-talk got so convoluted and unintelligible that I found myself saying "Excellent, excellent," and not understanding a thing he said. The gist of his message was that headquarters, for some reason, was overjoyed about what we were doing, as it related to Snowcap.

That made no sense. The old Mexican had indicated that Snowcap was a worthless and dangerous waste of time. How could that make them happy?

I should have known then, I was crossing into the area where sense—and an agent's life—meant nothing.

TWO

NORIEGA-LAND ADVENTURE

On November fourteenth, a steamy, tropical afternoon, we arrived in Panama. Before leaving the plane I instructed that we immediately split up into two teams. Urquijo, Wheeler, and I were the undercover team, Ross and Hoopel the surveillance team. The plan was that neither team would ever be seen in public speaking with the other. From the moment of our arrival the only people we could turn to for help in an emergency would be the two DEA agents assigned to Panama—Fred Duncan and Rene Delacova. Traffickers on that level were known to have eyes and ears everywhere, and "Noriega-land" was easy pickings to buy any kind of connections.

We were still three months away from the Miami Florida federal indictment accusing General Manuel Noriega of drug trafficking.

As we lined up for immigration checks, a Panamanian *coyote** (after eyeing me for a moment) approached. Sixty dollars later the undercover team had bypassed the immigration lines. The *coyote* slipped the immigration officer our passports, he stamped them quickly, and we were on our way.

---

* Roughly, a middleman for bribes to officials.

Country Attaché, Alfredo "Fred" Duncan, DEA's "man-in-charge" of Panama, who was said to have an outstanding relationship with Noriega himself, had not made any of the "plush" arrangements Hoopel had said he'd promised. In fact, he made no arrangements at all. He seemed to want to distance himself from the investigation as much as possible. He did, however, make one recommendation that almost cost us the case before we got started: He recommended that we stay at the Marriott hotel.

The teams traveled to the hotel in separate cabs and registered without so much as a nod of recognition.

By the morning of November sixteenth we still had not heard from the Bolivians. Wheeler telephoned his contacts in Mexico. By midafternoon we learned that the Bolivians had been in Panama for at least twenty-four hours, but did not contact us.

At eight P.M., Wheeler telephoned Méndez's room and was told that the Bolivians thought we were DEA, because we were in the one hotel in Panama known as a "DEA hotel." Wheeler was as white as a sheet when he and the others came to my room.

I exploded. "Call Méndez and tell him to go fuck himself; that Luis is leaving." *I could already feel that old stomach-twisting "Roberto Suárez feeling." Why would Duncan, who'd always struck me as being so smart, do something so foolish? The case was already in deep trouble, and maybe we were too.* "Nothing to die over," *I kept thinking.* "Nothing to die over." *But how could I tell this to a couple of scared-looking Boy Scouts without making them crap their pants?*

"Why don't we wait 'em out?" asked Ross, pale and nervous. "We came this far. . . ."

"Because only a fucking agent would wait them out! A real doper would get mad after coming all the way to Panama, and then to be kept waiting—red-*hot* fucking mad. They are playing cute. If they really wanted to leave they would have fucking gone. Believe me, now is not the fucking time to wait for anything. Now is the time to act like a real doper."

I was angrily pacing the floor. I hated the feeling. I was too close to retirement for this shit. I was as worried about why Duncan had sent us to the hotel as I was about Méndez and the Bolivians. I looked at the faces around me—they were innocents.

"But if you piss them off," said Wheeler, "they'll leave."

"Listen to me, you sonofabitch!" I was right in his face. "You fucking tell them I'm as mad as I really am!"

They all looked at me like I was crazy. For a few moments I probably was. In any case, it was done my way. Wheeler told Méndez that Luis was packing to leave. I ordered all of them to *really* pack their things. We had gone too far to bluff and not follow through. If we had tried to cajole them into meeting us, or wait them out, they would know we were DEA.

The ploy worked. Méndez called Wheeler's room to say that the Bolivians wanted to meet with me. I told Wheeler, "Luis said, 'Go fuck yourself!' Tell him Luis is leaving because he does not do business with people who play games."

This time Ross, Wheeler, and even the very mild-mannered Hoopel lined up against me. Urquijo kept silent. "You're really going to piss them off," said Ross.

"I am sticking to the role of a real doper." I was weary of giving the guy on-the-job training, but I also wanted to get our asses out of Panama the way they came in—alive. "A guy as big and important as I'm claiming to be would not just turn around and meet these bastards after all the Mickey Mouse shit they put us through. I say we pack up and leave, and if they *are* for real, they'll be begging us to come back—and when we do, we'll do the deal *our* way."

After much arguing it was decided that Wheeler and Urquijo would meet with them and explain, "with sincerest regrets," that Luis no longer wanted to do business and was leaving for the States.

At midnight the four of them woke me up; they were almost breathless with excitement. The Bolivians had asked Wheeler and Urquijo to "please" try and stop me. They wanted the opportunity to explain that it had all been a "misunderstanding" brought about by our using the one hotel in Panama that all drug traffickers *"know"* is a "DEA hotel."

"They want to invite you to lunch tomorrow to make amends," said Wheeler, his beady little eyes bigger and wider than I had ever seen them. "Christ, you were right. But don't overdo it."

They all watched me expectantly. I looked at their faces. They had no idea how dangerous a situation they might be getting into—even Wheeler somehow looked blissfully innocent. I thought of some of the DEA agents who had been killed working overseas. I had been given the "Octavio González Award," by the International Narcotics Enforcement Officers Association, named for a DEA agent who had been gunned down in his office in the American embassy in Colombia. Kiki Camarena had been "arrested" in front of his office by *Mexican police* and then tortured to death. Death had come in the most unexpected form in the least expected places.

"I guess these guys are really serious," I said. "At least they're in the right frame of mind. Fuck it! Let's do it!'"

On November seventeenth, in the afternoon, we met Méndez and his Bolivians at the Balboa Yacht Club, a ramshackle, hip little dive that Wheeler said he knew from his dope-trafficking days. It was the kind of place where millionaire yachtsmen, drug runners, and seamen from every port in the world could drink together, while they waited their turn to move their boats through the locks of the canal.

The place was crowded when we entered. I wore tinted Ray-Ban glasses with sun-sensor lenses—I wanted to affect a distant, cold look; I wanted *them* wooing me.

The undercover seduction process began.

I spotted Méndez immediately. He had a deeply worried look on his face that he quickly forced into a smile. The two men with him stood as we approached the table, their eyes riveted on me. Thousands of undercover assignments had taught me that the first moment was everything. Among drug dealers, who live by their instincts, first impressions die very, very hard.

The moment I shook hands with the Bolivian who introduced himself as "Jorge" I knew that everything I had heard was for real. A man who could produce and control hundreds of millions of dollars' worth of a product—of which less than twenty dollars' worth had cost people their lives in our country—had to be an unusual man, and Jorge Román was. There was nothing special about his appearance, other than his intense dark eyes. He was short, square-shouldered, and barrel-chested, typically Bolivian. His ruddy complexion, black wavy hair, and clean-shaven features might easily have been taken for European. He looked to be about my age, in his mid-forties. What I could feel immediately was his power of concentration.

Jorge Román was a man who studied situations and people with the attitude of a scientist—nothing was missed. Everything said, even in jest, was weighed and examined carefully. He was the kind of man I could understand very well—a man like me. My act had to be flawless. Román was going to be a very attentive and critical audience seated only inches from my face. He had one fear: that this new customer who said his name was Luis might be exactly what I was—an undercover DEA agent.

I felt myself come alive with the challenge. I was undercover in Panama with one of the biggest drug dealers in the world, doing what I did best; and I was going to win.

Mario Vargas, the second Bolivian, was Román's mild-mannered, soft-spoken partner. He had a pleasant smile that seemed to slip out into the open and vanish quickly with the changes in Román's mood. It happened twice during the quick exchanges before I took my seat. Jorge Román was definitely the key—the one to be seduced.

Lunch was not going to be a business discussion. It was going to be a period of examination. Every time a drug dealer meets a new customer, he lays his life on the line. A simple conversation is enough to be indicted and found guilty for conspiracy and sent to jail for the rest of one's life—something Román's eyes told me he was acutely aware of. He spoke very softly. Later he would tell me of an incident in Brazil where a hidden recording device had failed to pick up his soft voice, saving him from arrest.

"The Marriott is a DEA hotel," said Román, after we had ordered drinks and lunch. "You must never go there again, Luis. Right now there are DEA agents registered on the third floor." He studied my reaction closely.

I felt myself go cold, but held his gaze. He had identified the floor that Hoopel and Ross were staying on. I could not afford the slightest glance at Wheeler or Urquijo. Apparently Román had not wasted a moment of the past forty-eight hours. I wondered if

Wheeler and Urquijo knew how close to death we might be at that
moment.

"How could I know that, Jorge?" I said with mild impatience.
"I have only been to Panama once before in my life, and that was
not to do business. I came as a guest of the Panamanian government
in 1974, to fight in a karate tournament."

I was aware that I had contradicted one of the many statements
the out-of-control Wheeler had made about me—that I had many
business and banking connections in Panama. I had specifically
warned him about making any claims or statements that could not
be backed up by fact, or at least knowledge. I had very little experience with or knowledge of the Panama banking system and I suspected that Román did. But it didn't matter. I was sure that Román
had already figured Wheeler to be a phony, albeit a phony with a big
connection—me. In any case, I knew I could not count on the DEA
Panama office to back up any fiction I came up with. Duncan, the
agent in charge, had had nothing to do with us since our arrival and
seemed, for reasons I did not understand at the time, to want to
distance himself from the investigation. I would have to stick as
closely to the truth as possible and mold it to my purposes.

The karate story captured his interest. I told him of my mem-
bership in the U.S. karate team that had fought in the South American–Caribbean championships, gently steering his concentration
from focusing on our flimsy background stories. I told him of the
week of partying, the busloads of women brought in, and my resultant bout with gonorrhea. He loved the stories. I also discovered
something that I would use as a psychological button to get him off a
subject at will—he had a morbid fascination with and fear of AIDS.
The mere mention of the disease sent his mind reeling and his eyes
rolling.

Jorge questioned me closely about my fictitious Puerto Rican–
Italian background and my ties to organized crime. I mixed as much
reality with the fiction as I could. We talked at length about Argentina, where I had lived for three years. I told him I had smuggled
drugs from there. When he heard that my father was a loan shark he
really started to warm up to me. He had known loan sharks in
Bolivia and had an abiding respect for their keen knowledge of hu-

man nature. He told us a story that gave me a good insight into the man.

"In Santa Cruz," he began, "I knew a loan shark who knew people better than any psychiatrist or psychologist ever could. A woman came to him to borrow money. He asked her how much she needed and she told him. The man took the money out, without counting it—he knew how much he had—and placed the stack on the table before her. 'Shall I wrap it for you?' he asked. 'No,' she said, taking the stack and putting it in her bag. She thanked him and started for the door. He stopped her. 'Give me the money back,' he said. 'But why?' she protested. 'Because you do not intend to repay the loan. . . . You did not count the money.' "

We drank and laughed and I answered his questions easily. I had been doing the act for so many years that my undercover identities had become as real to me as my own. Urquijo was fantastic in his role as one of my California employees. He quickly filled every silence with jokes, tales of his own, a quick smile, and a disarming laugh.

Wheeler was who he was—he could be nothing else. At times he would babble on in his gringo Spanish and Román would look from him to me with the unspoken question clearly on his face: *How could you employ such a clown?* In any case, the clown was clearly my "employee," and that was enough for him. Román gradually relaxed and let his guard down—but never one hundred percent.

Every now and then my "rap" would falter slightly—no big deal, maybe just a hesitation in my voice, an answer that didn't sound entirely natural. Román would pick up on it instantly, his coal-black eyes sparking into alert. He would shoot a quick questioning glance at Méndez that would remind me of the deadly spot we were in.

All I could do was smile and continue to sell myself. All I was armed with was a bullshit story and my acting ability. I had to make the man like me. Not far behind *like* is *trust,* and no seduction will work without trust. And undercover work, no matter what the media try to make of it, is really just that: a seduction.

Several hours into our lunch the rhythm of the conversation, the smiling, relaxed faces and frequent laughter, told me what I wanted to know—we were "getting over" on them. I had success-fully given Román the impression that he had learned enough about me to trust me, when in reality he had been much more enlightened about karate and AIDS. The crafty Bolivian finally manifested his growing trust by turning the conversation to business.

Román and Vargas owned a cocaine laboratory that manufac-tured two hundred to four hundred kilos of cocaine a day. Roman was sure that his laboratory was big enough to meet the demands of any customer, but if for some reason he could not, he and Vargas were members of a much larger combine of Bolivian cocaine manu-facturers who could. "Have you ever heard of the Corporation?" he asked.

"No," I lied, hoping my excitement would not show. *La Corporación* was one of those almost mythical drug-dealing organi-zations, like the Medellín cartel, believed to rule whole countries and control millions of lives, yet evidence of its existence was rarely more than unsubstantiated rumor. It was the way the American Mafia used to be. It was rare—if not impossible—to find an admitted mem-ber. I had never heard of an undercover narcotics agent dealing directly with a member of the Corporation.

"We are members," said Román. "It is a group of many dealers, just like us. If you, for instance, want more than Mario and I can supply, I call another member and you have it immediately. Between us we control all the merchandise in Bolivia. For instance, I under-stand you have been buying from Colombians?"

"Yes," I answered, immediately on edge, anticipating another test.

"How much are you paying them per kilo?"

"I'd rather not say."

He smiled as if he understood my reason for not answering. The truth was that I had no idea what a reasonable price for cocaine was when you were buying thousands of kilos at a time in Colombia. I don't think anyone in DEA did. I simply did not want to say any-thing that would alert him to the fact that I was not "for real."

"Forgive me," he said. "We have never dealt with Americans before. All our customers are Colombians, with a few Brazilians. The Americans think we supply the Medellín cartel with seventy to eighty percent of their base [cocaine base]. The true figure," he bragged, "is more like ninety percent."* *If Román's claim was true, the Corporation was indirectly responsible for more than ninety percent of the cocaine entering the United States.*

"Why are you taking the risk of coming here to deal with Americans?" I asked.

His face darkened. "The Colombians think they own us. They pay what they want and then overcharge the Americans. If we could find the right American customers, we could eliminate them from the middle."

Again I felt sick with déjà vu. It was a replay of the Suárez case. I had heard the same words eight years before. I fought an urge to just call the whole damned thing off. Trouble was coming, I could sense it; and it would not be from the Bolivians.

I made a halfhearted attempt at getting down to specifics with Román. It failed, as I knew it would. He had had enough for one day and was content. He had wanted a free peek at our act and he'd gotten it. He was wise enough to realize that he'd had a lot to drink and had taken a liking to me—not a very prudent position to be in when one is conducting business, especially a drug deal. Román said that he wanted the night to rest and think things over and that we should do the same. In the morning we would begin to negotiate "seriously."

As we were saying our good-byes in front of the club, Román suddenly decided that he wanted to take a walk with me . . . alone. "Of course," I said, my heart suddenly hammering at my chest. He was not a man who did *anything* without a purpose. He led me out onto a narrow pier that had to be at least 150 yards long, jutting straight out into the bay. There wasn't another soul on it. We walked very slowly, all the way to the end, with the others following a distance behind us. I kept waiting for him to say something, but he never said a word. On the way back toward land, on a hill above us, I spotted Ross taking our picture. I looked at Román; he was staring

---

* It has long been known that the best way to close down Colombia as a cocaine source, is to shut down Bolivia.

off in another direction. Then it dawned on me. He had his own
people out there, somewhere, getting a good look at us.

That night none of us slept. We were to meet at eight A.M. to
begin our day of negotiating. I spent most of the early evening preparing a long list of business concerns a bona-fide buyer of tons of
cocaine would have during a negotiation, down to the most petty
detail—everything from price, to quality, to who would be responsible, and for how much, should something unforeseen happen. I
listed every probable—and even a few improbable—situations where
the cocaine and money might be lost or damaged before, during, and
after shipment. It was a list someone from Lloyds of London might
have prepared before insuring a business deal—a list of *real* concerns
a *real* drug dealer would have.

*I did not want to be like the woman in Román's loan-shark
parable.*

Long into the night we rehearsed our roles and contemplated
our futures—or possible lack thereof. The Panama DEA office had
still not contacted us, which worried me—not because of the lack of
such protection as they might have afforded us, but because of what
might be lining up against us.

Deep cover and *overseas* is an extremely vulnerable place to be
in. There's not much anyone can do to help you. We had no weapons
or cover other than Ross and Hoopel and their cameras, and there
was no doubt that the Bolivians had people watching us. We could
not trust the local government enough to ask for help. If we wanted
to do the case, we were on our own. It was going to be a personal
effort—not a DEA or Customs effort. It was like an old-timer had
once said about undercover work: "There just ain't no safe way."

On November eighteenth at eight A.M., with Wheeler driving
our rented BMW, we met in the parking lot of the Balboa Yacht
Club. Román, Vargas, and Méndez had arrived earlier in a taxicab.
The driver, a thick, hard-looking black Panamanian, turned out to
be one of Román's most trusted people in Panama. Méndez got into
our car and instructed us to follow the taxi.

The driver led us on a slow, circuitous route with one eye on his
rearview mirror checking for surveillance. We had already decided

earlier that it would be too risky for Ross and Hoopel to even attempt to follow, so we were on our own. Ironically, the driver led us onto a United States Air Force base,* to an almost deserted fast-food restaurant on the beach. Román said he liked to talk business there. DEA agents being trained for Snowcap were housed not far from where we stood.

After ordering sodas and coffee Román and I, followed by Wheeler, Urquijo, and Vargas (Méndez and the cabdriver had returned to the city on some mysterious errand), walked out to some picnic tables near the beach. I took out my list. "I have taken the liberty of noting down some of the concerns I think we should cover," I said to him. By the time I finished going over the list, his smile said I had hit a home run. He had made his mind up about me.

"This is no place to talk business," he said, getting to his feet. "Walk with me." Once again I found myself walking alone with him as the others followed some distance behind. He was silent for a long time. I thought it was going to be a repeat performance of yesterday, but then he said, "My wife died a few months ago."

"I'm sorry," I said.

"You know," he continued, as if I hadn't spoken, "we were together almost thirty years." He was silent for a long moment, then he said, "Life no longer means anything to me."

Jorge Román did not say another word. We continued along the beach, not speaking. I have since thought often of those words; I'll never know if he was warning me, or if he had some premonition about me.

Méndez and the cabdriver returned and Román once again asked us to follow. Minutes later we were following the speeding taxi along the Pan American Highway across the international bridge into Central America. After about a half an hour of driving along the deserted highway, the taxi left the pavement onto a dirt road. A few more bumpy, dust-billowing miles and the road disappeared. We were driving over a worn tire-track through an immense field of ten-foot-high weeds. I was suddenly terror struck with the idea that we

* Howard Air Force Base.

had been set up. My heart hammered in my chest. It had taken DEA almost a month to find Kiki Camarena's mutilated body in Mexico; they might never find ours.

We burst out of the weeds onto another dirt road; ahead we could see a little village of shacks lining both sides of the road. As we pulled into the village, I saw that it was populated by colorfully dressed Indians with gold rings through their noses and odd little hats. Ahead, almost as in a dream, an Indian, his face a mask of blood and gore, ran stumbling toward us. Behind him ran another, a big rock in his hand. The two floated past and disappeared in the clouds of dust kicked up behind us. None of us said a word. Méndez looked as though he hadn't seen a thing.

The taxi suddenly veered left. We followed. I could hardly believe my eyes. We were in the parking area of one of the strangest restaurants I have ever seen in my life. There, in the middle of nowhere, stood a long, low building with a thatched palm roof that extended out over a patio set with tables. The place looked deserted.

"This is a good place to talk business," said Román, grinning happily.

Before Román had started his second American bourbon, we had agreed, in principal, that I was going to buy five thousand kilos of cocaine at five thousand dollars a kilo. I was to purchase the first thousand kilos within two weeks, the remaining four thousand within fifteen days thereafter. If all went well, we were to meet again to renegotiate the purchase of an additional ten thousand kilos. The dollar value of the whole transaction: $75 million. The wholesale price in the United States: a staggering $3.6 billion.

It was by far the biggest undercover drug deal anyone had ever heard of. I was having a hard time acting as though I talked these figures every day. I looked at Urquijo. He was as unreadable as a cigar-store Indian.

As if reading my mind Román said, "Luis, I want you to come and see our facilities, with your own eyes. We have landing fields big enough to accommodate a 747. In the jungles, near the Brazilian border, we have built whole cities underground. I do not exaggerate, Luis. Come see for yourself."

"I may send some people," I said. Before we had left for Panama, headquarters had given approval to send Wheeler to visit Bolivia—should the opportunity arise. Sending an undercover DEA agent, without notifying the Bolivian government, would have been an extreme violation of international accords—it was something DEA no longer did. It did not matter. I was sure Román was not boasting.

Even so, it was, for an undercover agent, an exhilarating offer. The opportunity to see locations producing hundreds of kilos a day in cocaine—huge underground cocaine-producing facilities that armies of agents and Bolivian troops assigned to Snowcap had not been able to come near in a year and a half—was an opportunity that was more than golden. It was an opportunity to win the most complete victory in drug-war history—an opportunity to really turn the war around.

"They will be more than welcome, Luis."

I was in my glory. This is what I had trained all my life to do. This was how we were told the drug war was to be fought—smash the source at its highest level; and hitting the Corporation was as high as you could get. I could not resist pushing further. If these two dark little men, so comfortable in the jungle, could agree to supplying me with fifteen thousand kilos of cocaine without a blink of an eye, just what was their bottom line?

"If the first transaction goes well, my people might want to negotiate a contract for as much as twenty or thirty tons . . . only, at a better price," I heard myself say. Urquijo coughed again. I met Román's penetrating gaze and held it.

"Luis," he said, "if you bring a Boeing 747 [to Bolivia], we [the Corporation] will fill it with cocaine—as much as you want. You have only to prove yourself as a 'serious' customer."

"And how am I to do that?" I said, trying not to blink.

"You must buy the first thousand kilos, cash, after which we will know you are serious and proceed from there."

"Of course," I said, a plan formulating in my mind.

What would happen if I actually spent the five million for a thousand kilos of coke? This was an opportunity to put a whole drug-dealing country out of commission for a long, long time. It was the biggest case in history. Up to that point I had made them believe in me with nothing more than words. The kind of credibility spending five million bucks would give me would make them vulnerable to a lot of damage. The possibilities were staggering but I had to figure out precisely how to use the buy and exactly what damage it would do to the enemy.

"There's no way I'm going into Bolivia," I said, some time later. We had finished a long lunch and Román had begun sipping his fourth drink. The contract agreed on, Román was insisting that I come to Bolivia to pick up the first thousand kilos. He was acting exactly the way I had predicted he would. Bolivians never deliver large quantities of cocaine, anywhere. *You want it? You come and get it* is their attitude. That is why the Colombians have them tied up in economic knots. I glanced at Wheeler again, wondering about his story of a high-seas delivery.

"Ah, Luis," said Román, smiling benignly. "I can tell you have dealt with Colombians. You will be safer in Bolivia than in your own homes." Méndez and Vargas nodded in smiling agreement.

"The American press says that the DEA has sent many agents and military people there. According to our newspapers they are making it very hot for you," I said, referring to Operation Snowcap.

Román and Vargas looked at each other and laughed out loud. Méndez shook his head. His look said, *I told you so.*

"Luis," said Román, tears of laughter glistening in his dark eyes, "do you believe everything you read in your newspapers? Let me tell you about the gringos. They have a few helicopters. They go up, and they go down," His hand fluttered up and down illustratively. "That is all they do. They do nothing. We control them." They laughed again. "Please do not be offended, but Americans are such simple people," he added, causing more laughter.

Once again DEA's "big gun" in the war on drugs was being laughed at by those it was aimed at. I laughed with them, a sick feeling in the pit of my stomach. Méndez had not exaggerated. The money spent on this massive operation was not even effective enough to provide me with a goddamned undercover excuse *not* to go into Bolivia.

Román drew a map on the tablecloth representing the vastness of the Bolivian wilds, laughingly pointing out the tiny areas where the Americans were positioned, the small range of the aircraft at their disposal, and the almost comical hopelessness of what they were trying to do. It occurred to me that a similar conversation might have happened at the very beginning of the Vietnam war.

When Román had finished ridiculing DEA and its operation, I said, "I believe you, but it makes no sense putting the money and the merchandise in the same location. If something goes wrong, I lose everything. It makes much more sense that I send my plane to Bolivia. You put the merchandise on board. The moment it leaves I will pay you in cash, right here in Panama, or in some other country."

Román paused and studied me for a long moment. His wide face broke into a grin. "There is no doubt whatsoever, Luis, that you are the son of a loan shark." He put his hand out. "Agreed." I shook it, my plan for the destruction of the Corporation already clear in my mind. It was a dream case, and it was about to get better.

Later that day Urquijo and I accompanied Román and Méndez to the Las Vegas Apartment Hotel, a small, neat, out-of-the-way place. In the lobby we were closely scrutinized by a security guard and two men in dark glasses and *guayabera* * shirts that barely concealed the guns in their waistbands. Román had the run of the place. He went behind the desk to use the phone.

Minutes later we were in a suite that occupied half the sixth floor, being introduced to a dark, educated, soft-spoken Bolivian named Remberto. "This is the man who moves most of our money in Panama," explained Román. "He will receive the first five million dollars."

Whatever fears I had about the case were suddenly forgotten. I had just lived out an undercover narc's fantasy of fantasies. I had made the biggest undercover drug deal in history and met the biggest money launderer in Panama, obtaining more than enough evidence to convict them twice over for conspiracy, and had done it all in one day. Adding to my glee was the fact that the whole deal had been arranged by high-level, corrupt Mexican government officials

---

* Loose-fitting shirt worn outside the pants, a favored garb for South American secret police for its ability to conceal guns.

who would also be indicted. We had managed to strike at top-level drug traffickers in three countries at once. It was like winning a trifecta at the racetrack, only we had a long way to go before we could cash in our ticket.

When we left the hotel, Méndez explained that Remberto not only handled all the Corporation's money, but much of the Colombian cartel's as well. "His brother [Remberto's] is one of the top members of the Corporation," said Méndez.

I was ecstatic. Drug cases didn't get any bigger than this one. I wondered to myself, how it could be possible for Remberto to operate in Panama on that grand a scale, *without* being tied to Noriega? It would certainly be something to consider when it came time to make the arrests. *It was a thought that I should have kept in mind throughout the rest of the investigation, but didn't.*

Román would not go near the Marriott hotel, not even to bid us good-bye. "No problem," I told him. "We'll take a taxi." The four of us hugged and shook hands. We agreed to maintain contact via the radios and that Wheeler and "my organization's pilot" would be visiting the Corporation's facilities in Bolivia within two weeks. As we separated I could see real affection in Román's eyes.

I wanted to hurt these bastards who laughed at my country, and worse, at my street brothers, in the worst way. With a little bit of planning and luck we could set up a sting operation the likes of which had never been seen in law-enforcement history. At the end of it I would take out my badge and stick it right up their asses. "See, you sonsofbitches," I would say, "I *am* a DEA agent, like the ones you laughed at. This is one helicopter that went up and came down on your head." For once we would have a *real* drug victory for the suits to announce.

That night I began to draw up the game plan for "Operation Trifecta," designed to smash the top drug violators in three countries with one blow.

The first step was to make the buy—actually spend the five million dollars for the first thousand kilos of cocaine. This at first glance might seem like a lot, but alongside the two hundred million we were already spending on Operation Snowcap it was nothing.

The buy would do a lot more than get a thousand kilos of coke off the streets; it would give me the credibility I needed to demand another meeting in Panama with the top members of *la Corporación*, to negotiate a much bigger deal. I was sure that Román, Vargas, and Méndez would back the meeting a hundred percent. They already believed in me and I hadn't spent a dime.

I would then, with the Mexican presidential election over, be able to offer sizable bribe money for the safe passage of my cocaine shipments across Mexico. I would demand, through Méndez and Girón, that the highest Mexican officials, who up to that point had managed to stay in the background, come to Panama and negotiate with me, face-to-face. Knowing these money-hungry bastards as I did, I was sure that five million dollars' worth of credibility would bring them running.

The top money launderer in Panama was already there.

It would be a meeting from which none of them would ever return—they would all be arrested, and that would end phase one of the operation.

Phase two, which I dubbed "Trojan Horse," would commence simultaneously with the arrests in Panama. DEA and Bolivian military elements assigned to Operation Snowcap would arrive in the planes that the Bolivians would believe were coming to pick up the massive load of cocaine. Also simultaneously, whatever other locations we had identified via Román's invitation to tour the Corporation's cocaine labs would also be attacked. When the hammer fell it would be delivering the most devastating blow in law-enforcement history.

I had been around too long and seen much too much to believe the operation could win the cocaine war, but it certainly would give us an edge. It would be the first *really* damaging blow to the prestige of the cartel, and its international influence, in drug-war history. It would cost *them* billions of dollars, for a change, instead of us. The edge the case might provide could lead to some very real controls on the overall production of cocaine base in Bolivia, which meant the first *real* controls on a significant portion of the world's cocaine production. And it would inspire awe and respect among nations to whom our war on drugs had become the object of ridicule.

The plan was simple and direct. It was like two boxers circling each other looking for an opening. The Bolivians had flinched and left themselves wide open for destruction. If DEA didn't do it now, it would be a long time before there would be another opportunity like it—if ever. Aside from the logic and appropriateness of the plan, it was something I had much experience doing. In the past ten years I had done a series of successful undercover cases with the biggest violators in South America without a single failure. *I could not conceive of the plan being turned down.*

Once again, memories of the Suárez case fought their way to the surface of my brain. I buried them quickly. Nothing like it could ever happen again. It had been a fluke, an aberration. If the drug plague had been bad then, it was now a nightmare. The American people would never tolerate a repeat.

A friend once said to me, "Mike, for a guy who's been around, you really act like you haven't been around." How right he was.

THREE

PALACE
OF SUITS

And so it was in some idiotic state of naive ecstasy that I boarded
the Eastern Airlines shuttle for Washington, D.C., on November 22,
1987, a draft of Operation Trifecta prepared on my Macintosh home
computer—I would not even trust a DEA secretary with the information—in my attaché case, and visions of drug-war victory in my
brain.

On November 23, 1987, in a soundproof conference room in
DEA headquarters, I passed out copies of Operation Trifecta and
repeated the results of the investigation to DEA's grim-looking top
management. Also in the room were Jim Ross, Hubert "Helmet
Head" Hoopel, and "Fast Albert" Scuzzo.

The suits sort of ho-hummed through all of this.

When I repeated Román's words of derision, complete with my
imitation of his fluttering hand as he described the "up and down"
of American helicopters, the masterminds of narcotics enforcement,
as I had hoped, grew livid with anger. Only, their anger was not
directed at the Bolivian cocaine dealers, the Panamanian money
launderer, or the corrupt Mexican officials—it was directed at me.
They reacted as though the words attacking DEA's "baby" were
mine.

"We know it hasn't been effective. You are not telling us any-thing we don't know," said Staff Coordinator Art Egbert angrily. He was directly charged with the running of the operation.

"This is the direction the agency has chosen to go," he contin-ued, "and anyone who doesn't believe in it does not belong in the agency.* What you don't understand, Levine, is that Congress asked DEA what our answer to the cocaine problem was. Snowcap *is* our answer. If Snowcap fails, DEA is down the tubes."

"It's the Bolivians—not me!" I persisted. "They are saying Snowcap has no effect whatsoever. They say they've got landing fields that planes land on every ten minutes around the clock, pick-ing up cocaine."

"We know they are laughing at us," snapped Egbert angrily. Then, instead of making a case for DEA's huge investment in Oper-ation Snowcap, he proceeded to bury it. He said that almost every-thing the Bolivians had claimed was "on the money." That DEA did not have aircraft with "near enough range" to reach the cocaine labs, and that the corruption problem was "insurmountable." That the Bolivian cocaine traffickers were warned three days before every recon flight and that every cocaine seizure that Snowcap did make was "a gift, to keep us happy." And then, as though he were some-how proving the Bolivian a liar, he said that according to DEA's estimates the Corporation was producing *more* cocaine than Román had claimed.

Finally, he said the most incredible thing I have ever heard in all my years in narcotics enforcement: "They are making so much cocaine down there that just seizing another ten, twenty, or thirty thousand kilos isn't going to make any difference whatsoever. There are probably a hundred fifty or two hundred guys like Román down there. It's just not worth making a buy."

I wanted to scream, "Why the fuck have two DEA undercover agents died this year going after ounces of cocaine? Was it for noth-ing? And why are you sending agents into the jungles like an invading

* A threat that was later issued to every agent in DEA, backed up by a Teletype from Administrator John Lawn, stating that talking an agent out of volunteering for operation Snowcap would not be tolerated.

army, like Vietnam? FOR NOTHING?" The words were on the tip of my tongue. Only the realization that it would have meant an instant end to Trifecta silenced me—but not completely.

"You know," I heard myself say, "I would like to take the total amount of cocaine seized by Snowcap and divide it by the amount of money spent and see if DEA wouldn't do a lot better just letting me buy the shit at five thousand a kilo."

Egbert stared at me as though I had insulted his mother and said, "We've got a bunch of guys down there on TDY doing the best they can. Snowcap may not be the best game in town, but it's the only game."

The whole bureaucracy had been gambled on Snowcap; alongside of that the drug war, Operation Trifecta, taxpayers' money, agents' lives, and Mike Levine's career meant nothing. I decided I would still push for making the buy. I still had two weapons on my side: truth and logic. And from the look of the vacant stares I was getting from Hoopel and his supervisor Fast Albert Scuzzo, that was all I had.

I peered down the long conference table at the office-pallored faces in control of international narcotics enforcement and realized that I was surrounded by bureaucrats and politicians, not one of whom had ever drawn a gun in fear and anger in this war they were directing. They had no idea of what they were doing or of how it affected the lives of the men and women they controlled. DEA was no longer even a semblance of an enforcement agency—it was a political tool. Maybe, in truth, that's what it had always been.

Glaringly absent from the meeting was Dave Faro, a very sharp-minded, experienced street agent who had worked undercover with me many years before. He was on assignment in headquarters, in charge of some ambitious undercover endeavors; an unusually high position for a nonsuit. In earlier conversations with headquarters I had been led to believe Faro would take charge of Trifecta, a job perfectly suited to a man of his experience and talent. However, in a recent telephone conversation he had hinted that he was being edged out of the picture. "The cocaine desk wants the case," he had confided. *It was the new "improved" FBI organizational structure in action.*

One of the first of the so-called sweeping changes made by the FBI after its takeover of DEA in 1980, to "improve and streamline narcotics enforcement," was the creation of the desk concept. The newly appointed FBI/DEA administrator, Francis Mullen, decided that DEA headquarters would be more efficient if divided into sections, or "desks," charged with the control and oversight of all narcotics investigations according to the type of drug involved (heroin desk, cocaine desk, marijuana desk, and so on), as opposed to the previous geographical organizational structure, with a South American division controlling all investigations and operations in that area, a European division, a Middle East division, et cetera. This one move effectively destroyed even the notion of effectively and centrally controlling an international narcotics investigation and threw DEA headquarters into an irrational, illogical, bureaucratic mess from which it has never recovered.

Drug dealers don't separate their organizations according to drug category. A Colombian drug organization might deal in Quaaludes, cocaine, heroin, and marijuana, thus putting them under the jurisdiction of four separately managed divisions in DEA headquarters. This means four separately run investigations; four times the amount of man-hours spent on one target; four times the amount of paperwork; four times the amount of expenses; and bureaucratic infighting for control of cases (particularly those that have the promise of media attention) that is nastier, dirtier, and more underhanded than a Chicago election.

Faro was working under the heroin desk directing an operation similar to Customs's Operation Saber, aimed at uncovering corrupt Mexican officials. Since Trifecta hit both corrupt Mexican officials and Bolivian cocaine dealers, it fell under the jurisdiction of both the cocaine and heroin desks. I was ecstatic about Faro taking over Trifecta. We had had several telephone conversations on my return from Panama. He was as enthused about the operation and making the thousand-kilo buy as I was. Then the cocaine desk (charged with the running of Operation Snowcap) began lobbying for the case. From Faro's absence at the meeting it seemed that they had been successful in removing him.

Over the next hour the discussion grew heated. I pressed for making the buy. Egbert must have repeated a dozen times that he didn't care how many tons of drugs were seized, with the other suits nodding in agreement. "Numbers are meaningless," he kept repeating. "It's the people we want to get . . . the top people." I kept countering with the fact that the buy would give me the credibility to invite *the top drug dealers of three countries* to a business meeting in Panama, or some other location, and make it possible to arrest them all. It was almost as if I were speaking a language the suits did not understand. I was trapped in a bureaucratic madman's debate where the rules allowed those of higher rank to ignore any point they chose to. Instead of answering me Egbert would launch himself on long-winded tirades defending Operation Snowcap. Around and around we went; we began to sound like a broken record.

It was then that Fast Albert Scuzzo spoke up. "Uh . . . uh, I agree with Mr. Egbert," he said, getting shakily to his feet, as fidgeting and nervous as a first grader asking permission to go to the john. "I . . . uh . . . think we should do a buy-bust operation."* He glanced around the table for the approval he thought he would get.

I felt a sinking sensation in my stomach. I had prepped Scuzzo over the phone for two days prior to meeting in Washington. It was a case he had "inherited" as a result of his recent transfer to San Diego. He had little knowledge of the investigation and none of South American cocaine trafficking. We had agreed that we would push for the buy option, but apparently something had happened.

Egbert's reaction surprised me. "I am tired of going after the mother lode of drug seizures," he snapped impatiently. Scuzzo flushed a violent red and took his seat as though he had just pissed his pants. "We know the Bolivians have all this cocaine, big seizures just don't matter anymore. I want *people*. If we can get some of their top people, *that* would be something."

"That is why the buy option is the thing to do!" I said, quickly grabbing the opening again, wondering if I was going mad. *Couldn't these people hear themselves?* "If we just do a buy-bust on this one,

* A buy-bust operation is a tactic employed by narcotics enforcement wherein the money is shown to the violators as though a buy were going to be made. Instead of paying—once the drugs are delivered—everyone is arrested.

not only will we only end up with just another load of cocaine, but
there is no guarantee that we'll be able to con the Mexicans who set
the deal up in the first place, out to a place where we can arrest
them, or that all the Bolivians—or any of them, for that matter—
will show up for the money in Panama. I was instructed to pay the
money launderer. He may end up being the only arrest we make.

"On the other hand," I continued, not liking the desperate
sound of my voice but sensing that it was now or never, "I can make
the buy. With the kind of credibility that gives me, I can order up
ten, twenty, or even a hundred tons of cocaine. . . ." I pressed
home each of the points of Trifecta again, watching the deadpan
faces of the suits around me.

"You are right," I concluded. "A buy-bust operation gets us
nothing but dope. The buy option will not *just* get us people—it will
get us the *top* people in three countries." I hit Egbert hard with his
own logic. He stood there blinking, unable to talk for a moment; he
had proved my point for me. I noticed Scuzzo fidget uncomfortably.
Hoopel had sunk so low in his seat that his eyes looked just visible at
the top of the table. Ross, the Customs agent, looking like a rabbi at
a mosque, looked on with nervous interest.

Scuzzo suddenly blurted, "Uh, so you think getting people is a
better idea than drugs?"

Egbert, ignoring the remark, came alive. He asked me detailed
question after question about the buy plan, pointing up every possibility that *might* go wrong. The other suits soon joined in—*What if
the bad guys want you to bring the money to a bad location? What if
they want a hostage? What if they want you to bring the money to
Bolivia? What if . . . ? What if . . . ? What if . . . ?* I had prepared myself well for the meeting and quickly described all the alter-
natives we could take. I pointed out that I had already been successful at executing more complicated undercover and deep-cover
operations, like the Suárez case, Operation Hun,* and others, and
that while there could be no guarantees of success—there never are
—there was certainly a very high likelihood of it.

---

* A three-month deep-cover assignment that ended with the indictment of Luis Arce-Gómez,
the Bolivian minister of the interior.

It was all to no avail. They were clearly focused on building a case *against* making the buy. As they continued their attack it gradually became clear that not only were they against the buy, they were against the entire investigation. They did not want Trifecta to succeed; only, they had neither legitimate reason nor the gall to just veto it. It was too logical and just too appropriate. At that moment the best they could do was filibuster it to death.

"You know," I said finally, to all present, "This whole discussion may be moot. The dopers have given us a deadline. They think I'm a dope dealer, not a DEA agent. If we procrastinate enough, they just won't do the deal."

Once again the reaction around the table told me that I had made no friends. Egbert glared at me with barely concealed dislike. "This agency," he began slowly, not taking his eyes off me, "on Snowcap, is way the fuck out front. If [Snowcap] doesn't work, this agency is down the tubes. Within the federal law-enforcement community, and with Congress, [Snowcap] was sold up and down the Potomac. Snowcap is going to be successful, one way or the other. It *will*"—he slammed the table—"be successful." He went on to tell me, in warning tones, that "Snowcap is Mr. Westrate's† baby and nothing is going to jeopardize it."

Once again my head swam with the double-talk. We had come full circle to the beginning of the meeting. Snowcap was their primary concern—not Trifecta. In their minds Trifecta's existence was a threat to Snowcap, and no investigation or operation was going to be permitted that in any way would make Operation Snowcap appear ineffectual; not even one that could turn the South American drug war around.

Egbert suddenly had to leave. Two hours had gone by and nothing was resolved. Another highly ranked suit from the cocaine desk said, "Mr. Westrate is going to give you a half hour of his time this afternoon. He is very busy, so if you really want to sell your operation, you better get a good presentation together. It's going to

---

† Dave Westrate, assistant administrator for operations of the Drug Enforcement Administration.

be your only chance . . . short and sweet. And if I were you," he added, "I would prepare some charts. . . . Mr. Westrate likes to see charts." He left my Macintosh-computer rendition of Operation Trifecta on the table and left.

Sell my operation, I thought, watching the rest of the suits file out of the meeting room. *My* operation? My only chance? . . . Was I in this drug war by myself?

"We better make s-s-some charts," said Scuzzo, his face flushed, his hands trembling with the sudden realization that he was in the Palace of Suits, where pissing off the wrong guy could turn your career trajectory on a sharply downward incline—and Egbert had seemed very, very angry.

"Yeah," I said, feeling a pain that seemed to stretch from the middle of my brain to the pit of my stomach. "Mr. Westrate likes charts."

"You know," he added as I got up to leave, "I, uh . . . don't think they'll go for the buy. I'm just gonna draw up a buy-bust plan."

"You do that," I said wondering what the hell my next move would be. I noticed Ross, the Customs agent, watching me, a strange smile on his face. I could not read him at all.

"Uh . . . you know where I can find charts and crayons?"

■

"There's no way in hell they're gonna go for a buy," said Faro in hushed tones, watching the doorway of his office as though expecting a raiding party at any moment. "Your case is going to make Snowcap look like a fucking waste."

"No, it won't!" I protested. "It'll make it look good."

"Tell it to them," said Faro. "They put the agency's record and reputation on the line with Congress. Nothing's going to make it look bad."

"What about Mr. Westrate?"

"Are you kidding me? Snowcap is his baby," he said, echoing Art Egbert. "You wouldn't believe how the whole fucking thing began."

"Try me."

"One of these Intelligence analysts dreamed it up. The guy's never been out of the fucking office. He dreamed it up on paper and the suits bought it. They told Congress that Snowcap would cut cocaine production by sixty percent in three years. Can you believe it? Now they're stuck with it."

■

The afternoon meeting with Dave Westrate, one of the most powerful and influential men in the Administration, was, as had been promised, short and sweet. There was no debate whatsoever. Westrate, a fair-haired, pudgy-faced, rosy-cheeked man who looked more like an oversized choirboy than DEA's head of enforcement operations, swept into the meeting room escorted by a phalanx of suits. Everyone stood until he sat, then everyone sat—me included. He looked around the room imperiously, then nodded.

Scuzzo coughed, shuddered, and got slowly to his feet. With trembling hands and stammering voice he began to flip through and read about twenty hand-scrawled, barely legible flip charts that even had me confused, and I knew the case. I noticed some of the suits coughing and looking away to hide their laughter.

I could see Román sitting across the table from me, laughing with them. Can't these fools see that the joke is on us?

When my turn came I had to begin at the beginning. Once again I heard myself, in words that I will probably dream about for the rest of my life, try to "sell" Operation Trifecta. When I'd finished, the only questions Mr. Westrate had were technical questions about funding that he directed at some of the suits. I sensed that I was being "handled" very carefully. It occurred to me that someone might have recalled the Suárez case and warned him about me. No one would say anything against the operation. They didn't have to. The lowered gazes of the suits when I tried to make eye contact told me all I wanted to know: Trifecta's doom had already been decreed.

The meeting lasted about half an hour and ended abruptly with no decision being made. Mr. Westrate, who had "more pressing" matters, said he would "consider" the plan and quickly swept out of the room at the center of his wave of suits. I had an idea of what they were going to do. They would no-decision the case to death. I was afraid that by stalling their decision and keeping me from acting as a true drug dealer would, Román would get suspicious and refuse to deal with me. I could feel anger and frustration replacing the caution and wisdom of twenty-five years of spy versus spy. Bitter experience had taught me that you don't fight a bureaucracy by attacking wildly in anger. The big trick is to fight them without their realizing that you are. You keep your back to the wall and look for weaknesses and openings and peck away.

An opening presented itself right after the meeting.

"Do you mind coming over to Customs headquarters?" asked Jim Ross. "Mr. Rosenblatt* is on top of the case and he'd like to meet you and be briefed. [Customs Commissioner] von Raab has given the case number-one priority."

"Sure thing," I said. They might kill Trifecta, but I was going to make sure there were a lot of witnesses.

Ross, Scuzzo, Hoopel, and I taxied over to U.S. Customs national headquarters, arriving early in the evening. The office was closed, but Mr. Rosenblatt was waiting for us. William Rosenblatt, the second-in-command of the Bureau of Customs, a big, powerful, no-nonsense type, read my game plan for Operation Trifecta slowly and carefully as the four of us sat in silence watching him. When he'd finished reading he had a few questions about strategy and technical problems that indicated that he knew what he was talking about. As I answered the questions, he watched me closely.

Rosenblatt did not equivocate. He loved the idea. He thought enough of it to immediately (with a little urging on my part) telephone Dave Westrate to tell him that he was "very impressed" with the plan and thought it "the appropriate action" to take. Then he almost knocked my socks off by offering to put up half the buy money, $2.5 million, from Customs's allotment of "trafficker funds."† Westrate told him that the idea was under consideration.

---

* William Rosenblatt, assistant to the commissioner of Customs for enforcement.
† Monies seized from narcotics traffickers that can be converted to use by federal enforcement agencies. One of the many ways to circumvent budget or funding problems.

We sat there listening as Rosenblatt tried to push Westrate into making a decision, telling him that he had been sufficiently convinced and could see no reason for delaying. For several minutes the two men explored how the operation might be funded, but Westrate refused to commit himself.

The move, nevertheless, had been a good one. DEA and Customs would rather trust the Bolivians than each other. Now DEA was on alert; they couldn't kill Trifecta without worrying about Customs's reaction. DEA might end up not looking too good in the media—the only battleground they really worried about.

The next problem was Román's deadline. After the Panama meetings the Bolivians expected me to contact them within a week to visit their landing fields and laboratories. A real drug dealer about to enter into a transaction as big as ours would not delay. An American agent cannot enter a foreign country in an undercover capacity without notifying that country's authorities. To do so is a violation of most international accords. It is something I and other DEA undercover agents have done in the past; however, the risks usually far outweigh any benefits. Thus it was decided that Wheeler and a private contractor—a trained civilian informant/pilot (to be furnished by DEA) would travel as my employees.

The chance to actually see the massive jungle cocaine laboratories and landing strips that Román had spoken of was an opportunity one would expect the Drug Enforcement Administration to take advantage of, yet it was not until mid-December—when we had run out of excuses to the Bolivians and Mexicans, and had made dozens of nagging phone calls to headquarters—that they finally supplied us with an undercover pilot.

The pilot, Jake Sales, had come highly recommended by Mike Powers, a Tampa, Florida, group supervisor whom I had known, worked with, and respected for many years. Mike told me that Sales had experience flying for both the CIA and DEA on air missions in both South America and the Far East and that his words could be as trusted as those of an agent. That was more than enough for me.

Sales and Wheeler would go to Bolivia as "my eyes" to verify Román's assertions.

Up to that point Urquijo and Wheeler, from the undercover house in La Jolla, had been in constant radio and telephone contact with the Bolivians and the Mexicans, convincing them that my delay in coming was due to the extremely cautious nature of my organization. We did not know it then, but this psychological groundwork would later help rescue Trifecta from almost certain doom.

On the tenth of December I flew out to San Diego to rehearse Sales and Wheeler in their roles as part of my mythical organization. Their solid performances not only meant the success of the case, it meant their lives. Incredibly, DEA had still not made a decision about the buy option. During the two-day rehearsal I learned from Customs supervisor Arnie Gerardo (an ex-FBI agent, newly assigned to Customs and the investigation) that Customs had grown so "disgusted with DEA's inability to make a decision" that they had withdrawn their offer of half the buy money.

Fast Albert Scuzzo informed me that he had been told by headquarters that the decision whether or not to make the buy was to be made on the basis of what Sales and Wheeler actually saw in Bolivia. "If it's what Román said it is, they'll go for it," he droned. On that basis, at a meeting with U.S. Customs officials in San Diego, December eleventh, I convinced them to keep their money offer open a while longer.

The tentative plan for Operation Trifecta was now to be accomplished in four movements:

> Phase one: As soon as Sales and Wheeler had visited the Bolivian cocaine labs they would return to Miami, where they would report to "Luis." If I was happy with what they saw I would dispatch them, in one of "my planes," to Curaçao, where they would await the arrival, from Bolivia, of one of the Corporation's pilots. The pilot would then guide them to a clandestine landing strip in the jungles of Bolivia, where they would pick up my first thousand kilos of cocaine.
>
> Phase two: I would then fly to Panama with five million dollars, which would be paid to Remberto, or whomever else the Bolivians instructed me to pay, the moment I received word that my planeload

of cocaine was safely in the air. This would be accomplished through coded radio contact.

Phase three: George Urquijo, who would remain in the undercover house, would call the Mexicans to San Diego to get their "commission."

Phase four: If DEA decided against the buy, the case would end at that point with the arrests of whoever showed up in Panama and San Diego to collect.

The fact that both the Bolivian and the Mexicans might send low-level employees or innocent couriers to pick up the money, making the case a total failure, did not seem to bother anyone.

I asked Scuzzo to contact headquarters and ask for permission for me to use two agents assigned to my New York City group, Luis Pizarro and Gene Blahato, to pose as members of my criminal organization during the operation in Panama. "I'll need them to protect the money," I lied. *What I really wanted were witnesses, and agents I could count on to protect my back.*

On December thirteenth I flew back to New York, the Vietnam of narcotics enforcement, to rejoin my group, and Wheeler and the pilot left for Bolivia. I told Pizarro and Blahato to get their things in order, we would be going to Panama in a few days.

On December fourteenth, at twelve noon, I received a call from Scuzzo, who told me, in his incessant code-sprinkled drawl, that Wheeler had lost his money and his airline tickets in Bolivia, but that "our man [Sales] had some extra change" and was going to help him out. Wheeler's story was that someone had gotten into his bag while it lay at his feet in a Bolivian airport, and had only taken his money and airline tickets. Scuzzo had more more good news. "Headquarters has some new hoops for us to jump through," he said. "They are trying to force us to flash the money in a bank."

The Bolivians, in a recent telephone conversation with Wheeler and George, had said, "Tell Luis, no banks." The suits were well aware of it.

"They're going to kill the case," I said. "You've got to tell headquarters we have to flash the money in a villa, or some kind of rented house or something." Scuzzo said he would convey the message; better him than me. I did not want the suits to perceive me as a threat. Up to that point I had been successful in getting others, like Customs, to apply the pressure. I suggested that Scuzzo also call Fred Duncan in Panama and ask for his help in renting a villa or getting us a safe place where, if necessary, we could show the Bolivians our money. I was really curious as to how DEA's top agent in Panama would act, considering his strange behavior in November. If he was going to be an enemy, it would be better to know *before* we left for Panama with five million dollars.

Later that day I called San Diego to find out what progress they had made. "You know," said Hoopel in a hushed conspiratorial voice, and more emotion than usual, "Customs actually offered to put up *all* the buy money."

"You're shitting me." I was shocked.

"Five million dollars . . . and headquarters turned them down."

"What? Did they give a reason?"

"Nope."

I hung up the phone, happy that I had a raid to go on that night. The action would take my mind off Trifecta.

At ten P.M., after a car chase under the East River Drive, I arrested a heroin dealer named Mike Crespo and his Chinese connection.

On December fifteenth, at twelve noon, Scuzzo called. "I've been kind of arguing . . . I guess, with headquarters," he said dully. They were now requesting that Scuzzo use some sort of "wire transfer" of money to Panama that Scuzzo did not fully understand. He rambled on for a few minutes in his curious code before I realized that we both had no idea what he was talking about. It was no wonder headquarters was happy with him running the case.

"You have any luck with Panama?" I asked, both curious and hoping that a change of topic would make the conversation more intelligible.

"I can't get this guy Duncan to do anything. I didn't want to argue with the guy, so I just called the cocaine desk and told them . . . 'Let's talk about reality.' We're talking about being big-time fucking operators and merging with the FBI . . . and we can't even go out and rent a house for a week. . . . The fucking people know that the Marriott is the U.S. government hotel, and yet they [DEA headquarters] are forcing us to go back in there and use it. . . ."

He had to be mistaken. Not even the suits would make a move that blatant and that dangerous to agents' lives.

At nine P.M. the phone beside my bed rang. I picked it up and found myself on a long-distance conference call with Hoopel and Ross. Hoopel's voice was so animated that for a moment I didn't recognize it. Wheeler had called in from Bolivia and said that what they had seen "was incredible"; that it was "everything Román said, and more." He reported having seen seventeen landing fields with at least five tons of cocaine at each. There was a total of 105,000 kilos of cocaine—more than twice the amount of cocaine DEA had seized in all its years of existence.

But there was a problem. Wheeler and Sales had seen too much. There was a possibility that Wheeler would be held in Bolivia as a hostage until the transaction was completed.

"What about the buy, now?" I snapped. If the buy wasn't made now, it might cost the man's life.

"They are still discussing it," said Hoopel.

I was furious but unable to show it. This stammering, frightened man was the case agent of the biggest, most far-reaching case in drug-enforcement history. "Lay it on headquarters," I said, afraid of alienating him. If I lost him, I had nothing. "They have hamstrung us every step of the way. Let *them* make the decision!"

"Uh . . . the pilot [Sales] is coming out [of Bolivia] the seventeenth, maybe we should play along with their scenario . . . and at least hold them off until then. The pilot will give us a lot of information. . . . If we have to go in there and get him out . . . you know what I'm saying?"

I kept silent.

"Maybe we are better off playing along with this scenario, and get the pilot out of there for intelligence purposes, because Wheeler mentioned . . . he said the pilot can retrace the route to everyplace they had been. . . ."

I flipped. "He said that? He said that on the telephone?"

"Er . . . yes. . . ."

"What a schmuck! What a dumb thing to say over the phone." The Bolivians were certain to be monitoring telephone conversations.

"They said a lot of things over the phone," said Ross.

I was furious. "If Bolivians are listening on the phone, they'll know he is talking like a DEA agent."

"Er . . . they're not," stammered Hoopel.

"Are you sure?" I asked. The idea of the most powerful drug-dealing organization on earth giving two American informers a glimpse of their innards without protecting themselves was ridiculous.

"They are in a hotel room," said the man called Helmet Head.

I wanted to cry. All I could do was laugh. I remembered Román in Panama telling me what floor our agents were registered on in the Marriott. How clever the suits had been. How incredibly clever.

"Don't you think the Bolivians have control of the hotel?"

"No," said Hoopel.

My mind reeled with the hopelessness of the situation.

"Er . . . maybe we should get the pilot out and debrief him on the situation," babbled Hoopel. "Then we can decide whether to make the buy or not."

"Hoopel," I said, "I think we should lay this right on the suits. Let one of them make the decision, finally."

"Uh-huh," said Hoopel.

"This is not our decision to make."

"Uh-huh."

"You're dealing with people's lives. In my opinion, I think we should go ahead and buy it."

"Uh-huh."

"That's my opinion."

"Uh-huh."

"You've got an organization with seventeen landing fields, five tons [of cocaine] seen at each. A sophisticated operation like that and all we want to do is take off [seize] one ton without trying to get deeper into the organization? It doesn't make sense!"

"Um-hm."

I suddenly felt despair about what I was trying to do. I wanted to inject the rage I felt into the mild-mannered, almost catatonic Hoopel, who, through no fault of his own, was sitting at the controls of a jumbo jet of a case that headquarters wanted to see go down in flames. I wanted *him* to attack the suits for me because—and it was a hard truth for me to admit—I was afraid. I already knew how dangerous they could be when cornered.

"Is that a good point to bring up, that he's in too deep and they might want to kill him?" asked Hoopel. I started to feel sorry for him and angry at myself.

"Yes," I said, "that's part of the rationale for making the buy. But look, we can't make this goddamned decision. These people [DEA headquarters] have hamstrung us, they've put us into corners and boxes, they don't make a decision. . . . At this point I think it is up to them. You have to make it clear to them that guys' lives are on the line."

"Yeah," said a somewhat more resolved Hoopel.

"And force *them* to make a decision!"

"Right!"

"There's no case worth this poor guy's life," I said.

Feeling tired and desperate, I discussed alternative plans of getting Wheeler safely out of Bolivia, with them. "We ought to consider calling the whole thing off," I said, mentally conceding victory to the suits. "It has to be put to headquarters that we either call the whole thing off or buy the stuff."

"Uh-huh," said Hoopel.

"We've got to be real careful backing out of the deal," said Ross. "They [the Bolivians] already don't trust us since Wheeler mentioned doing it in banks."

You could thank the suits for that one, I thought, and Wheeler, Mr. "high level" drug dealer, for repeating the idiotic plan. Ross was right. If I suddenly backed out of the deal it might cost Wheeler his life. There was nothing we could do. The Bolivians were allowing Sales to leave, so I had to assume that things were still reasonably cool. We still had some time, but not much.

"If I were the case agent," I told Hoopel, "I would call Mr.

Westrate himself. If necessary, call him at home. This is way out of
our hands."

Hoopel said he would report everything to Scuzzo.

The suits had to be enjoying this one.

On the morning of December sixteenth, unable to sleep all
night, I decided to call San Diego and find out what had been done.
Scuzzo put me on a conference call with Hubert Hoopel who said
that Urquijo had received a couple of phone calls at the undercover
house, from Wheeler, and that apparently the Bolivians were very
cool. Jake Sales was trying to get reservations for Miami, to arrive
on the seventeenth or eighteenth.

"Wheeler must feel comfortable or something, talking to these
people," said Fast Albert. "He sounded very up today. . . . He's
concerned with the way things are going to go in Panama. He said
something to the effect that we can't approach these people the way
we did last time in Panama. . . . He said, 'Things aren't going to be
that way.' He said something is going to be 'different . . . really
different.' "

"Well, somebody has to tell us what the hell he's talking
about," I said, wondering why Wheeler hadn't. He certainly had not
censored anything else he said over the phone. The man always had
some private angle going. I began to wonder whether the whole
thing about him being held hostage was more of his bullshit.

"He said," continued Hoopel, " 'we all have to go back to Panama to renegotiate the deal . . . and then I can go back to Bolivia
and put this deal together.' "

Neither Scuzzo nor Hoopel had any idea what Wheeler was
talking about. And with no one there to control him, his mouth was
as dangerous as a bottle of nitroglycerin on a motorcycle.

"Well, if we have to go to Panama," said Hoopel, "like Albert
was saying, we'll just arrest everyone on sight."

It was Scuzzo's turn: "I think what's happening is, all these
deals always end up havin' hitches in 'em. . . . They always think
. . . you know, they have the appearance like they're gonna be a
slam dunk and then they start changin' up. . . . You know what
I'm sayin'?"

Once again, I had no idea.

He went on: "I think right now they . . . uh, they feel more secure having a hostage-type situation . . . and if that doesn't work for whatever, they're gonna likely expect a 'front.'* So, so, what I'm thinking . . . an alternate course of action—"

"We front a million?" I said, unable to stand the slow drone of his voice and at the same time immediately wanting to bite my tongue off. Any utterance while Fast Albert spoke seemed to derail him and send him rambling off on coded verbal tangents.

"I uh, uh, don't know what we'll do." *Honesty at last.* "I mean, I'm talking about the bottom-line, last-resort kind of thing, so that we can get some success out of this thing. . . . In other words dope. . . ."

Schmuck! The suits said they want people—not dope.

"Yeah," I heard myself say.

"It's basically . . . uh . . . take the CI† that we're expecting out soon . . . and have him go down and meet with some other people . . . and have him identify the locations they visited . . . and have him get hit . . . and you know, bust a few of the people . . . that's as a last-resort kind of thing."

He was back into his code again, which really worried me. Then he suddenly veered off in another direction and began talking about arranging for planes and "flash rolls" in Miami, for either a meeting or a buy-bust operation in Panama. And then he totally confused me by telling me to cancel my flight reservations.

I tried to get Scuzzo back onto the subject of the buy, reminding him that headquarters had said we would go ahead with the buy option if Sales and Wheeler saw "something significant." Even my reference to a buy frightened him. He immediately changed the subject and rambled off in another direction.

"Here's what we're doing," he said. "You know. . . . What we're gonna do . . . and I'm sure they're gonna do it. . . . You know they are really delighted with our first mentionings of intelligence. . . . You know they're gonna meet us in Miami." *He'd forgotten he had just told me to cancel.* "Gospadarik [Ron Gospadarik,

---

* Money paid out "front."
† Confidential informant. In this instance, Jake Sales.

staff coordinator, cocaine desk] is gonna be there. There are gonna be some people there. . . . I think that our hand is getting stronger . . . we can make it like a military-type operation. Only, we can't do it over the weekend. In fact, maybe we ought to put it off until after the first of the year. I know a lot of people will be jumping for joy with that decision."

Scuzzo finished the conversation by once again telling me to cancel flight reservations.

After hanging up the phone, for the first time in my career I wanted to surrender. I could handle a sleazy runaway informant like Wheeler and the constant feuds between Customs and DEA. I was a veteran of years of battling the suits, the bureaucracy, and special interests. Incompetent DEA supervisors—especially those serving overseas, where you won your assignments based more on *who* than *what* you knew—were a given. But Trifecta had brought me all of the above in one big ugly package, and it was becoming too much.

At one P.M., during a raid on a Bronx heroin mill, special agents Luis Pizarro, Willy Gray, and I were attacked by a German shepherd guard dog. The dog narrowly missed taking a chunk out of Pizarro's groin. Willy and I shot it. The incident depressed me. I used to be a sentry-dog handler in the military. The dog was only doing what it was trained for; there wasn't an ounce of treachery in him—it's a shame people aren't like that.

At three P.M., while I was still in the middle of the myriad of reports that have to be filed every time an agent fires his gun, Hubert Hoopel called to tell me that the operation was "on." "It has been decided," he said with a sudden uncharacteristic resolve, "that we are going forward with this thing, until it is done! No putting off nothing. Whether it goes through Christmas, or whatever."

I was to join with the rest of the Operation Trifecta team in Miami the next day. Hoopel was not sure of exactly what our plan was. All he would say was "We are going to get everything [the five million dollars] on site, in Panama, and we'll see what happens."

"Where are we going to be staying in Panama?" I asked, holding my breath.

"They [the Panama DEA office] have some kind of penthouse set up for you."

"In other words it won't be a hotel," I said.

"No," said Hoopel.

I breathed a sigh of relief.

At about four P.M. Hoopel called back to tell me that everything was very cool in Bolivia. "They're letting Wheeler go," he said. "He's going to meet us in Panama."

Once again I hung up the phone bewildered. All I knew was that I was going to be part of a DEA enforcement team going to Panama with five million dollars, under the command of Fast Albert Scuzzo. The only thing I was sure of was that, at that moment, no one had any idea what we were going to do when we got there.

FOUR

MIAMI

The Frying Pan

On the morning of December seventeenth I made my final flight reservations to arrive that same evening in Miami, and to continue on to Panama on the nineteenth. The forty-eight hours in Miami was for a final undercover planning session. The dynamic duo of Scuzzo and Hoopel was already on their way there, from San Diego, to pick up five million dollars in cash for the operation in Panama. DEA had still not made a decision; I didn't know if I was going to spend the money or flash it. All I knew for certain was that the Bolivians were expecting me in Panama on the nineteenth with five million bucks to buy their drugs.

Jake the pilot, just arrived from Bolivia, would be at the Miami meeting, along with a couple of suits from headquarters who were to give us our ultimate marching orders. The final decision—whether to buy the drugs or not—was to be based on what Jake and Wheeler had *actually* seen. Up to that point all we had were Wheeler's cryptic telephone reports, and truth and accuracy were not among the informer's most notable virtues. Jake, on the other hand, had flown many missions into South America for DEA and had a solid reputation. The suits had said they would take his word for what was seen.

That morning I had also been informed that Lydia Soto would be part of the undercover team, and that she had already arrived in New York ready to join with me for the trip to Miami. Customs wanted one of their undercover agents present in Panama, and DEA had aquiesced. A deep-cover assignment in a drug-trafficker-controlled country like Panama is not a situation of "the more the merrier," but the decision had already been made. I had no idea what I was going to do with her, but then again, I had no idea what *I* was going to do when I got there either. What I *did* know was that I wanted some people there whom—when push came to shove—I could count on to back me up.

I called special agents Gene Blahato and Luis Pizarro into my office. Both men, though relatively new agents, had been through a lot of hairy and violent experiences with me in a short period of time. *It doesn't take long in New York.* Gene was a quick-thinking, aggressive undercover agent with three years street experience. Luis, a native Spanish speaker of Puerto Rican descent and a onetime collegiate boxer, had less than a year on the street but had proven his mettle in dozens of violent street incidents. They were two men whom I felt I could count on. I had already mentioned to them the possibility of accompanying me to Panama, but now it was real.

"Gentlemen, you're about to learn what deep cover and *real* international narcotics enforcement is all about."

"You're kidding," said Gene.

"I wish I was. I just want you guys to take notes on everything you see, hear, and do . . . everything. You're my witnesses. I think you are going to be quite amazed."

That would turn out to be my understatement for the year.

Gene and Luis made reservations to leave New York on the nineteenth. Their flight would make a stop in Miami, where I would join them so that we would arrive in Panama together.

■

Lydia Soto and I arrived in Miami late that evening to find that Hoopel and Scuzzo had ended up in the wrong hotel. They were supposed to be at the Miami Airport Marriott, but had instead wound up in the Dadeland Marriott, about twenty miles away. When I finally got Hoopel on the phone he blamed it on the cabdriver. If they couldn't communicate with a Miami cabdriver, I wondered, what the hell were they going to do in Panama?

This was deep cover in the land of Noriega and these men were supposed to be my lifeline.

On December eighteenth, at about ten A.M., I arrived at Scuzzo's room in the Dadeland Marriott. Soto had stayed behind to take care of some personal business, but the rest of the cast had already assembled. Hoopel, Scuzzo, and another San Diego agent named Bill Brown—who, according to Scuzzo, was joining the expedition because he had "a lot of South American experience" and could speak Spanish—were deeply engrossed in planning the movement of the five million dollars from a Miami bank vault to an undercover Customs jet that would fly them to Panama.

The two suits from headquarters—Bob McCall representing Operation Snowcap and Ron Gospadarik from the cocaine desk were the only two men actually wearing dark business suits in the ninety-degree Miami heat—had obviously not come to stay. They, in fact, could not have been less interested in what was going on in the room. Gospadarik, at the moment, was monopolizing the one room-phone in an attempt to get the earliest possible reservations, that day, back to Washington, D.C., for the DEA Christmas party.

Scuzzo, waiting for Gospadarik to finish with the phone, complained that DEA in Miami was refusing to help move the money. He was upset and, despite the early hour, already drinking and rambling on in incomprehensible monologues.

Jake the pilot was also there, along with another CIA pilot whom I'll call Smilin' Jack. The two were to fly the mission to Bolivia to pick up the thousand kilos of cocaine—*if we ever got that far.* Smilin' Jack wore a green one-piece flight suit and—I swear to God—a silk scarf tied around his neck, an Australian bush hat, and an exotically curled pipe stuck in his mouth. He kept rushing busily in and out of the room to use an outside telephone. Arnie Gerardo, the San Diego Customs supervisor, winked at me from across the room, looking like an oasis of normalcy. A decision had apparently already been made. I pulled Jack aside.

"What did you see?"

"I still don't believe what I saw," he told me excitedly. "I saw so much that, for a while, I didn't think they were going to let me out of there. And that Wheeler, running his goddamned mouth—it's a miracle he didn't get us killed."

"What exactly did you see?"

"All told, we saw seven landing fields."

"How much coke, would you estimate?"

Jake was thoughtful, "I would say about five thousand kilos at each, maybe more. Mike, I'll tell you what," he continued. "You can ask Mike [Powers]—I've been flying these missions into Colombia for years; this is the mother lode. For years they've been talking about finding the guys who supply the Medellín cartel—well, this is them."

"Did you tell them about it?" I nodded at the suits. It wasn't the exaggerated hundred thousand kilos of cocaine that Wheeler had reported, but thirty-five thousand was certainly good enough. If the Bolivians were *showing* that much, they had to have a hundred times that amount hidden in those jungles.

Jake shook his head. "I don't understand these guys, Mike."

"Did they say *anything* about making a buy?" I asked anxiously.

He shook his head negatively. "I hate to tell you this, but I think they had their minds made up before they got here. I just don't understand DEA. The Bolivians had a military-industrial setup that was right out of a West Point textbook. It's unbelievable." Jake went on to describe a massive, sophisticated jungle cocaine-manufacturing complex with heavy armaments, radio communications, and landing fields that could accommodate a modern jumbo jet. "It is without a doubt," he said, "the General Motors of cocaine."

Arnie Gerardo had moved alongside and was listening. "My agency [Customs] withdrew its offer," he said, speaking softly, eyeing the suits, who were just out of earshot and still intensely engrossed in the getting their flight reservations. "My people just got tired of DEA not making any decisions. There's no arguing with them," he told me with finality.

He need not have bothered.

Gospadarik finally finished with the telephone (which was immediately grabbed up by a panicky Scuzzo). He had apparently been successful in getting reservations; he and his companion were now in a rush to get back to Washington. The Christmas party was scheduled for that evening, and as everyone in DEA headquarters knew, if you wanted a promotion or a choice assignment or post of duty, the Christmas party was where the best connections were made.

"What about the buy?" I asked. Gospadarik's face foreshadowed his answer. The room was silent except for Scuzzo's droning monotone complaining to someone in the Miami DEA office. Everyone else already seemed to know the answer.

"The buy is out," he said flatly. "Mr. Westrate wants a buy-bust operation."

"I don't believe it. What about all that shit about basing the decision on what the pilot sees?"

"That is what has been decided," snapped the pale, angular man. The smile on his face told me that he was just dying for me to make an issue out of it.

This meant that the pilots would fly to Bolivia to pick up the thousand kilos of cocaine and that the whole operation would end in Panama with the arrests of anyone who showed up to collect for it. George Urquijo, who was staying in telephone contact with Pablo Girón, the Mexican *federale,* from his post at the undercover house in La Jolla, would con him into returning to California for the "finder's fee" I had promised him, where he, too, would be arrested. Operation Trifecta would have ended—effectively destroyed—and no one would be the wiser. We would lose the opportunity to penetrate, identify, and destroy the organization that supplied as much as ninety percent of the cocaine on our streets, along with the chance to uncover their highly placed Mexican government partners. And the suits, as they have always done, would turn the outrageous fraud into a media success.

Customs Commissioner von Raab would have the well-publicized arrest of a "high-level" corrupt Mexican official; and DEA would tell the public—via the ratings-hungry media—of the heroic derring-do of the undercover agents in making the thousand-kilo seizure and arrests in Panama. *The suits, of course, would graciously*

and modestly accept all credit for the cleverness of the sting. The
DEA administrator and the commissioner of Customs would hold a
joint press conference and congratulate each other in a show of
unity. The suits would then go to the politicians and request even
more funding for *more* operations like Snowcap—and get it.

I did not know Gospadarik, but it seemed that he had been well
prepared to "handle" me. Before I had a chance to react he slammed
home the kicker: headquarters had ordered that the operation was to
be carried out at the *"Panama Marriott hotel."*

The satisfied looks on both suits' faces told me that they knew
exactly what they were doing. The ball was in my court. The Bolivians were expecting me in Panama on the nineteenth. If I refused to
go—as I am sure DEA expected me to—the case was over, and they
hadn't risked anything. If I did go, there was little or no chance of
its being a success.

*As the man in Washington had said: Operation Snowcap might
not be the best game in town, but it was certainly going to remain the
only one.*

My twenty-five years of this sleazy, double-dealing life—barely
surviving with my health, life, family, and job intact—screamed at
me to keep my mouth shut. Somehow I was going to disappoint
these bastards. The war on drugs was no joke to me—it had been my
whole life. I swallowed a lot of bile, kept silent, and returned to my
hotel to prepare to leave for Panama.

■

Alone in my hotel room I could not stop pacing, punching at
the air, and cursing to myself. My mind was reeling with pent-up
rage and frustration. I've always been a fighter, but who was there to
attack? *Who the hell was the enemy, anyway?* I turned on a radio and
forced myself to sit down and write out every word of the earlier
conversations—who said what to whom, when, how each was
dressed—every detail that I could remember. I had to keep busy or I
would explode. My hands would not stop trembling. I realized I was

keeping the kinds of undercover notes that I would if I had just left a meeting with drug dealers instead of government agents.

Why was this happening to me, again? I was suddenly conscious of the radio playing a rock song that had been popular seven and a half years before, when I had come to Miami from Argentina to finish the Roberto Suárez case. The memories came rushing back.

"I rule Bolivia more than its president," Roberto Suárez had told me in the spring of 1980. I was then living in Buenos Aires, Argentina, posing as a mixed Italian–Puerto Rican representative of the American Mafia. Suárez wanted me to guarantee that my organization would buy a thousand kilos of cocaine a month. It was the end of a decade when the largest cocaine seizure on record was two hundred kilos at a border-patrol checkpoint; when our government believed that the drug-trafficking problem was limited to organized crime; and when Peter Bourne, President Jimmy Carter's advisor on drugs said, "Cocaine is probably the most benign of illicit drugs currently in widespread use."

"You're full of shit," said one of the top suits in headquarters when I telephoned headquarters for authorization to set up a sting operation. "His name's not even in the computer. What are you trying to scam, Levine?"

Six months later, when Mike Wallace, on national television, was calling Suárez the "biggest drug dealer alive," we would learn that—while we did not know who Suárez was—he had copies of the official State Department files of every DEA agent stationed in Bolivia, complete with photos and family medical histories.

I pushed like a wild man to do the case, bombarding headquarters with phone calls and cables. DEA fought against it. At the time I could not understand why. I finally got a very grudging authorization to go ahead and set up the operation, along with a warning from a top-level suit who for reasons of his own began to support the case. "A lot of people in headquarters want to see this fail," he said. "Just watch your butt." The words just went in and out of my ears like wind of the Pampas. I was setting up the biggest undercover sting in history. Why would anyone in my government want it to fail?

The plan was for an undercover plane to travel to Suárez's jungle landing strip and load up with the first shipment—a thousand pounds of cocaine. When it was safely in the air I was to pay nine million dollars to Suárez's men in Miami.

In spite of questionable decisions made by the DEA suits that could have destroyed the case—such as forcing the undercover agents to use an airplane that had been used only months earlier in Bolivia as an *"official" DEA plane,* to name just one of many—the case was brought to a successful conclusion on May 13, 1980, when our undercover plane took off from an airstrip in the jungles of Bolivia laden with almost nine hundred pounds of cocaine. The largest undercover drug buy in history had been completed.

That afternoon, in a Miami bank vault, I paid Alfredo "Cutuche" Gutiérrez and José Roberto Gasser, two of the biggest drug dealers in history, nine million dollars, after which they were both arrested. "The biggest law-enforcement sting in history," the media called it. Before Operation Trifecta it was the biggest fraud.

José Roberto Gasser—the son of Erwin Gasser, powerful Bolivian industrialist and right-winger—was almost immediately released from custody by the Miami U.S. attorney's office, *without* the case being presented to a grand jury. *I was beside myself; there was more than enough evidence to indict him.*

A short time later—*precisely as my South American informants predicted*—Miami federal judge Alcee Hastings reduced Alfredo Gutiérrez's bail from three to one million dollars.* Gutiérrez was allowed to post his bail and walk out of jail. In spite of my furious phone calls from Argentina begging DEA headquarters and the Miami office to put him under surveillance, nothing was done. Within hours he was on a plane back to Bolivia. The biggest drug sting in history was left without any defendants.

From their stronghold in Bolivia, Suárez and Gutiérrez put a two-hundred-thousand-dollar price tag on my head. They called me *"El judío trigueño de Argentina"*—the dark Jew from Argentina.

My sting operation never could have happened without help from an antidrug faction within the Bolivian government—a faction

---

* Judge Hastings was later, in an unrelated case, indicted for accepting bribes and was found "not guilty" after trial. On 10/20/89 Judge Hastings was impeached by the United States Senate and removed from office.

that Suárez's organization had to obliterate. If the cocaine economy of Bolivia was to prosper, the Suárez organization had to have complete control of the government. Within weeks of the Miami arrests, with the financing of the Suárez organization and Erwin Gasser, and the support of our CIA, a bloody coup was begun. It was the 189th revolution in Bolivia's history and one of the bloodiest ever. Our State Department called it "the cocaine revolution." Thousands of innocent people were tortured and killed. It ended with the Bolivian government coming under the complete control of the Suárez organization. Bolivia soon became the principal supplier of cocaine base to the then fledgling Colombian cartels, thereby making themselves the main suppliers of cocaine to the United States. And it could not have been done without the tacit help of DEA and the active, covert help of the CIA.*

I felt responsible for every life lost—and still do. From my post in Argentina I orchestrated another deep-cover probe into Bolivia, resulting in the arrest of Hugo Hurtado-Candia and information that indicated many key members of the new Bolivian government should be indicted for violations of our drug laws (including José Roberto Gasser). Instead of DEA and the Department of Justice (already in bed with the likes of Manuel Noriega) pursuing the investigation and indictments, evidence began to "mysteriously" disappear and pressure was exerted against me to "back off." I was ordered to open my office files to the CIA.

"Why don't you take it easy," one of the suits cautioned in a phone call to my office in the American embassy. "You're in Argentina, no one expects much from you down there; it's not a source country. Why don't you travel around awhile and visit the countryside."

Instead of taking it easy I turned to the media. I wrote a letter (return receipt requested) to a pair of investigative reporters who had written one of the typical DEA-manipulated stories about what had happened in Bolivia for *Newsweek* magazine. In the letter I listed all the "mysterious" events of the Suárez case that indicated

---

* A State Department diplomat in La Paz, Bolivia, said that it was the first time in history that an entire government had been bought by drug dealers.

that our government was not only protecting the biggest drug traffickers in the world, but had helped them to take over a government, and offered my cooperation in any investigation. I never received a reply. Instead, within weeks, I was put under investigation by DEA's feared Internal Security Division.

The investigation, which lasted over a year, invaded every corner of my professional and private life. I was accused of, and investigated for:

—fraudulent travel vouchers
—black marketing
—having sexual relations with a female undercover agent
—personal phone calls from the American embassy
—playing rock music too loud on my radio in the American embassy
—not knowing the location of the CIA office, in the American embassy
—excessive absences from my post of duty
—failure to keep proper records of my undercover expenses

I, along with everyone I worked with, was frequently called in for interrogations. I was followed, my phones tapped, and undercover Internal Security agents were sent to Argentina to contact my neighbors in an effort to find something—anything—derogatory. Ironically, more taxpayer's dollars were spent investigating me than were spent on the entire undercover phase of the Suárez operation.

I was soon transferred from Argentina to DEA headquarters, where I was kept on a tight rein. While the Internal Security investigation of me continued, they used me in one of the most dangerous deep-cover assignments of my career, called "Operation Hun." I was suddenly more concerned with my own survival than with justice. I stood by in silence as the media eagerly repeated every lie the suits told them about the courageous uphill drug war they were fighting. I was eventually "convicted" of not keeping the proper records for my undercover expenses during the Suárez case, and suspended for five days.

Lawyers advised me to sue; that it was one of the most obvious cases of "witch-hunting" they had ever seen. But I had all the fight

taken out of me. The suits won; they had frightened me into silence
—*something for which I have never been able to forgive myself.*

As I lay staring at the ceiling of my Miami hotel room, I realized that it was happening again. The suits were doing all they could
to frighten me out of the operation. *This time,* if I let them, there
would be no way that I could live with myself. My life, my career,
would have been meaningless—a fraud; as much a fraud as they
were. *This time,* I was going to treat them as if they were just as
much an enemy as any drug dealer.

From that point on I was undercover *all* the time.

I was not sure what action I would take once in Panama. It
seemed that the case was headed for certain failure. The only clear
plan I had in mind was to make sure that I documented everything
that happened. The suits might destroy Trifecta, but I was going to
make sure there were witnesses to the crime.

On December nineteenth I spent most of the morning getting a
false Florida state driver's license in the name Luis García-López, to
match my undercover passport. I returned to my hotel room at
about one-thirty P.M. and began to pack for the five P.M. flight to
Panama.

The phone rang. It was Lydia. Hoopel and Scuzzo were in a
panic and had been trying to reach me all morning. The dynamic
duo had neglected to get the "official" headquarters authorization
for the operation.* "Not only that," she said, "but they can't get
Miami DEA to help them move the money, and they want *us* to help
them."

"I'll handle it," I said. "You just head out to the airport. I'll
meet you there."

I got Hoopel on the phone.

"We've been trying to get somebody on the phone from headquarters all morning," said the man called Helmet Head. "The trouble is, they had the Christmas party and everyone was out partying
all night. And we have another problem. Did Lydia tell you?"

---

* An overseas operation of that magnitude requires the "personal" approval of either the
administrator himself or one of his deputies.

With my jaws clenched I said, "Look, it's kind of ridiculous that we take a chance on missing our flight to help you move money. Miami has a couple of hundred agents. If you can't get two to help you, shame on you.

"And about the authorization: Why don't you call Lawn or Westrate at home and leave a message that they forgot to authorize the biggest case they ever had."

Hoopel was silent. I hung up and began to pack.

At four P.M. I arrived at Miami International Airport. I immediately telephoned Homestead Air Force Base, where Hoopel, Scuzzo, and Brown were supposed to arrive with the money. To my surprise they were there. "We got the money here by ourselves," said Hoopel. "Can you imagine, we couldn't get one Miami agent to help us."

"Yes," I said. "I can imagine. What about the headquarters authorization?"

"I finally got Gospadarik. He got a verbal okay from Westrate, but he made a big point of it: We're *only* authorized to do the deal at the Marriott."

"See you in Panama," I said, and hung up.

At five P.M. Lydia Soto and I boarded Pan American flight 977 bound for Panama City, Panama. Gene and Luis were already on board. I was relieved to see them.

"Don't forget what I said about taking notes," I said, before getting into my rear seat and immediately falling into a fitful, dreamless sleep.

FIVE

PANAMA

The Fire

I awoke with a start as we bumped down for a hard landing in Panama. It was already dark outside. As the plane taxied to a halt at the terminal, the tropical heat began seeping into the cabin and steaming the windows.

As the four of us moved through the passageway leading toward the terminal, I said, "From this point on it's got to be real, guys. Anything can happen, and I mean anything. You are my employees." Pizarro and Blahato smiled. Reality still had not set in. In about five minutes it would.

From the moment we descended a long escalator to the end of two long lines to immigration checkpoints, I could see that we were being watched. As we inched our way on line toward the desk, I picked out at least four plainclothes security men watching us. Their actions were too obvious. I already knew they were going to grab us. I said nothing. There was no sense letting the others react any way but naturally when we got hit.

When my turn came one of the security men moved behind the immigration counter and took my passport. He examined it carefully. It was in the name Luis García-López and showed my place of birth as San Juan, Puerto Rico.

"Would you come with me please, Señor García," he ordered in staccato Spanish.

"Of course," I said, following. Behind me other security men were taking Lydia, Pizarro, and Blahato into custody. They looked at me questioningly. All I could do was shrug my shoulders and smile. "It's like I said, guys, anything can happen."

After they had searched our bags thoroughly and made Xerox copies of all our documents, I asked what the problem was.

"We are the antinarcotics police," said a dark, squat man with wide Indian features, who seemed to be the senior man. He had not taken his eyes off me, from the moment I got on line. I got the distinct impression that he did not like my face.

The idea of their being suspicious of people smuggling drugs *from* the United States to Panama seemed too ludicrous to mention. So I said, "Well, we have nothing to hide, so do whatever you have to do."

We were interrogated for over an hour. What business are you in? Why are you here? Where are you going to stay? Et cetera. Our answers were so phony and unprepared that they had to know we were lying, but lies did not seem to worry these men; the only thing that did was whether or not we were American undercover agents.

After the long interrogation they still seemed unsure about something. They conferred in hushed tones, one of them eyeing Lydia hungrily. The senior official said something and a decision was made. Gene Blahato was taken into a back room and strip-searched.

"What the fuck was that all about?" asked Gene later, when we were finally settled into a taxi and speeding through the wild maze of nighttime traffic toward downtown Panama.

"The Bolivians are already here," I said. "I would say they're behind this."

"Holy shit!" said Gene.

"Don't say anything," I cautioned, watching the cabdriver. My guess was that he was a security agent. The Corporation handled more money in cash each month than the total budgets of DEA, the

FBI, and Customs combined. That bought a hell of a lot of security. It was a strange moment for me. I had worked undercover posing as a cabdriver at New York's JFK Airport, picking up drug smugglers and taking them to their contacts. The driver's mannerisms were the same as mine, his eyes going from side-view to rearview mirror, making sure he did not lose the tail, and at the same time listening to our conversation—not an easy job.

By the morning of December twentieth, my forty-eighth birthday, the entire Operation Trifecta team was assembled in the Panama Marriott Hotel. Lydia Soto and I were installed in a top-floor three-room executive suite. Gene and Luis were on the same floor in smaller rooms. Scuzzo, Hoopel, and Brown were on one of the lower floors with the five million dollars. Wheeler had already arrived the day before and was waiting for us.

At seven A.M. I had him meet me for breakfast; I wanted to speak to him before we spoke with Scuzzo and company.

"I don't fucking believe it!" said Wheeler when I told him that we were going to have to do the operation right there in the Marriott. "You know they're liable to fucking kill us?"

"You want to back out?"

"Are *you* going over there with me to tell the Bolivians?" His look was a challenge.

"Of course."

"Shit, I wouldn't miss this for the world."

It was the only moment that I could remember, since meeting the man, that I kind of liked him.

At eight A.M. Wheeler and I went to Scuzzo's room; Brown and Hoopel were already there. From the moment we entered the room Scuzzo began to babble confusedly about the difficulties he had had moving the money and the total lack of cooperation from DEA in Miami and Panama. I noticed a couple of empty beer bottles and an open whiskey bottle and decided that I would not even mention their covering us for our first undercover meeting, scheduled at nine A.M.

The Bolivians were staying at the Las Vegas Apartment Hotel, where we had met the money launderer in November. Once we were inside that place, with all its security, there wasn't much the best of narcotics agents could do to help us if we got into trouble, not to mention this hapless trio. Our only defense was going to be the same thing that had gotten us there—our act.

"Oh, yeah," said Scuzzo as we were about to leave the room. "At this point I'm not even sure we got a plane, or pilots, to fly the fucking mission."

"You gotta be kidding," I said.

"No, I'm not. There's some trouble with headquarters and Smilin' Jack. He says DEA owes him money for his last mission and he ain't flyin' this one till he gets paid. All I know is, as of right now, we do not have a fucking plane."

"I don't believe this," said Wheeler as we hustled toward the elevator.

"Believe it," I said. "Believe it."

"What do they wanna do, get us killed?"

Before leaving the Marriott I told Gene and Luis to make sure they were at Scuzzo's disposal. I knew I didn't have to say, "I want you to observe him." They would not be able to avoid doing that.

At nine A.M. Wheeler and I arrived at the Las Vegas in a taxi. There were a uniformed security guard and three men in civilian clothes who looked right out of the cast of *Scarface*. They were expecting us. We were admitted quickly. As the cramped box of an elevator groaned and creaked slowly to the second floor, Wheeler looked at me and smiled. He looked very pale for a man who had just spent a week in the Bolivian jungles. I could see the whites of his eyes gleaming with fear. My own heart was thumping out a pretty good rhythm. I'm sure I looked just as frightened.

The door to room 116 opened and Jorge Román stood there beaming. He gave me a welcoming hug and admitted me to a small, cramped room with two beds, a table, and a kitchenette. Many years of dealing with the biggest of South American cocaine traffickers had taught me the ironic difference between Hollywood's concept of a drug deal and the real thing. In real life the bigger they are the more anonymously they travel; out-of-the-way places with tight security and no records are par for the course.

A dark, clean-shaven Mexican in his early thirties stood to

greet us as we entered. As he shook my hand, he said his name was Jesús but that we should call him "Chuy" (Chew-ee). His mouth smiled amiably, but his eyes were piercing instruments of examination. I did not need Román to tell me he was a bodyguard, probably one of the legion supplied by Mendez.

Román offered us a choice of breakfast—to be cooked by Chuy —or coffee, juice, or drinks. I accepted coffee. The room was already heating up. There were only two small windows—not big enough to crawl through—which were wide open, and no air-conditioner. The thought that it was about to get even hotter occurred to me.

"We have a problem," I began, deciding to get right to it. "When we arrived last night we were questioned and searched by the antinarcotics police at the airport. I came with two employees and my woman. . . ."

As I told the story I watched Román closely for a reaction— there was none. I thought I saw a faint smile flicker at the corners of Chuy's mouth but could not be sure. I went on to describe, in great detail, our interrogation and the photocopying of our documents. Román still had no reaction. His eyes examined me closely, which was precisely what gave him away.

He was about to do a five-million-dollar drug deal with me; the incident at the airport should have had him wary of the police having me under surveillance at that very moment. He wasn't, and there could only be one reason behind that. It was he who had had the police question and interrogate us. I now had him by the balls.

"So I had to go to the Marriott," I finished.

"You what?" He jumped to his feet as though he'd been hit with a cattle prod. "How could you do this, after everything that happened?"

"That is the address I put on our immigration documents. I am sure the police had us under surveillance. We had to go there. They have copies of all our documents. Not only that, my investors are terrified. They had the money brought to the hotel by others who came in a private jet."

"You mean the money is in the hotel?" Román's eyes were bugged wide. For a moment his squat face looked like Kermit the Frog's. I fought the urge to laugh.

"What was I supposed to do, Jorge? My investors trust me. It was my duty to report what happened. One of them has a very big financial interest in the Marriott company. He insisted that the money be brought there too."

Román was beside himself. He began pacing the floor. "How could you do this, Luis? After everything that happened last time. I told you, anywhere *but* the Marriott. How in God's name could you do this?"

"Please do not be offended, my friend," I said, "but my investors are very suspicious. They think that you might have been behind what happened at the airport."

"You have no idea how I am sticking my neck out to do this transaction," he said, ignoring my statement. There were many members of the Corporation who said that we should not do it. They said the whole deal smells like a DEA trap."

The trap he was referring to was the one I had sprung ten years earlier on Roberto Suárez. The suits had pushed us into doing an almost duplicate operation. And I was well aware of the pressure Román was under from the Corporation. By bringing the two informants to visit their landing fields and cocaine labs, he had exposed the entire operation and made it vulnerable to destruction. *If only we were* really *fighting a drug war.* He had to be under heavy criticism and scrutiny. At that moment there was no one alive to whom the success of our transaction was more important than Jorge Román—a fact that I was going to exploit to the hilt.

"And we have another problem, my friend," I said, deciding to push as hard as I could. "Since the Mexicans could not give us safe passage for this transaction, I had to make arrangements for the merchandise to enter Miami on Christmas day. That is the day that most of our government employees are on holiday."

Román paused to consider this, nodding in appreciation.

"The arrangement has already cost us quite a bit. The Customs people with whom we are dealing said that we *must* enter on that day. If we are late, they will not be responsible. This means that David [Wheeler] must leave for Curaçao no later than tomorrow evening to meet with my plane. And your pilot must also be there."

I remembered Scuzzo's earlier words and said a silent prayer that there was a plane. "If the timing is off, the whole deal is off."

"Everything on our end is ready," said Román. "He was almost frantic. "Our pilot is ready to leave with one phone call. All your merchandise is ready and waiting. We simply cannot do it in the Marriott. If I tell my people they will want to call the whole thing off."

"It is out of my hands, my brother," I said, shrugging my shoulders, praying that our end was as ready as the Bolivians'. "Last night one of the investors said, 'If we can risk sending our plane to Bolivia and our money to Panama, they can risk going to the Marriott for their money.' I could think of nothing to say to refute him." And neither could Román. This was going to be the basis of my stand, which would be repeated a dozen times over the next twenty-four hours.

Román and I went around and around for hours with both the room and the discussion heating up. There had to be some way, he said, of doing the transaction "other than at the Marriott." He had suggested we use the home of his taxi driver, whom he described as "a man of trust."

To illustrate how trustworthy the cabdriver was, he told us the story of another five-million-dollar transaction he had done at the Marriott that had ended with DEA seizing two million dollars. "It was only with the help of the cabdriver that I escaped with the other three million," he said. He described how he and the cabdriver had stayed with the money for two days until Román was able to change it to checks, using his banking contacts. The procedure, he said, had cost him two percentage points.

As I listened to Román, I realized that, in spite of DEA, I had not lost the most important asset I had—his trust. I knew that, somehow, this case was going to be made.

"I am sorry, my brother, but I am sure my investors—after everything we have already been through—will not authorize the use of a cabdriver's home to transfer that amount of money."

Román would not give up. He could understand our fears; but he could not understand my refusal to move to *any* other location. It did not make sense to him, as it well should not have. He came up with suggestions ranging from doing the transaction in bank vaults, to the homes of Panamanian friends, to changing the money to checks—all methods and places he had used in the past.

At one point, in frustration, he showed me a check for sixty thousand dollars drawn on the Iberoamerican Bank of Panama, as an example of his money-laundering operation. I calculated that the man must have done hundreds of millions of dollars in drug trade, in Panama alone. He had to have enormous influence there. Whatever happened with the case, the intelligence we were gathering at the moment was invaluable.

To keep him talking I told him that I would go back to my hotel and convey these other possibilities to my investors, but that I doubted that they would change their minds. "These people are very cautious, Jorge," I said. "It is for good reason we have never been caught."

At about twelve-thirty P.M. there was a lull in the conversation. The four of us, wilted by the tropical heat, sat drenched and exhausted around the table. I decided to test Román. "You know, my friend," I said, putting my hand on his shoulder, "no matter what happens, you are a good man, and I consider myself lucky to have met you. I think it might be better that we call the whole thing off, so that our friendship is preserved. I am sure that, someday, we will do business."

Jorge looked at me for a long moment. His drawn, tired face seemed to come alive in a smile. "Luis, I have said this before. There is no doubt that you are the son of a loan shark. . . . That is why we call you *Tiburón.** Go, go to your hotel, call your people. I will call Bolivia and talk to mine. We are here, now. There must be a way to complete this business."

We agreed to return at three P.M.

As we were about to leave, Wheeler suddenly said, "Why don't you have Pato call me the moment our plane is in the air, and we'll just pay you."

The son of a bitch had taken a giant leap out of character. He

* *"Tiburón,"* Spanish for shark, was the radio code name the Bolivians gave me for the shortwave radio conversations between Bolivia and San Diego.

was referring to Pato Pizarro, the Bolivian reputed to be the head of the Corporation, whom he had been introduced to by Román. I could tell by Román's face that the remark was way out of line. Pizarro had had virtually no conversation with Wheeler. The only reason for the remark that I could deduce was that he was trying to prove to me that he had in fact met the man. It was no secret that I doubted many of his claims, but this was no time for those kinds of games.

I gave Wheeler a wicked look (that did not take much acting) and said, "You take care of your own business!" It seemed to satisfy Román, who I was sure—after spending a week in Bolivia with the man—realized he was a braggart. It had been a long, hard morning.

Outside, I jumped all over the six-foot-four-inch beanpole of a man whom the Bolivians dubbed "Antenna" in their radio code. "You are my fucking employee, you son of a bitch. . . . You got that straight?"

When Wheeler and I got to Scuzzo's room it was already a mess. Beer bottles were strewn all over the place and the whiskey bottle was half empty. Both Scuzzo and Brown showed signs of heavy drinking, while Hoopel, as usual, sat in a corner and said nothing. In a far corner of the room, alongside the bed, sat two suitcases filled with five million dollars in cash.

Wheeler and I brought them up-to-date on the meeting. Scuzzo was livid that he might have to stay in Panama past Christmas. I told him that I did not think he had anything to worry about. "This deal is not going to go, unless we agree to change locations," I said.

"Well, these fucking guys are gonna have to do it our way!" roared Scuzzo. "Just bring them the fuck over here and show them the fucking money. If they're for real, they'll do it."

"Maybe they can't even do it," said Brown, red-faced, a drink in his hand. "I spent a lotta years in South America. I think they can't do it and they're just fucking stalling."

"Yeah," I said, fighting to hold my temper, "They show our guys about forty tons of cocaine and you think they are stalling."

"Well, headquarters says we gotta do it fucking here!" Scuzzo belched loudly. "And that's where we're gonna do it!"

"Is there any news about the pilots and our plane?"

"As of right now," said Scuzzo, "as far as I know, we have no plane."

"No plane," echoed Wheeler in amazement.

"Read my fucking lips!" roared Scuzzo. "No plane." Wheeler shook his head wearily. No one was giving him any respect here either.

"Just bring these guys over here," slurred Brown. "Just shove their fucking faces in the money. That'll make 'em get off their asses. Just show 'em the fucking money. If they're for real, they'll do it."

Wheeler looked as if he were about to speak again. I grabbed his arm to quiet him. "What about Duncan, where is he?"

No one had any idea where DEA's Panama attaché was, or where he could be found.

Before leaving the room I asked Scuzzo to keep on top of the plane situation and to try and get headquarters to let us move to another location—any other location.

"I'm gonna blow this whole deal off!" I said to Wheeler the moment we were outside the room. "This is getting too dangerous." Wheeler mumbled something about going to Senator Helms. I said nothing. He was, after all, an informer—in the DEA scheme of things, the lowest form of life. But at that moment we were one mutual protection society.

We checked upstairs in the suite and found Lydia with Luis and Gene. The three were staying away from Scuzzo's room because of the drinking. I could not blame them. Just the fact that they were aware of it was enough for me. In a quick aside to the two New York agents, I reminded them to "keep taking notes."

Lydia informed me that she was in constant contact with the Customs people in California, where George Urquijo was waiting in the undercover house, keeping in telephone contact with Pablo Girón in Mexico. I realized then why the Customs bosses had insisted that she be included on the operation: She was there to protect von Raab's interests in the Mexican-corruption aspect of the case.

The drug case was starting to look like it would collapse and Customs was getting worried. I could not blame them.

At about two-thirty P.M. Wheeler and I checked back at Scuzzo's room to see if there was anything new they could tell us. Scuzzo said he had checked with headquarters and that our orders had not changed—we were to do the buy-bust operation in the Marriott; *no other location would even be considered.*

"And at this point I have no idea if we even have a plane either," he added. "The fucking pilots say DEA owes them for some other trips they made, and if they don't get paid they're just not going." I looked around the room that now looked like a veritable beer-bottle forest, and was somewhat relieved to see the five million dollars still in the same place.

At three P.M. a shirtless Chuy admitted us to a room that felt like oven temperature. A drained-looking Jorge watched us from the bed. "My people want me to call the whole thing off," he said almost before the door had closed. "They think something is very suspicious. You know, DEA agents are in your hotel right now."

I was not surprised by the last. At the rate Scuzzo and company were going, I figured their presence in the Marriott was going to be front-page news.

"My brother," I said, meeting his level gaze, "I think I agree with your people. We should call the whole thing off. There is just too much distrust to do business. My people are on the verge of ordering me back with the money." I again rehashed the airport incident, using it like a club on him. "They said exactly what they said before. If we can risk our plane in Bolivia and our money in Panama, they cannot understand why you can't come to the Marriott and walk out with two sixty-pound suitcases that look like any of the other suitcases seen all over the lobby."

Román shook his head wearily. "You know, Luis, the one thing I am sure of is that you are not DEA. This whole affair is so stupid that it could not be DEA. And if you were, you would be shoving money at me, which you are not."

I smiled and said nothing. It was a line I would never forget.

"Luis, we have come so far," he continued wearily, his voice tinged with desperation. "I do not want to let the opportunity get by. If you could convince your people to do the transaction in any location—anyplace but the Marriott—I will convince mine."

"Anyplace?" I asked.

"I have an idea," he said suddenly, moving to a wall telephone. He dialed a local number. In a moment he was speaking to someone named Manuel. From the conversation I could tell that whoever was on the other end was fully aware of everything that was going on. Román asked the man if we could use his house. He really had to be desperate to commit a faux pas of this magnitude. I started shaking my head in disgust. Román quickly hung up the phone.

"How is it that people I am totally unaware of have knowledge of our transaction?" He stared at me, thunderstruck. His mistake was a godsend; I had him solidly on the defensive. "I am surprised at you, my brother. What does this man have to do with me? Why does he know about me?"

Román's chest heaved with anguish. He looked as if he were about to cry. "You are right, Luis. I am not thinking. This whole thing has me crazy. . . . You have no idea how I stuck my neck out for you. The man I just spoke to is a banker. He can be trusted." He saw the look on my face. "But you are right. It was a mistake."

"If I told this to my people, I am sure they would order me to leave immediately," I said.

"I am asking you to please trust me, Luis. This man is no threat."

"I trust you, my brother, or I would not still be here." I could see that the man was at his breaking point. I wondered what would happen if he finally agreed to come to the Marriott and headquarters had still not straightened out the plane-and-pilots mess. I could not risk it. "I think it best that we call the transaction off. There is too much against it now. Perhaps some time in the future . . ."

"No," he insisted. "We are still here. I am sure we can work this thing out."

"It will soon be too late," I reminded him. "We have the Christmas deadline. And the last flight to Curaçao is tomorrow morning."

"Leave immediately for Curaçao," he said to Wheeler. "I am

sure we can work it out. If you can get your people to agree to someplace other than the Marriott, we will do it. Why don't you tell your people that I will even stay with you as a hostage until your merchandise is safely in the air."

"We are not gangsters, Jorge." I smiled as benignly as I could under the circumstances. "If something happened, what do you think I would do, kill you? That is not my business. We are not killers, we are businessmen," I said, employing my Bolivian "killer" speech.

I had used it many times over the years in the chess game of undercover. It never failed. One of the main reasons these gentle country people were constantly straining to get away from the Colombian "yoke" was their distaste for the Hollywood-gangster style of doing business that the Colombians seemed to love to emulate. I knew there was no way he was going to let me leave after that. Even Chuy was smiling.

Román suddenly looked at his watch and excused himself. "I must go upstairs to call Bolivia." He hurriedly left the room. His haste told me that the call was going to be a preset incoming one; and "upstairs" had to be Remberto's suite. We had furnished Fred Duncan [DEA country attaché] with Remberto's location two months before, so I was sure they had to have the phone tapped. A wiretap was par for the course in almost every overseas investigation. If Román was making all his calls from Remberto's suite, we had to have a good idea of everyone involved in this operation.

While Román was gone Wheeler and I made ourselves at home. Chuy served Wheeler some tequila and me some orange juice. The heat was brutal. I stripped out of my shirt, shoes, and socks and stretched out on Román's bed.

I don't remember how it began, but the three of us ended up trading stories of derring-do, shootouts with the police, and other tales that ended with each of us barely escaping with our life, with Wheeler telling some of the most outrageous stories since *Indiana Jones and the Temple of Doom*.

Chuy, not to be outdone, suddenly turned his back, pulled up his T-shirt, and lowered his pants, exposing his buttocks. His back and rear end were splattered with huge ugly scars that were the unmistakable result of the almost half-inch-in-diameter .45 caliber slugs—the much favored weapon of the Mexican *federales*. He had been shot trying to escape a drug deal gone bad.

"They got me five times," he said casually. "Then they tortured me. I did seven years in prison, but I never talked."

Wheeler was suddenly quiet. I could not help but look at the man who had betrayed his old friendships to save his own ass; he was staring at his drink. I wondered if he felt any remorse. I had worked with thousands like him—too many—and despised them all. I wondered what internal price I had paid in concealing that hatred and manipulating the slime for my own purposes. At the moment the price seemed to be in the energy that had suddenly drained out of me. I closed my eyes.

In the silence I could hear a breeze stir the trees outside, but nothing seemed to enter the little room. Somehow, the silence seemed to make the heat more bearable. I fell into a dreamless sleep.

When I opened my eyes Román was already in the room. I stretched, looking at my watch, and was amazed to see that I had slept almost forty-five minutes.

"My people think it is very suspicious," said Román. "They want me to drop everything."

"Brother, I agree," I said, sitting up groggily at the edge of the bed.

"But I don't! It is too close. We are here. We cannot give up until we have exhausted every possibility."

"Very shortly, it will no longer be possible." I reminded him of Wheeler's reservations for Curaçao and our Christmas deadline. I prayed that he would call it off. Even if he agreed to accept payment at the Marriott, I *still* did not know if we had pilots or a plane to fly the mission. What an incredibly ironic position to be in—both the Corporation and I wanted Román to give up. But he would not.

"Try to get your people to agree to another location. I am sure mine will come around." I agreed to speak with my investors. It was almost five P.M. We agreed to meet again at eight-thirty P.M.

As Wheeler and I were about to leave the room I offered my hand to Román. He refused to shake it. "That is saying good-bye, brother. I am not saying good-bye yet." He was smiling broadly, an odd twinkle in his eyes. His trust in me was complete. I suddenly had a queer sinking sensation in the pit of my stomach. I liked and respected this man—whom I was doing my best to destroy—a hell of a lot more than the people I was about to face in the Marriott.

Such is the life of an undercover narc.

When Wheeler and I arrived at Scuzzo's room, everyone was gathered there. The cigarette smoke was suffocating; the number of empty beer bottles had doubled. Lydia sat in a corner, glaring at Fast Albert and Brown, both of whom were in a semicoherent manic state. Hoopel, as usual, sat quietly in another corner. When Wheeler and I told them of the results of our meeting, Brown raged, "They are not for fucking real. These guys can't do the fucking deal."

Scuzzo was suddenly on his feet, moving toward me. "What if they take Wheeler hostage? Huh? What the fuck are we going to do then? Did you ever think of that?"

"I am trying to call the deal off," I said as quietly and as calmly as I could, not even trying to make sense out of what he was saying. "The man won't let me."

"We can't call the fucking thing off!" raged Scuzzo. He reminded me of the drunken cartoon characters with X's instead of eyes, except that his X's were blood-red. "We've moved too much equipment. We spent too much to call the fucking thing off."

"We are doing everything they want," added Brown. "They aren't doing a fucking thing we want. I don't think these guys are for real."

"They're not for real," I repeated angrily. "We're trying to get them to do a five-million-dollar drug deal in the one place on the face of the earth they said they don't even want to visit, and *they* are not for real."

I was disgusted with myself the moment the words were out. I was trying to reason with a wall—a drunk wall. I glanced at Luis and Gene, happy that they were there to witness what was happening to the biggest case in DEA's history. "Román said that he would do the deal if we would move to any other location," I said. "What do I tell him?"

"Well, tell these fucks that we will," Scuzzo was almost shouting. "Let's call their fucking bluff."

"I don't think they can do it," said Brown, undaunted. "I think they're stalling for time."

"I don't want to interrupt anything," said Wheeler suddenly, a wary eye on Scuzzo, "but do we even have a plane and pilots?"

"That's being taken care of!" shouted Scuzzo.

"Are you sure?" asked Wheeler. "You know, my ass is on the line."

"Read my fucking lips!" shouted Scuzzo, moving menacingly toward the tall, skinny informant. The two were about the same height, but Scuzzo had to outweigh him by at least sixty pounds. Wheeler flushed and cowered back a step.

"How many drinks have you had?" asked Lydia in a sudden burst of anger. "I counted about twenty." The room was suddenly hushed. I saw real fear in both Scuzzo's and Brown's eyes. Lydia was a senior Customs agent and not beholden to cover up for a drunken "brother" DEA agent. The specter of an OPR [Office of Professional Responsibility] investigation suddenly loomed real and frightening.* The discussion continued at a much calmer level, with both Scuzzo and Brown keeping a wary eye on Lydia.

They should have been watching me.

Scuzzo was saying that he thought he could get headquarters to authorize a change in locations, when there was a sudden light tapping at the door.

Alfredo "Fred" Duncan, DEA country attaché to Panama, had finally arrived. I was glad he was there. For reasons known only to himself he had been keeping his distance from the whole operation. It was curious that he was staying away from a case of this magnitude—in a country where he was the recognized DEA representative.

While Scuzzo attempted to make some long-distance phone calls and Brown babbled on about his years of experience in South America and how "these guys are just stalling," I tried to get some information from Duncan. We already knew each other; he had

* The Office of Professional Responsibility replaced the old Internal Security Division.

worked for me for a short period of time in Argentina. I repeated Román's story of having lost two million dollars in the Marriott. Duncan immediately recognized the incident but had nothing more to say about it. I told him about Román's telephone conversations with Bolivia in the suite on the sixth floor of the Las Vegas. He said he would have the phone tapped immediately.

Suddenly Scuzzo's booming voice dominated the room. Whoever he had on the other end had to be thoroughly confused by his telephone code: ". . . and once we get the thing to the people down there, what we have to know is, do we have a bird? . . . a metal bird—and these people want to play in a different playground—we have all our things right here . . . our things . . . our paper things . . . you know, the things you use to buy things with. . . ."

Duncan looked at me and smiled. His smile said it all.

By seven P.M. we had agreed that Wheeler and I would tell Román we were looking for a villa or an apartment that we might use, and would have something by the next day. Duncan was going to help us locate a place by noon. Scuzzo said he was sure he would get headquarters approval for the change in plan. I asked him about the plane and pilot and he said, "We'll have a fucking plane. It will be ready. We moved too much paper and equipment to let this thing go now."

"What if they take Wheeler as a hostage?" I said, unable to resist. He looked at me blankly. "Never mind," I said.

Upstairs in our suite an angry Lydia told me that not only had Scuzzo no idea if we had a plane ready but that he had stopped communicating with her people in Customs, who were now afraid that they were going to lose their Mexican defendants. The Mexicans were calling Urquijo in the undercover house, wondering what the delay was, and he had no idea what to tell them.

"Lydia," I said, feeling sorry for her, "I am only supposed to be doing the undercover. If I were you, I would call my bosses." I prayed that she would.

Luis and Gene were astounded. I was glad they were. Astounded people make good witnesses. When this case was over and the smoke cleared—and I had my ass well covered—I was going to take some action. I had no idea what that action was going to be, but I had to do something.

At eight-fifteen P.M. I returned to Scuzzo's room, alone. Wheeler wanted to wait for me in the lobby. How ironic it was—I had three times as many notes written on my meetings with Scuzzo and company as I did with the drug dealers. My years with DEA had made me the perfect undercover weapon. I knew how to put on a flawless acting performance and at the same time gather and document information, evidence, and statements with the efficiency of a human vacuum. And there, in Scuzzo's smoke-filled, beer-reeking room, I found myself turning those talents against the people who were supposed to be my partners and protectors—and doing it with a vengeance.

Scuzzo, Brown, and Hoopel were still in the room. I asked if there was anything new. "Tell the guy you're going to find another place," said Fast Albert. "Everything is falling into line. I been on the phone with people from Washington and they are really behind us. We're going to do the whole thing by ourselves in the morning. Mrs. García [as he had begun calling Lydia] and your employees will rent a place. In fact, we have a place in mind that belongs to a real doper."

"If these guys aren't full of shit," added Brown, "now they'll do it."

I bit halfway through my tongue as I listened to Scuzzo launch into another tirade about how much time and money had been expended in the case. "What about the plane and pilots?" I asked finally. "Are they going to be in Curaçao if Román agrees?"

"Headquarters told me that everything is set," said Scuzzo.

"Great," I said, feeling uncomfortable with just myself and the three of them. I checked my watch; I had wasted ten minutes. "Then I guess there's nothing else to say." My rush to leave seemed to bother Scuzzo.

"Wait," he said. "Do you want us to keep the money here, or should we stick it in the safe at the embassy?"

I looked at the two money-laden suitcases that I had almost forgotten. I had no idea what Román might say or do. "I think you better keep it here. Why take a chance, after all this, on not having it available?"

"Okay," said Scuzzo, patting one of the suitcases. "It'll be right here."

At eight-thirty P.M. Wheeler and I were knocking on the door of room 116 again. A different Román opened the door. He seemed fresh, resolved, somewhat distant, and a lot more suspicious than when we had left him. Something had happened. He wanted Wheeler to leave immediately for Curaçao, yet he refused to say that he would complete the transaction at any location of our choosing. "I am sure we will work it out" was all he would commit to.

Sensing that there was something in the air, I said, "It does not make sense that Dave leave until we are one hundred percent in agreement. I would rather call it off."

Román, seeing that I would not be moved, tentatively agreed on completing the deal in a "suitable" location. "But I must get a final approval from Bolivia," he said finally.

He had backed off quite a bit from "anyplace other than the Marriott." He had also made inquiries and found that there was one more flight to Curaçao in the morning. "Find the place," he said. "I am sure, by morning, that I will have the final approval." He had a strange, distant gleam in his eyes as he looked from Wheeler to me. I was sure we had failed some sort of test prescribed by the Corporation. If I were a real dope dealer, I suppose—after all the time and expense we had gone through—I would have immediately dispatched Wheeler to Curaçao on a promise—but I wasn't.

"I will call David the first thing in the morning," said Román, leading us to the door. His handshake was cold and limp. The undercover meetings for December 20, 1987, were over. I looked at my watch and realized that the meeting had lasted less than a half hour.

"Something is up," said Wheeler the moment we left the Las Vegas. "He smells something."

"You felt it too."

"Yeah, and I don't like it."

Wheeler accompanied me to Scuzzo's room. For the first time that day the big man seemed somewhat composed. He was dressed in an electric-blue floral shirt that looked like it glowed in the dark. The stale beer and cigarette odor had been overpowered by a strong cologne that we could have followed blindfolded from the elevators. Scuzzo was alone and I could understand why.

"Something is up," I said. "I don't think it's going to work." Wheeler cautiously seconded my opinion.

"Bullshit," said Scuzzo, shoving money into his pocket, checking his room, in a rush to leave. "Everything is falling into line. Headquarters is behind us now. We'll have a new place by tomorrow. . . . I'm gonna meet the guys now. We been cooped up in this fucking room all day. We spent too much time organizing this thing to stop it now" were his final words.

Wheeler and I rode silently up the elevator to the suite of rooms on the top floor. Gene Blahato had told me of seeing CBS television newsman Ed Bradley, staying on the same floor with us. For a moment I thought seriously of paying the man a visit. Then I remembered how I had turned to the press during the Roberto Suárez fiasco, and how badly I had been burned. This time I would have to come up with something new.

When we arrived at the suite I was pleasantly surprised. Gene, Luis, and Lydia had prepared an impromptu birthday celebration for me with little cakes and candles. For a while we had a few laughs and tried to forget about what we were living through, but there was just no way we could. My worst suspicions were confirmed when Lydia told me that Scuzzo still had no idea what the status of our pilots and plane was, and that he hadn't even discussed looking for an alternate location. There was no way that we could be ready by morning. And as if that weren't bad enough, Gene and Luis informed me that the moment I had left for the final undercover meeting, Scuzzo had the five-million-dollar flash money transferred to the embassy vault so that they could go out on the town the moment we returned.

There was no doubt in my mind that if Román had wanted to see the money, and it was not available—for any reason whatsoever —all possibilities of doing an undercover case against the Corporation would have been destroyed forever. Scuzzo had to know that, and so did whoever was pulling his strings at headquarters.

No one could be that dumb.

It was close to midnight of my forty-eighth year on this earth. I again made a vow that, this time, some way, somehow, I would shine a blinding white light on the bastards who were losing us the drug war. But at that moment all I could do was take notes.

On December twenty-first, at about one A.M., my room phone jangled me awake. It was a furious Lydia. Customs was in an uproar, she said. My refusal to do business anywhere but the Marriott had reached all the way to Mexico. Pablo Girón was very suspicious. The Mexican federal cop had called Urquijo and told him that he could not understand why I was behaving in such a strange manner. He and Hector Alvarez refused to come to California until the situation "cleared up." And that was not all.

"Scuzzo told my boss," she fumed, "that Mr. García [my undercover name] was making all the undercover decisions and that he [Scuzzo] was in charge of the administrative decisions and that 'everything was under control and going well.' " Customs had also learned that the pilots were *still* refusing to fly the mission because DEA owed them too much money from previous missions.

Customs had to be in a panic. Commissioner von Raab was planning a major press blitz on the arrests of Girón and Alvarez, and now he was about to lose them. The telephone lines in Washington must be sizzling. "I'm sorry," I told Lydia. "It's out of my hands." I hung up the phone and wrote down the time of the call, and what was said; then I tried to get some sleep.

At nine-thirty A.M. I got a panic phone call from Scuzzo. He wanted me to come to his room immediately. Román had telephoned Wheeler and told him to come to his hotel, "alone."

When I got to Scuzzo's room I found a frightened Wheeler and a raving Scuzzo. "That fucking Duncan hasn't done anything," he raved. "I told him to lead, follow, or get out of the way and we'll do it ourselves." *I had no idea what he was talking about, but then I rarely did.*

"What do you think?" asked Wheeler, ignoring Scuzzo.

"I think the Bolivians are suspicious, but I don't think they suspect us of being agents yet, or they wouldn't be calling."

"You think I should go?"

"If you go," said Scuzzo, "we can't be responsible for you."

"I can't make that decision for you," I said, also trying to ignore Scuzzo. "If he called for me, I would go. I don't think there's anything to fear."

We left Scuzzo's room and I accompanied a pale-looking Wheeler to the lobby. "I mean it," I said, "I would go. If Román was really upset we'd have been long dead—you and I."

I watched him get into a cab and drive off. I turned and headed straight for the hotel gym. At that moment, I felt, the only thing that would keep me from punching Scuzzo's front lights out would be a good workout.

At eleven forty-five A.M. I returned to my room and found a message: "Call Mr. Scuzzo—urgent."

"Get your guys and check out of the hotel right away," said Scuzzo, the moment he came on the line. "They suspect you are an agent. I'm ordering you and your men to check out right now and move to the hotel out by the airport."

I was not going to argue. As soon as I hung up I called Wheeler's room. As I suspected, he was there. I asked him to come to my suite and fill us in on what was going on. Lydia, Gene, and Luis were with me. From the moment he entered the room he began babbling excitedly, "I only have two minutes; they want to get me to a secure phone at the embassy."

"Well, all I know is, I've been told to pack up and leave the hotel," I said. "Can you tell us what the hell is going on?"

"The main guy from Bolivia [Pato Pizarro] called Jorge [Román] last night at two in the morning and woke him up. They don't understand why we are insisting on the Marriott. The guy said that they know who I am but they don't know this man Luis. He said that your insistence on the Marriott was insulting and inconceivable. The guy [Pizarro] has a numbered account here in Panama—protected by Noriega—and he told Román to have us to put the money in it. They've given us an ultimatum. We either do it by tomorrow or go home."

"I recommended that we put the money in the account," said Wheeler, "and I think they are going to follow my recommendation."

"You mean we are going to make the buy?" I asked, looking at Lydia, Luis, and Gene, their mouths agape. It was reassuring to see that the others were as shocked as I was. I was beginning to think I was losing my mind.

"Who the fuck knows," said Wheeler, throwing his arms up in the air. "They [Brown and Scuzzo] said, 'Maybe we'll do that, put the money in the account and try to trace the thing out, because the agency [DEA] and the Company [the CIA] in Washington, D.C., want to do that, they want to put the money in the account and trace it out.' But they don't know if they can get approval.

"And I got the Mexicans all calmed down also. At first they were suspicious, because of us insisting on the Marriott, but now they are cooled down and ready to come to California for their money."

This was illogical. Wheeler spoke to me as if I hadn't met the Mexicans. They had been keeping abreast of everything that was happening in Panama. And if they were the same men I had met in California—which they were—they would be in no rush to walk into so obvious a trap. Real dope dealers do not pay a commission until a deal is complete. And it is usual for the people owed the commission to be pursuing the debtors, not the reverse. Once again I had cause to wonder about Wheeler's personal agenda.

Wheeler then began talking wildly about other recommendations he had given Scuzzo and Brown, about fronting half the money, or just showing up at the Las Vegas Hotel with all the money and staying there until the deal was done. I saw Gene look toward the ceiling and roll his eyes. I did not think Wheeler was crazy—far from it—he, like DEA, had his own agenda. But at that moment I had to find out what was going on.

"I still have no idea what I'm supposed to do," I said, cutting him off. "I'm going to Scuzzo's room."

Moments later, my stomach churning as it had on any one of the thousands of undercover assignments I've carried out with some of the deadliest criminals in the world, I was knocking on Scuzzo's door. Brown opened it. The two men were stone sober and watching me very closely.

"Can you tell me what's going on?" I asked as calmly as I could. "All I know is that I'm supposed to pack up my guys and get out of the hotel immediately."

"Well," began Scuzzo, even more slowly than usual, "we plan to get permission to let some of the money walk."

I looked at the two of them, trying to determine whether they were incredibly stupid, or dangerous. The notion of giving Román money out front—after first refusing to even leave the Marriott—was ridiculous. The Bolivian would immediately know something was wrong. These men were a real danger to me.

"Just tell me what to do and say," I said, "and I will do it."

"You don't really have to do anything," said Scuzzo, "except get out of the hotel. . . . By doing that we can sort of restructure the whole thing. You know, what they told Wheeler . . . basically, they want . . . within the next twenty-four hours, basically a 'front.' And the Mexicans were not going to move until something was deposited here. You know the UC* in California is trying to suck some big officials across the border."

"Look," I said, "I have no idea what you're talking about. The only problem with this thing was, and has been, the fact that I have been forced to stay in this hotel. If that had not been done, this case would have been closed by now."

"Do you realize what we're trying to do now?" persisted Scuzzo.

"I haven't the slightest idea," I said, wishing that I were in a karate tournament and that these two were my next opponents.

"Get permission to front the money . . . let it go."

"I hope it goes," I said, wondering whether the great taxpaying American public would believe any of this. "I swear to God, I hope it goes."

"We've got a plane en route to Curaçao, and basically, we put a lot of effort and money into this."

"What you have," I said, fighting a losing battle with my tem-

* Undercover agent.

per, "are a lot of suspicious people because we insisted on doing a deal in a DEA hotel."

Brown suddenly jumped into the conversation. "If we give them some money," he said, "we're gonna buy a lot of credibility."

"I really hope it works," I said, "but at this point I just don't think anything will." I wondered how much of a role Brown was playing in the decision making. He had suddenly appeared in Miami, prior to which he had had nothing to do with the case. He said he had served a lot of years in South America, yet I had never heard of him, and his Spanish—from what I heard—was very basic and almost unintelligible.

"We're going to send Wheeler over to the Bolivians," said Scuzzo, "with part of the money—I don't know how much yet; I don't know what the number is, but whatever the number is—and say, 'Here! Let's do it!' I think we can put life back in this thing if we give them money."

"I hope so," I said dully, trying to put what these two semicomatose men were saying, together with what I had just heard from a hyper Wheeler.

"I'm not so sure the Bolivians have got their shit together any better than we do," droned Scuzzo. "I talked to people who did a lot of these deals. . . . If you think you're going to go to Curaçao and be home for Christmas, you don't know what you're talking about."

I did not know what *he* was talking about. I suddenly flashed back to my days in the Air Force. I had once—due to lack of hospital space—spent some time in a ward that was shared by both medical and mental patients. I remembered a card game I had gotten into with two guys who seemed normal at first, but as the game progressed began making up strange rules and speaking in their own private language. They began to look very big and very dangerous to me. I was too afraid to quit, so I just kept playing and inventing my own rules and language. The only way I knew that it was my turn to play a card, and say something, was that the two would get very quiet and just stare at me. With Brown and Scuzzo I still couldn't tell when it was my turn.

"Look," I heard myself say, "I am totally bewildered by what is going on. If you just tell me what you want me to do and say, I will be happy to do it."

"You don't have to say anything," said Scuzzo for the second time. "You just have to get out to that hotel. Basically, right now, it's failing. . . . It's dying by itself. The only way we'll get life back inside of this is you walking in there with one or two suitcases and sitting down until the deal is done."

By the time I left Scuzzo's room, the only thing I knew for sure was that he wanted Luis, Gene, and myself to register at the Airport Continental Hotel, where we were to stand by until we heard from him.

Scuzzo's final words were: "Just stay there till we find out what we're doing. I don't know if we're going to get a villa, an apartment, or what."

Brown's parting words were: "You're just gonna be out there hiding out, waiting till we go back to plan A, or B." Then he gave me a curious look and said, "It's down to the nut-cutting time."

I looked at him. He had no idea how right he was. I doubt that he could read the rage twisting inside of me. I had too many years of undercover to show anything but a disarming smile. I laughed and said, "Let's cut nuts, then."

An hour later Luis, Gene, and I were packed into a taxi and on the way to the Airport Continental Hotel. Lydia—perhaps on orders from Customs to keep an eye on their interests—stayed at the Marriott. I looked back at the Marriott Hotel disappearing rapidly behind us and laughed out loud. Gene and Luis looked at me. There was no way I could explain the feeling of freedom I had at that moment.

At five-thirty P.M. Scuzzo called me at the Airport Continental and said, "Get the family out of here, the case is over."

"Does that mean we should make reservations to return to the U.S. ?"

"Yes," said Scuzzo.

I tried to find out what had happened. Scuzzo would only say that "the people on our side want us to pull out of here."

By seven P.M. we had reservations for the morning flight to Miami with connections to New York. I taxied over to the Marriott, alone, to pick up my official passport, DEA credentials, and other identification that I had left with Hoopel before leaving Miami. I found everyone—Lydia, Hoopel, Brown, and Scuzzo—in Scuzzo's room, where the drinking had begun again. Feeling very uncomfortable, I quickly got my belongings from Hoopel and made arrangements for him to ship my gun (which he had also brought for me) back to my office in New York.

"You know, they [the Bolivians] don't trust Luis anymore," laughed Brown.

"Yeah," I said, turning to leave, "I guess I really fucked this one up."

"You know," continued Brown, "maybe the Bolivians set this whole thing up as a test, and we're passing it."

At about midnight Wheeler called. "Everything is changing," he said excitedly. Scuzzo had told him that everyone was going to get arrested. He said that the Mexicans, "including a general," were coming to California and that they, too, would be arrested. "There's a whole new game plan," he said. "You'll be hearing from Scuzzo."

As soon as I hung up I tried to call Scuzzo; there was no answer.

At eight-thirty A.M., December 22, 1987, Hubert Hoopel called to tell me that I might be needed to do some more undercover with the Bolivians. "Headquarters is thinking of locking up everyone, on a 'no-dope conspiracy.' "* Hoopel had no more information other than that George Urquijo had, somehow, miraculously enticed the Mexicans to come to California for their arrests. "We're going to arrest the Bolivians right here."

At nine-thirty A.M. I received a call from Scuzzo ordering me to cancel our flight reservations. He said, "They're all going to be arrested for a "no-dope conspiracy." He babbled on for a while in his coded gobbledygook, finally telling me to "stand by"—he would get back to me.

By eleven A.M. I still hadn't heard from Scuzzo, so I telephoned

* "No-dope conspiracy" is an arrest or indictment charging an individual with "conspiring to possess and/or sell drugs," without actually seizing any.

his room. Brown answered the phone. Scuzzo was at the embassy making telephone calls on the secure phone, he said. Then he knocked my socks off:

"Lydia and Dave are out looking for a place for you to show them the [money]."

"Do you mean this thing is still going to go as planned?"

"I think so," said Brown. Then he blew my mind even further. "You know, their [pilot] arrived last night and they gave him a big reception. He's staying out at the airport."

"You mean in the same hotel we are?"

"Yes, I think so."

The presence of the Bolivians in our hotel, without anyone warning us, was a violation of the most basic principles of an undercover investigation. A chance encounter—the odds against which were very high, as there were few people registered in the hotel—could have resulted in a number of different tragedies, not the least of which might have been my own early departure from this earth.

I was reaching a point with these men where I could no longer trust myself to speak without blowing my cool and screaming. Instead, I kept hearing myself muttering inanely along with a stupid little guffaw, "Holy shit! *Ha, ha.*" As much as it was tearing me up, I had to avoid having them perceive me as an enemy, no matter what the internal cost—a cost that was about to escalate to the breaking point.

By three P.M. I had received no further word from Scuzzo and company, so, together with my two "witnesses," I grabbed a taxi and headed back to the Marriott.

Scuzzo's room was once again a forest of empty beer bottles, along with a couple of bottles of Scotch. Smoke and the acrid odor of stale beer and whiskey hung heavy in the air. The whole cast—Wheeler, Lydia, Hoopel, Scuzzo, and Brown—was gathered.

A slightly tipsy and very surly Scuzzo said, "The Bolivians are blaming this guy Jorge for the screwup. Everything is changing. Méndez is on his way here from Bolivia. These fucking people are so desperate to sell us the stuff . . . I'm telling you, they're gonna end up fronting us the coke. . . ."

Wheeler began an explanation of his own. Scuzzo shoved his

face nose to nose with Wheeler. "Read my lips!" he raged. "They are blaming Jorge for the screwup!" He turned to me. "If it doesn't work this time, we'll just put the whole thing on the back burner." Wheeler backed off, a quick smile flickering at the corner of his lips. *What game was this man playing?*

"I just don't understand," I said, "why they are blaming the whole thing on Román." *Duncan must have had Remberto's phone tapped as he had said he would. How else could they have that information?*

"There's things I'm not fucking telling you!" shouted Scuzzo. He looked like he was about to lose control. A part of me prayed that he would. "I'm not telling you everything. There's other things I'm not telling you too!"

A wise decision, I thought, only it's a little too late. "What about the villa, or the apartment?" I asked, deciding to change the subject.

"We don't have it yet! So you just don't tell them anything!"

"You're in charge," I said, looking from Gene to Luis. "Like I said before, you just tell me what to do and say, and I'll do it."

"If this doesn't work," he slurred, "we'll just fall back out of here."

Precisely what I had in mind as I got to my feet, signaling Luis and Gene to follow.

At seven-thirty P.M. the explosion finally happened. When I returned to my room there was an urgent message to call Mr. Scuzzo.

"Hey, how long you wanna stay in town?" said Fast Albert when he came on the line.

"As long as it takes to finish this thing."

"Have you had dinner?"

"No, not yet," I said, immediately regretting not having lied.

"Well, why don't you come on down to the hotel," he said, and then launched into his telephone code. "As you know, we've massaged this thing a little more, and everybody is going to be in town, today . . . tomorrow morning, from down south. And I wanted to talk to you about, er . . . this morning, early tomorrow morning, showing them the equipment. . . . I figure it'll take about two or three hours to put it all together. . . . We can talk to the window people up north and tell them we have a solution to it all . . . and see if you think it's reasonable, in helping us. . . . But actually, basically, it's gonna keep us all in town until the twenty-sixth."

"Look," I said, totally bewildered, but wanting to keep him talking, "all I want to do is do the job." I had no idea what in God's name this man was talking about. His normal rate of speaking was so slow that on a telephone it was hard to tell if he was drunk or sober. "If you tell me to stay in town until *January* twenty-sixth, I'll stay in town."

"Yeah, well, I'll tell you what we can do. If you come down here, basically, I can tell you how . . . you and your partners. . . . You know that at about, like, one, they are going to be in."

"You mean tonight?"

"Yeah, in the morning."

"Do we have a place?"

"Well, let me explain that. . . . You know your partner . . . on the way in, picking up his friend, can stop off where you're at. . . ."

All I could decipher from that was that at least one of the Bolivians was coming to my hotel. "Look, I'm registered here under my correct name."

"Well . . . uhh, that won't be a problem for you because we'll be getting a brand-new place. . . . We're showing them all the wares."

"Yes," I heard myself say, thinking I was starting to understand him, and worrying about it. "When I left [Román] I told him I was going to look for a villa or a house to do the deal."

"That's gonna happen tomorrow," droned Albert Scuzzo. He rambled on for a few minutes about "the old guy" who was "coming in tonight." I finally deciphered what he meant: Efrén Méndez was to arrive from Bolivia.

That made sense. The two men who were being made responsible to the Corporation for this whole abortion were Román and Méndez.

I tried to explain to Scuzzo that the reason that the Bolivians were dealing with us in the first place was because Méndez had liked me, and was impressed by my act. And that since I had removed myself from the undercover negotiations, so much had gone on that I was not made aware of, that I could no longer effectively play that role.

"If I go out and meet this guy," I said, "I haven't the faintest idea of what's going on, and he'll know something is wrong."

I might as well have been talking to a third grader playing cops and robbers.

"Well, why don't you come in and sit down with them right now, and by the time they get there you'll be ready," snapped Fast Albert, speaking at his equivalent of three times the speed of sound. "Let me say this. All these people are coming to town . . . and they're not coming to fool around."

"I know they want to do it," I said, marveling at the sudden change in speed. "But the problem is, I'm the guy who's supposedly running this thing. I don't even know where the pilots are. I don't know if we even have a plane ready to fly the mission. I don't know what kind of a proposal I am going to offer them." Even as I spoke the words I knew they were wasted.

"Let me tell you something," said Scuzzo, heating up. "We're in a predicament. It's seven-thirty, and these guys are going to be in at two A.M."

"Oh, we're in a monstrous predicament, I would say."

"Let me tell you something else," continued Scuzzo. "The only way you are going to stay informed is if you communicate with us."

I felt an explosion somewhere in the middle of my head. The type of sensation akin to the first punch thrown in a fight. "Well," I began slowly, "we followed your instructions—"

"Let me tell you something right now," he said, interrupting me. "We have tried to contact you on several occasions, and you are either in the gym or not in your room. If you want to work this case, then work it."

By some miracle of self-control I calmly said, "I think I can document quite the contrary."

"All I'm tryin' to tell you, partner," he rattled off at incredible speed, "if you want to do it, then do it."

"All I can tell you," I said, "is that every time I'm around you, you are half in the bag, or you're *in* the bag. And that I'm holding my fucking temper. . . . If I got people that are covering me that are half fucking drunk or drunk, I'm going to call up somebody and just get my ass out of here."

Scuzzo was suddenly quiet. After a moment he said, "I think you should come down here and talk about it."

I said I would be right there and slammed the phone down, cracking its plastic cradle.

I quickly gathered Luis and Gene and told them what had happened, and that I needed them to accompany me as witnesses. Within minutes we were on our way back to the Marriott.

At approximately eight-thirty P.M. the three of us arrived at Scuzzo's room, to find a very sober and nervous Bill Brown and Hubert Hoopel waiting for us. Scuzzo was conspicuously absent. Brown asked to be allowed to speak for fifteen minutes before I said a word.

"We're all DEA here, so I can speak," said Brown. "That goddamned CI [Wheeler] isn't here either. If I were in your shoes, Mike, I would have packed my bags and left out of here forty-eight hours ago, but I'm begging you to stay. We need to stall for forty-eight more hours."

Brown went on to blame the catastrophic condition of Operation Trifecta on several things. He blamed Fred Duncan for not giving us any support. He blamed Wheeler for lying and misrepresenting "certain facts."

"Wheeler has been fucking with us," he said. "He [Wheeler] has been dumping on you behind your back because you have not had a full deck of cards to play with. But now, everyone is behind this thing. Calls have been made at the highest level," he said very mysteriously. *"This case goes to the top of three fucking countries."*

Brown finally got to the point of his speech. What he—and the rest of the free world, according to Brown—now wanted me to do, was simply stall Efrén Méndez and whatever other Bolivians showed up in Panama, for forty-eight hours. In that period of time Wheeler would be flown to La Jolla, California, from where he would make a phone call. On the basis of this phone call a Learjet would be sent to Mexico to pick up a Mexican general and two members of his staff (Girón and Álvarez) who—on Wheeler's word—would board the plane, which would then take them to La Jolla, where they would pick up Girón and Álvarez's "finder's fee" and make arrangements for the protection of some future drug shipments. They would be arrested for conspiracy to violate United States narcotics laws. At that point, whoever I had managed to stall in Panama would be arrested and extradited to the States to stand trial for the same charge.

Now that a Mexican *general* was coming, I theorized, Customs Commissioner von Raab had to be beside himself with worry. This was truly the kind of trophy he could shove right up the collective ass of Congress. The DEA suits were ready to do *anything* to please him—no matter what happened to the Bolivians. They were terrified that—if they didn't—Customs would reveal to the media how terribly they had botched the operation.

Brown had based his whole plan on Wheeler's promise that he could control the Mexicans. It amazed me that in one breath he had correctly recognized the man was a liar, yet he was still going to bet the last of his bankroll on the informer's words. But that no longer interested me.

What both interested and enraged me was the fact that Trifecta had been given up for dead. To the suits it was now just a red herring to get the Mexicans across the border.

What obsessed me was the continued documentation of everything to do with the case. I was going to go along with any plan they came up with, but first I wanted—on record and in front of my witnesses—some statement about everything that had happened to bring us to this point.

Brown finally got down to the specifics of his plan. When Méndez arrived at two A.M. Wheeler was going to pick him up at the airport and bring him to my hotel, where I was to show him the five million dollars. This, according to Wheeler, Brown, and Scuzzo's thinking, would mesmerize the man to the point that I could con him and the other Bolivians into hanging around Panama until the Mexicans were arrested.

"Wheeler has already told them he has a special problem with the refueling," said Brown.

I wondered what else he had told them. Wheeler was a lot smarter than they were and I was sure he, too, had his own agenda. It was a fool's plan, but at that point what did it matter?

Brown took a deep breath and said, "The final point I have to make is, Al [Scuzzo] is a unique person. He comes across like a stumblebum at times. But he doesn't miss a lick. I'm not trying to explain away some of his actions. But [Hoopel] and I have been with him for five days straight, and that man has been on the phone—"

"I'd rather not talk about him," I said, interrupting him. "What I've got to say, I'd rather say straight to his face."

"Wait," said Brown.

"I'll say this, though," I continued over him. I was back in control again. I wanted to heat the discussion to red-hot. It seemed that the hotter I made things, the more withheld information they revealed. But it had to be done slowly and with great deliberation. "Up to this minute there has been absolutely no leadership in this case, no plan."

"Let me say this: Lydia was sent down here to control the men in this room, because she's Customs. At three o'clock in the morning she had her ass rousted because Customs did not know what was going on." *So that's when this* new *plan was born.* "Intentionally, you guys were playing an undercover role and we did not keep you in contact as best we should have.

Intentionally? *That's interesting; just keep talking.*

"But there's been so many things going on, from dealing with the CIA in Panama and dealing with the CIA in Bolivia, and the fuck-faced pilot. . . . But I'm telling you, in the last two hours the plan is coming together. We are going to give you what you should have had forty-eight hours ago."

I was not to be sidetracked. Scuzzo was the main topic—a topic that seemed to result in all sorts of surprising information. I repeated what Scuzzo had said to me during our last telephone conversation. "I have gone to great lengths," I said, "to document everything that has been said and done in this investigation."

"I know what you're saying," said Brown, "You just happened

to be in the wrong place at the wrong time. He dumped on you. It was all the pressure he was under. Trying to keep this thing together."

"I'll tell you what we had decided," I said, deciding to go for the throat. "I'm going to ask for a Board of Professional Conduct investigation of the whole thing."

"I'm begging you not to," said Brown, squirming. "I'm begging you not to do that. I'm asking you to give us twenty-four hours."

I was starting to feel sorry for the man. I had a feeling that neither he nor Scuzzo had any idea of the real culprits behind the destruction of Operation Trifecta. The people who really ought to be investigated were at the helm of DEA, the CIA, and the Justice Department—the people running this bullshit drug war. *Who do you go to to complain about them?*

"Not only has there been no plan or leadership, but my men and I are in danger. If I am wrong, let DEA investigate and see if I'm wrong."

"I'm begging you not to do that for this very reason: A phone call was made thirty minutes ago at the highest level. A conference call. 'What are you fucking people doing down there?' It [the plan] was explained. We've got a Learjet standing by to pick up the three Mexicans."

"This is the first time since I got here that I've heard any plan that made any sense at all," I lied.

"The informer [Wheeler] has been dumping on you," said Brown, veering sharply off a topic he had already spoken too much about. "He's been blaming you for this, that, and the other thing, and Albert has defended you to the letter."

I fought the urge to vomit. The fact that Wheeler was "dumping on me" was no surprise; but the idea of Scuzzo defending me was too much.

"You know something, Bill, I really don't need anyone to defend me. I'm pretty good at defending myself."

"We're talking about three different countries," he continued. "We're talking about the top in Mexico, Panama, and Bolivia, and that's why the CIA is keen on this thing going. To the point where U.S. Customs is willing to walk two and a half million dollars, and

DEA didn't have the balls to match it. . . ." Brown continued to ramble in non sequiturs and eventually returned to his plan. "It's the best plan we've had, because even if it fails, it works for us."

A plan that works even if it fails—a notion that exists only in the drug war.

"I'll go in undercover," I said, ignoring the last. A week with Brown and Scuzzo had mercifully dulled my sensitivity to non sequiturs and nonsensical statements. "But I want to make sure that I've got a backup that is not only going to take appropriate action, but who's going to be sober, not drunk and not babbling incoherently. I do not trust the guy [Scuzzo]. It's not just me. You've got Lydia, who watched and counted the drinks. You've got a CI [Wheeler] who has watched you and counted the drinks. I'm telling you what they are telling me. I'm not here to watch and count the drinks. I'm telling you that all I know is that the man is drunk. . . . Now you are asking me to risk my fucking life."

I finally let Brown convince me to do the undercover work, in the plan that worked even if it failed. There was no point in dragging out the torture any longer. I was finally convinced that he and Scuzzo were just a couple of boobs who had been put in charge of Trifecta for precisely that reason.

In a few minutes a shamefaced Scuzzo arrived, followed by Lydia and Wheeler. I shook hands with Scuzzo and said, "Just forget about it. There's nothing to even discuss." I even felt sorry for him. We then spent the next half hour going over the new Master Plan. We were back to square one again.

I watched and listened to Wheeler closely, realizing that the once-rejected informer had manipulated himself into a position where he was actually calling the shots for DEA too. The conference call from the "highest level" seemed to have made eunuchs out of both Brown and Scuzzo. I said nothing. It was much too late now. There were new battle lines in this drug war and I was no longer on the same side with these people.

As soon as the opening presented itself, at about nine-thirty P.M., I signaled our departure.

It did not take long for the Master Plan to begin to come apart. At ten-thirty P.M. Lydia telephoned me in a panic: the Mexicans would not be coming. They were suspicious and were not going to come to California until after the first of the year. Wheeler's "control" of the Mexicans was not quite what he had painted it to be. I listened and said nothing. When Lydia was finished I said, "I'm really sorry. There's nothing I can do. I'm just the undercover in this operation."

At one A.M. on December twenty-third Wheeler showed up at my room, on his way to the airport to get Méndez. I made sure Luis and Gene were present. He was not at all upset that the Mexicans were no longer coming. He felt certain they would come to California "after the holidays." Méndez's flight was not due until two A.M. We made plans for him to pick the old man up and come to my room, where I would show him the five million dollars and tell him that, due to the delays, our preparations to bring the cocaine into the United States were no longer valid and we would have to begin new negotiations after the holidays.

Wheeler left for the airport at one-thirty A.M. Fast Albert, Bill Brown, and the five million dollars had still not appeared.

At about one forty-five A.M. Scuzzo, Brown, Hoopel, and a cadre of Panamanian secret police—whom I feared more than the drug dealers—appeared with the suitcases. I had to show them how to wire my room for sound. Scuzzo and company once again agreed that I would flash the money and call off the deal until after the holidays.

At two-thirty A.M. Wheeler appeared. "The old man's plane was delayed twelve hours," he said, with an odd smile. Instincts that had kept me alive for twenty-five years of this madness were now cringing every time Wheeler was around me.

By two forty-five A.M. everyone was packed up and leaving my room, when it dawned on me that Fred Duncan had not appeared. I asked Scuzzo about it. "The son of a bitch is out in the parking lot sleeping," said Fast Albert. Again the survivor instinct, deep inside me, jangled its alarm. Why was DEA's top agent in Panama staying as far from the center of the action as he could?

I spent the rest of the night lying on my back, my ears plugged into a Sony Walkman and a tape of Beethoven's Ninth Symphony, trying to wipe everything from my mind so that I could finally get some sleep. Dawn was just beginning to light the sky when the plan came to me. The suits didn't know it, but they had given me the opening to take full control of the case again, and I could make it work, no matter who was against it.

I jumped to my feet and began pacing. It was so simple, it was fantastic. The key to the whole thing was the old man. He was being sent here to find out what the problem was. All I had to do was to convince him that the impasse was Román's fault. If I could do that, then all I had to do was request a summit meeting in La Jolla, where both the Bolivian and the Mexicans would be invited.

Since my fictitious U.S. Customs arrangements had been ruined by the delay, I could now demand "safe passage" for my drugs across Mexico. I could also demand that the "top man" from Mexico come to meet me, in person, to guarantee the safety of my drug cargo. I was sure, with the promise of a one-million-dollar advance payment—whoever he was—he would come. And so would Girón and Alvarez, for their commissions.

I would request that the Bolivians come with their pilot, ready to leave immediately, aboard my up-to-now nonexistent plane, to guide my pilots back to Bolivia for the drugs. I would promise them advance payment of the five million dollars to be put aboard the plane immediately. Román and Méndez would have to agree to remain with me in California as hostages until my plane was safely on its return voyage. At that time I would pay Méndez his two-million-dollar commission. In all, it seemed an offer they couldn't refuse.

Of course, everything would be done before the hidden television cameras of the undercover house, and no one would be going anywhere but jail.

The final and most important part of the plan was that—*before* the news of the arrests was released—we could fly back to Panama and have Remberto the money launderer arrested, and even send in Snowcap troops to raid the locations visited by Wheeler and Jake in Bolivia. It would still be a grand slam of a no-dope conspiracy. All the defendants would be charged with conspiring to possess, sell, and transport sixteen tons of cocaine. Operation Trifecta would not result in anywhere near the smashing blow it might have been, but it would not be a total loss.

The beauty of the whole situation was that *I* could make it happen no matter who or what was operating against me. If DEA, the CIA, or anyone else wanted to kill the case now, they would have to step forward and reveal themselves—something they would never do. It was all in my hands now. It was going to be between Efrén Méndez-Dueñas and Luis García-López.

In the morning I called Scuzzo and laid out my plan. I could tell immediately that it was too much for him to comprehend. He had all he could handle with staying sober and safeguarding the money to even try and understand it. But he was not against it, and that was important. It again confirmed that he was not an enemy—just a boob intentionally put in way over his head by the suits.

At one P.M. Wheeler appeared at my room on the way to the airport to pick up Méndez. I again made sure Luis and Gene were present. I ran the new game plan down to Wheeler and was not surprised to find him dead set against it, and worried. I listened to his objections, which were only double-talk of the type he had been able to get away with with Scuzzo and company.

What bothered Wheeler more than anything else seemed to be the bringing of the Bolivian and Mexican contingents together in the same place at the same time. His opposition not only convinced me that the plan was the right thing to do, but that he did have his own secret agenda—an agenda quite different from that of the normal run-of-the-mill stool pigeon.

At approximately one-twenty P.M. a nervous and unhappy Wheeler left for the airport. Within minutes Scuzzo and company arrived with the five million dollars. We quickly wired the room. Luis, whom I had decided I would introduce to Méndez as my "nephew," and I sat down to wait for the old man's arrival.

At one forty-five P.M. the phone in my room rang; it was show time. I grabbed it.

"We're out front," said Wheeler, his voice tense.

"How does he look?" I asked.

"That's a very nervous and upset man."

"Take him to the restaurant. I'll be right there."

The moment I entered the restaurant I could see that Wheeler's description had been an understatement. The old man looked pale and as taut as piano wire. I sat down beside him and did not give him a chance to speak.

I apologized for my "organization's" paranoid behavior, repeating the story I had given Román. "It all began," I told him, "when the Panamanian police searched us and questioned us on our arrival." If Román was behind what had happened—as I still believed he was—the story would immediately set Méndez against him.

"The police asked where we would be staying. I said the Marriott. I knew they would check on me. From that point on my people insisted that I stay there, where they had connections."

Before he could say a word I hit him with other ace Román had provided me with. "And in my presence he told a complete stranger to me, everything about the transaction. His name was Manuel, some sort of banker, I believe." *It suddenly dawned on me that for all I knew he could have been talking to Noriega himself.*

Méndez almost choked on the last. His narrow face flamed with rage. "You are right, Luis," he said, his voice tight with anger. "The man is a close associate of ours, but you are right . . . you do not know him, and there was no excuse for Jorge to do this."

"It no longer matters," I told him. "We were counting on getting the cocaine into the United States by Christmas. All our arrangements with Customs are no longer good." The emaciated man looked as though the weight of the world rested on his bony shoulders. "But I think I have a way we can, once and for all, do business." His face brightened with hope. "Come to my room where we can talk."

Luis, doing his best *Miami Vice* imitation of Tubbs, checked the hallway as he admitted us to my room. Méndez barely glanced at the two large suitcases in a corner.

I immediately went to work telling Méndez my plan. "My brother," I said, "if you could get everyone to meet in San Diego, we could all sit down together and work out a deal so that there would be no mistakes or mistrust." After I told him that I would then front all the money, he smiled.

"But there are two requests I must make of you," I added.

"Yes?" He watched me closely.

"First, that for my five million dollars I get two thousand kilos of cocaine, instead of one. But I will pay you for the second thousand, once my plane returns safely to U.S. soil. . . ." *I had added this requirement at the last minute, with Román's loan-shark parable in mind.* "Second, that you and Jorge remain with me, as my guests, until the plane is safely off the ground in Bolivia."

Méndez's face slowly cracked to a smile. "Of course," he said. "We would be happy to." I knew I had him.

"Why don't you show it to him?" said Wheeler suddenly, nodding toward the two suitcases. Wheeler had sold Scuzzo on the idea of flashing the money to Méndez—whether the old man wanted to see it or not. I knew it was not the kind of thing real drug dealers at that level would do; it was the kind of thing DEA was famous for—a dead giveaway. Wheeler had pushed me into another corner.

I nodded to Pizarro, who put the suitcases on the bed and opened them. The emaciated Mexican gawked at what this whole business was all about—five million dollars in one-hundred-dollar bills.

"This is to show you we came as serious customers," I said, feeling lame.

Méndez looked like he would jump out of his skin. "You should not have done that," he said, moving to the door. He wanted to leave immediately. He was, of course, one-hundred-percent correct. For a moment it appeared that the case had been blown.

"I'm sorry," I said. "It is just that we have been through so much up to now, that I am not acting normally."

"I understand, Luis," he said as we walked through the long passageway leading toward the front of the hotel. Moments later, under the front marquee, we embraced. "Luis," he said, "your offer is agreed to. I guarantee it."

I watched Wheeler drive off with the old man in the same rented BMW we had used in November. I had played every card I had. It looked like Méndez would make the case for me. But I could not be sure until Wheeler reported back.

At about five P.M. Wheeler called and said, "You did it again." Méndez had gone crazy when he reached Román. According to Wheeler, the old man had to be physically restrained from choking him. Poor Román had to eat the whole blame for screwing up the transaction. And that wasn't all. Méndez had also called Mexico. Not only were the Mexicans in agreement with the plan but they wanted me, or Wheeler, to fly to Mexico and check some landing sites for my plane.

It seemed nothing short of miraculous, but Trifecta still lived.

SIX

SAN DIEGO SETUP

On my return to the U.S. I must have received a dozen phone calls on "the brilliance" of my plan. Méndez had reacted just as I had hoped by organizing the whole thing for me. He was hard at work convincing all the defendants that the whole Panama episode was a mistake due to lack of trust and also to come to San Diego for my "meeting."

The plan was for Méndez, Román, Vargas, and a Corporation pilot (none of whom, with the exception of Méndez, had ever been to the United States before) to come from Bolivia to pick up their five million dollars and guide my plane back to Bolivia to pick up the first thousand kilos of cocaine. Of course Méndez and Román would remain behind in California as my hostages, until the cocaine had been delivered. Girón, Alvarez, and some unknown "high-ranking Mexican army official" (one of my demands) were to come from Mexico to pick up a six-hundred-thousand partial payment (the full payment would be one million dollars) for Mexican military aid and protection for my cocaine-laden plane when it landed in Mexico to refuel. It was to be a meeting from which none of them would leave free men.

DEA was now solidly behind it, according to Hoopel and Scuzzo.

Trifecta was now more than just alive. If the setup of the San Diego sting was done right, and followed through by DEA and Customs, we could still strike at the heart of the Corporation *and* arrest Remberto the Panama money launderer. As much as the suits had tried to destroy the case, it still remained a danger to the image of Snowcap. They knew it, and I knew it. I still had more to fear from DEA than I did from the dope dealers. Undercover was no longer just a drug-war enforcement tool; I was now constantly undercover in my role as a group supervisor, pretending to be this docile company man from whom they had nothing to fear, so that they would keep their schemes and lies exposed to me.

I was also manipulating the suits to think that they had won. There was no longer anything to fear from Trifecta. The case had turned out in their best possible interests. It no longer jeopardized the image of Snowcap, *and* it was about to result in a great drug war "victory" that they could wave before the press, politicians, and public.

In the meantime, I still wanted to make the case much bigger and better than they thought possible and jam it up their collective ass—and I had the plan to do it.

By January 3, 1988, Efrén Méndez had done his job well. He, along with Hector Alvarez and Pablo Girón, had made arrangements in Mexico with General Poblano Silva for a section of Mexican road in the state of Puebla to be sealed off by military units under the command of Colonel Salvador de la Vega, so that my drug-laden plane could land and—under the vigilant eyes of Mexican soldiers—refuel, and then continue on its way to the United States. The price for that service was to be one million dollars cash paid to the general's bagman, Colonel Jorge Carranza. Ironically, Colonel Carranza was the grandson of Venustiano Carranza, an ex-president of Mexico and the author of that country's constitution.

The old man had called George Urquijo and Wheeler, both now living at the undercover house twenty-four hours a day, to tell them that he was now on the way to Bolivia to join with Jorge Román, Mario Vargas, and one of the top Corporation pilots for the trip to San Diego. Investigation had also established that the man the Bolivians were reporting to was definitely Pato Pizarro (the man with the Panamanian bank account protected by Manuel Noriega), probably the one most powerful drug dealer alive.*

I recognized immediately that while we had plenty of intelligence and circumstantial evidence linking both General Poblano Silva in Mexico and Pizarro in Bolivia to the conspiracy, we had no direct proof. No undercover agents had ever spoken to either of them directly, and Wheeler had lied so often and regularly that his claims (without corroboration) could easily be defeated by the greenest defense attorney. Anything less than a recorded conversation would be scoffed at by the Bolivian and Mexican authorities—especially the Mexicans.

Our "official" government position about Mexico, as expressed by the then Attorney General Meese, the State Department, and all the top suits and politicians, was that our relationship was a special one, and that Mexico was "fully cooperating" in our war on drugs. This entitled Mexico to special loans, grants, and antidrug funds that totaled, over the years, in the billions of dollars. A handful of U.S. politicians and bureaucrats called this absurd, making statements to the media that the Mexican military, police, and possibly the entire government were "rife with corruption" and involved in drug dealing.

The Mexican government had countered all such claims with *"Show us some proof."*

One of the loudest critics was Customs Commissioner William von Raab, who himself had been criticized by Congress for not being able to back up his assertions with proof. Thus the arrests in the Mexican portion of Trifecta† were looked forward to with great, and very enthusiastic, anticipation. It was my guess that the "highest

---

* There is some controversy over who is the one most powerful drug dealer alive. Most of the media usually credit one or more of the Ochoa brothers, of the infamous Medellín cartel, with that honor. But at the same time it is a well-known fact that Bolivia supplies the Medellín cartel with seventy to eighty percent of its coca base, and *that* was under the control of Pizarro.

† Customs still referred to that portion of the case as "Operation Saber."

authority" phone call that caused so miraculous a change in Scuzzo, Brown, and DEA's game plan in Panama, had originated from von Raab himself.

I remembered how Mexican police had "arrested" undercover DEA agent Enrique "Kiki" Camarena, and then tortured him slowly to death while they gleefully tape-recorded his cries. And how the top Mexican officials had almost laughed in the faces of the DEA suits while Kiki's killers were helped to escape Mexico. I could think of nothing I would have enjoyed more than repaying the bastards in kind with a recording of our own—a recording of a Mexican general doing a drug deal. That would be the kind of irrefutable proof that they couldn't deny. *And I had the plan to get it.*

The plan would also accomplish the same thing with Pato Pizarro and any other members of the Corporation involved with Román. We would have their recorded voices plotting to move tons of cocaine into the United States. F. Lee Bailey, Barry Slotnick, and Tom Puccio combined would not be able to get them off.

The other man I had not forgotten was the Panama money launderer, Remberto. From statements made by Méndez and Román and from the accent of his Spanish, I was sure he was a Bolivian, and therefore extraditable from Panama. He had done more than enough to be convicted for conspiracy. I pushed for the San Diego DEA office and United States attorney's office to have the international arrest warrant and State Department requests ready, so that Remberto might be immediately arrested and removed from Panama before he realized he had been "stung."

Scuzzo and Hoopel assured me that they had been in contact with Duncan in Panama and that Remberto was under surveillance. They also told me that the head of one of the Panamanian drug units, a "Captain Blackmon," had told them Remberto was "the key" to something they had been working on for a long time. That seemed logical. Duncan had told me that he was going to have Remberto's phone tapped; they must have found a wealth of information. I remembered Román, during the aborted Panama operation, running up to Remberto's suite to make and receive all his phone calls from the Corporation. *Somewhere in Panama they had to have tape-recorded conversations that were the key to the Corporation's entire operation.* I had a feeling that Remberto's arrest might turn out to be one of the most significant parts of the whole case. So when Scuzzo said it would be necessary for George Urquijo and me to fly to Panama immediately after the San Diego arrests to "positively" identify Remberto, I immediately agreed.

Nagging at me from somewhere in the back of my brain was Wheeler repeating the Bolivians' claim that Pato Pizarro's Panamanian bank account was "protected by Noriega." If this were true, how could we expect Panama to help us arrest Remberto, the Corporation's main money launderer? It did not seem logical. It had to be another case of Wheeler exaggerating. And if there was some "special" difficulty in arresting Remberto—such as his being a CIA asset or specially protected by some secret agency or other—Duncan, DEA's top officer in Panama, would have said something. I pushed Remberto from my mind to concentrate on the job at hand.

The final move that I had contemplated also hinged on the secrecy of the operation and was the most ambitious. The Bolivians believed that after the meeting they would be taken directly to my plane accompanied by Jake the pilot, Wheeler, and the five million dollars, to fly directly to Bolivia to pick up my first thousand kilos of cocaine. Instead they were going to be arrested. They almost certainly would be in some sort of telephone or radio contact with the Corporation (perhaps with Pato Pizarro himself) up to the last minute. If we could create a believable scenario for them, complete with five million dollars *and* a plane *and* pilots ready to fly to Bolivia, their final contact with the Bolivian Corporation—which would be tape-recorded, *or so I thought*—would indicate that they were on their way and nothing was wrong. Then, all we would have to do was keep the news of the arrests from the media for two or three days; that would be enough time for the Bolivian military elements of Snowcap to finally become useful, by raiding the jungle sites that Wheeler and Jake had been shown. The members of the Corporation and the landing sites would be there waiting to be busted like sitting ducks. It would also give Urquijo and me the time we needed to get to Panama and arrest Remberto.

On January fourth Hoopel called me in New York to tell me that in Bolivia, Román had been turned down for a visa to the United States, but that Méndez was going to take him to Mexico to get one there.

"How come we didn't just call the consular section?" I asked. "Just one phone call and they'd give it to him." I had worked overseas for many years. A DEA agent could arrange a visa for *anyone* with nothing more than a phone call. The idea of one of the biggest cocaine dealers alive not being given a visa to come to the U.S. for his own arrest would have been laughable on a movie screen, but in real life it was both frightening and tragic. Hoopel, as usual, had no answer that I could make any sense out of.

"It doesn't matter anyway," he said. "Méndez is bringing him to Mexico. We can wave him through, across the border."

After hanging up, my instincts told me that the suits were back at their dirty dealing again. I called Hoopel back; as case agent the undercover preparations were his job.

"Listen, Hubert," I began the moment I heard his voice. "I had a lot of thoughts about this thing since I talked to you."

"Okay."

"There's some real important stuff that has to be done."

"Okay."

"One is, talking to the U.S. attorney and getting a wiretap order on the phones of the undercover house. What I'm going to try and do is get these people to telephone their bosses back in their own countries, who you will indict. In other words, if I can get Román to call Pato Pizarro—under any pretext—you'll have his voice on tape."

"Uh-huh."

"If you don't have a wiretap on the phones, let's say I get the colonel to call his general, or some other big shot—you lost that guy."

"Okay."

"You follow me? . . . It's really, really important. The same thing happened to me in the Roberto Suárez case. He called me in my own undercover house in Miami, from Bolivia. I spoke to him with his right-hand man standing next to me, staring me in the face. I couldn't record the conversation, and because no one thought to wire the phone, we lost those conversations. So I'm speaking from experience."

"Uh-huh."

"You follow me?"

"Yes," he said, but I wasn't too sure. I continued to press the point that unless we recorded all calls from the undercover house, we would lose the chance to get direct evidence against both Pato Pizarro and General Silva.

Hoopel agreed to go to Assistant U.S. Attorney Paul DiPaolo with my request. Then he want on to tell me that "according to the latest calls from Mexico, everything is a go." The Mexicans were standing by, waiting to cross the border as soon as we were ready.

"Great," I said. "Luis [Pizarro] and I will be out there in two days.* This thing is not going to be the ground ball it looks like. It's going to take a lot of choreographing."

After I hung the phone up I spoke with Luis and told him to put his "witness hat" back in his overnight bag. "We're going to be doing some deep cover again."

We made reservations to leave for San Diego on January sixth. I wanted to be there to witness as much of the development of this case as I could. I had a feeling it was going to be very important.

On January fifth, when I got into my office in New York, there was a simple message from Scuzzo: *Don't come!* I dialed San Diego immediately. The moment the slow-talking Californian got on the phone I felt my teeth grinding in my jaw.

"Uh, Méndez is delayed in leaving where he's at to go south," he began, using his ridiculous code again, "and get with the people. Méndez is just leaving Mexico today to go south—and the one guy has a visa problem . . . but that was resolved. We had a message sent to the guy to just come to Mexico and we'll get him in."

Scuzzo said that he did not want me just "sitting around wait-

---

* Gene Blahato had court cases, and Luis Pizarro, the Spanish speaker, had already been introduced to Méndez as my nephew.

ing for these guys to show up." And that when he knew "for sure" that they were coming, he would call me.

"I don't mind hanging around," I said. "Besides, we could use the time to choreograph the whole thing." Luis and I had reservations for the next day. If I was going to document the destruction of Trifecta, I had to be there. Scuzzo finally agreed. Luis and I would be in San Diego the following evening.

Before hanging up I asked Scuzzo about the telephone taps. He said the house was being wired so that all calls could be tape-recorded from the attic. "I think we should get a pen register* put in," he said.

"No, we need a full Title 3 wiretap," I said, wondering for the hundredth time if he really knew that little about the basic tools of law enforcement or if it was all an act.

After a long pause he said, "I agree with you."

After I hung up the phone my knotted stomach gave me a hint of what the coming weeks were going to cost me.

By January 7, 1988, I was back in San Diego, accompanied by "nephew" Luis, attending a series of planning sessions at both Customs and DEA headquarters. The Customs agents were almost feverish with excitement. Commissioner von Raab himself was very "enthusiastic" about the case and was being kept apprized of every development. *The grandson of the writer of the Mexican constitution was on his way to San Diego to be bribed. What was Congress going to say now? Was that enough proof of Mexican corruption?* If ambitious Customs agents had wanted a piece of the case before, now they were scrambling over each other like a school of hungry piranhas.

At a planning session that same day, before the growing group of people now "in charge" of Trifecta, including Jim Ross, Arnie Gerardo, Albert Scuzzo, Hubert Hoopel, the newly promoted Lydia Soto, and the respective chiefs of each agency in San Diego, Ken Inglesby (Customs) and Charlie Hill (DEA),† I made these requests, wanting as many witnesses as possible:

---

* A device hooked to a phone line that gives a printout of every telephone number called.
† There were other Customs people present whom I did not know.

1. That a Title 3 wiretap be placed on the telephones in the undercover house in La Jolla.

2. That a flash roll of five million dollars be obtained in order that the Bolivians might be led to believe—up to the very last possible moment—that the deal was for real.

3. That an undercover aircraft be parked at San Diego airport, in case the Bolivians came with orders from the Corporation to verify everything before going through with the deal, which—considering what they had been through in Panama—should not surprise anyone.

4. That a private jet be made ready so that Jake, Urquijo, Wheeler, and myself, accompanied by other agents of both Customs and DEA, could leave for South America immediately after the arrests—first stop, Panama and Remberto; second stop, Bolivia and an attack on the Corporation.

A very disturbing event happened after the meeting at Customs. Jim Ross showed me his report of our undercover activities in Panama. The reason he had listed for the operation's failure was *"unreasonable demands on the part of the Bolivian cocaine traffickers."*

"This is bullshit!" I said, putting the report down in front of him. Both Hoopel and Luis Pizarro were also there. "This is pure unadulterated bullshit, and not true," I repeated, making sure Pizarro heard it loud and clear. I quickly rattled off the true reasons for the operation's failure, not the least of which was our being "forced to use the Marriott."

Neither Hoopel nor Ross had a comment—their crimson complexions spoke eloquently enough. What really disturbed me was that I had been toying with the idea of using Customs to blow the whistle on DEA and now could no longer even count on them to tell the truth.

Everybody was screwing the American public.

Another interesting development began to take shape. Ever since I had met Wheeler, back in September, he had made comments about how corrupt he thought DEA was. The comments had been made in the presence of almost every DEA and Customs agent assigned to the case, including Gene Blahato and Luis Pizarro while we were in Panama. Suddenly, it seemed that Wheeler was not only making his comments more frequently, but they were becoming more explicit.

"I wouldn't trust DEA in Miami for anything," he said in front of a roomful of DEA and Customs agents. "The whole office is on the take. I paid them off myself." He went on to describe how the DEA agents were dressed and the kind of car they were driving.

I found myself in a curious position. I, too, believed that DEA was corrupt, but in a totally different way. Wheeler believed the whole agency was taking graft and selling drugs. I believed the suits were lying to the American public to perpetuate the funding of the agency and its programs and, of course, their jobs; not to mention parlaying their easy access to the media into more lucrative careers in the private sector and politics; along with a host of other reasons that had nothing to do with winning a drug war.

I was ripping mad. The sonsofbitches were destroying everything I had been, and believed in, for the past twenty-five years, and tying my hands behind my back while they did it. All I could do was continue to document every move that was made and hope for a chance to someday use it. But the kind of thing Wheeler was spouting about was another story.

DEA had very stringent rules about reporting allegations of corruption. When an agent hears an allegation of corruption against another DEA agent, he is duty bound to report it immediately. Since Wheeler had been working as an informer for quite a while before I stepped into the picture, and was not inhibited in the least about spouting his allegations in front of any and all DEA and Customs agents, I had assumed that "someone" must have already made an official report. There was only one conceivable reason that the allegations would not be reported: fear of what an investigation might reveal.

Well, I was not afraid of an investigation—I was hungry for one. For months I had also been toying with the notion of going to some politician to start an independent investigation of both Operation Trifecta and Snowcap—but what politician could I trust? Most of them were supporting Snowcap in the press. And who knew what other special interests I might be treading on? I was sure the calculating beanpole of a man had something up his sleeve, but I was tired of trying to figure him out. I had enough to contend with fighting my own agency.

Suddenly his allegations gave me an idea. There was a way I could use them to start an investigation.

Late in the afternoon the whole team met at the house on the cliffs of La Jolla to begin rehearsing the undercover scenarios. Present were Wheeler, Ross, Hoopel, Luis, myself, some of the technicians who would work the cameras and recording equipment, and hosts of others who floated in and out. Before we began Hoopel gave me some bad news.

"Headquarters isn't going to authorize a five-million-dollar flash roll," he said, looking like he wanted to duck me. "They said all we needed was one million."

"Great," I said, the overtness of the suits' opposition to Trifecta no longer surprising me. They were still afraid that big, bad, uncontrollable Mike Levine would harm the image of their baby, so they were cutting my balls off before I began.

"And they aren't giving us an undercover plane either," said Hoopel.

"What the fuck do they think I'm going to do, jump in and fly to Bolivia myself? Got any more good news?"

He smiled. "Not yet."

There being not much else that I could do, I got down to the business at hand. Méndez had called Wheeler earlier and played right into our hands by requesting that the Bolivians and Mexicans not meet each other. The old man was probably afraid of losing his power as the main connection between the top criminals of both countries. He was the only one who knew both, and he wanted it to stay that way. That made the undercover scenario easy for us. There would two separate meetings, each culminating in an arrest. We planned to "entertain" the Mexicans first.

We rehearsed positioning the colonel before the hidden cameras; the kinds of conversation we would have—each of us staying in character in the best acting-school tradition—squeezing them for as much information about Mexican corruption as we could. (I had worked as a professional actor and was really enjoying the role of

Undercover in Panama, first trip, planning session.
Levine (standing), Urquijo (sitting).

Levine, with four other agents and
the five-million-dollar flash roll in Panama.

Levine as "Luis" just before first undercover meeting
in Operation Trifecta.

"Trip to Las Vegas." Left to right, Carranza, unidentified woman,
Hector Álvarez, Pablo Girón, and Jorge "George" Urquijo.

Arrest and press "ambush" of Pablo Girón.

Arrest of Colonel Carranza in San Diego.

Levine, undercover on day of arrests, as "Luis."

During trial, Urquijo and dummy dressed in Carranza's uniform.

Efren Méndez (The Old Man) after his arrest.

Jorge Román, after arrest.

Colonel Jorge Carranza after arrest.

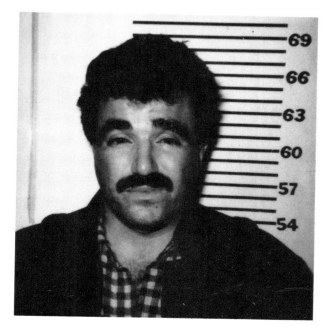

Mario Vargas after arrest.

Rolando Ayala (the Corporation's pilot), after arrest.

"Just what does an undercover agent do?"
President George Bush and Urquijo at luncheon.

Plaque received by Levine for participating
in the vice president's task force.

director.) When I got to the point where I would request the colonel to call his general to "make sure there were no problems" (our tape-recorded irrefutable evidence against the Mexican high command), Wheeler objected.

"What if he smells a rat?"

Ross nodded his agreement.

"What difference does it make?" I said. "By the time I get to the phone call, we'll have had more than enough conversation to convict him ten times over for conspiracy. If he smells a rat we just arrest him."

Nothing further was said about the matter, but his objection was enough to make me suspicious. There was no logical reason for it, but maybe there was a hidden one. I noted later that whenever I would mention the general, Wheeler would react in a way that reminded me of the sentry dogs I used to handle when I was in the Air Force. He would go on "alert." As we got closer to zero hour—if the sneaky sonofabitch did have something up his sleeve—I would know it.

After the Mexicans had left—thinking they were being driven back to the border—and been arrested, we would then bring the Bolivians to the house for act two.

The rehearsal for the Bolivians was a bit trickier. They were bringing a pilot who thought he was going to guide my pilot and plane back to Bolivia. To perfect a conspiracy case against him we needed someone to play the role of my pilot and discuss the flight plans on camera. I was told that Jake the pilot would be arriving shortly to play that role, which was fine with me. The Bolivians had already met him. The more comfortable we made them, the more they would talk.

Another problem we now had to overcome was the money. Thanks to the suits we only had one million dollars to show the Bolivians—not the five they expected to see. I was sure that if Román had any doubt about anything—after what he had been through in Panama—he would not make that final everything-is-okay call to Bolivia. We would lose both the final recorded conversation to Pato Pizarro (or some other Corporation big shot) and all chances at a military strike in Bolivia. But I had a plan that not even the suits could stop. Poor Román had been right about me; I *was* the son of a loan shark and I knew how to make a million look like five.

My plan was to have Luis Pizarro, whom Méndez had already met in Panama, show up—after we had milked them dry before the camera—to take the Bolivians to the airport, carrying the one million dollars. I would tell Román that the rest of the money was already on board the plane, but to save time, he should count this million in the house before leaving. It would be great evidence before the camera and hopefully would fool him long enough to make the phone call before he left for his final ride in this world as a free man.

I was an undercover specialist. The actual arrest plans did not concern me; that was for the conglomeration of DEA and Customs supervisors to work out. *Another mistake.* The only thing I was told was that each group would be arrested on the road somewhere, a distance from the undercover house.

It was close to midnight when Méndez called the undercover house. Wheeler answered the phone. The Mexican enforcer had finally arrived in Bolivia and had taken the Bolivians to La Paz to try and get visas. They had been turned down a second time. He was unsure of what they were going to do.

Wheeler suggested that he go to Mexico and cross the border on foot. The old man did not seem too keen on the idea of risking an arrest as a "wetback" in the middle of a multimillion-dollar cocaine deal. He sounded worried and said he would call back when they decided what they were going to do.

"I don't understand it," I said to Hoopel, trying to control my temper. "You told me that they had agreed on crossing the border on foot."

Hoopel glanced at Wheeler and Ross and said, "That's what I was told."

The look was enough to tell me that Wheeler had lied again. But why? And more important: Did Ross know he was lying?

"Christ, Hubert," I said. "I told you, all we had to do is call DEA in Bolivia and they would have gotten their visas right away." The room was silent. I was pissed. Scuzzo had worked many years in Thailand, he should have known better. There had been dozens of cables sent to Bolivia outlining everything that was happening in the case. The greenest of agents reading the cable traffic could have picked up a phone and arranged for the visas. Had Hoopel not told me that they were going to cross the Mexican border, I would have called.

January eighth was the day I would ambush Wheeler. At eleven A.M. he telephoned my room to tell me he had been called by Chuy in Bolivia. Méndez, Román, Vargas, and the pilot had taken off at five in the morning "for São Paolo" and would be calling the undercover house when they arrived.

I noted that Wheeler had said, after his earlier call with Méndez, that they were headed for Rio. I decided not to mention it; the time was not right, yet.

Wheeler then said that he had called Hector Alvarez in Mexico and that Alvarez had said that our deadline to pay the general was Monday (January eleventh). "The general has decided," continued Wheeler, "that in order to legally seal off the road our plane will be landing on, what he's going to do is order the resurfacing of two and a half fucking miles of road."

"That's great," I said, wondering how many phone calls the freewheeling informer had made that no one knew about. I decided to use the phone call to my own advantage for documenting a few more lies.

"You heard me call [Ross's] report, about everything that happened in Panama, 'bullshit,' right?"

"Oh, yeah! You know what [Customs] told me? They said, 'It's politics, don't worry about it, we'll iron it all out in the end,' but right now they want the thing to keep on going smoothly."

Wheeler and I made arrangements to meet within the half hour, at the house in La Jolla. As soon as I hung up the phone I called Pizarro in his room and we headed over there.

At the house Hoopel, Wheeler, Ross, and Lydia Soto's boyfriend, DEA agent Tommy Sharp, were already there. Sharp was fluent in Spanish and, this time, I was happy he was there. He would turn out to be useful.

The first order of business that concerned me was having Wheeler corroborate my report covering our aborted negotiations with Román in Panama—which directly contradicted Ross's report.

My report went into great detail about our conversations in that hot little hotel room, and how the case had nearly been destroyed by the suits. My only real witness was Wheeler. His telephone agreement that Ross's report was "bullshit" was not enough for me. I wanted him to say it in front of live witnesses—as many as possible—so he couldn't deny it later.

With a well-coached Luis looking over his shoulder, the lanky informer seemed to fold himself around the twenty-five-page report, as he read slowly and carefully, line by line, pausing only to pencil in some minor changes. From time to time he would glance at Ross. When he finished he said, "That's the way it happened," and handed the report back to me. I glanced significantly at Luis as I stuck the report in my attaché case.

We then sat around a while engaging in some small talk. When the time seemed right, I brought the subject around to Miami, and sure enough Wheeler attacked the bait.

"That fucking Miami DEA office is all bad," he said. "I paid off three agents myself."

I sprung my trap: "Did you ever make an official report of any of this shit?" Wheeler gaped at me as if I were speaking in a language he did not understand. *"I said,* did you ever make an official report of what you just told me? Did anyone, any official from any agency, ever write down or investigate what you are claiming?"

"I tried," he said, looking around the room at the four of us. "DEA just wasn't interested." Wheeler said that after his arrest in Oklahoma, he had tried to tell a DEA agent about corruption, but that the agent had said he wasn't interested.

"Well, I am very interested," I said, pulling out a pad and paper, unable to keep from smiling at the shocked expression on his face. He looked at Ross for help. Wheeler did not understand the bureaucracy. Within a bureaucracy a man on an anticorruption investigation is on a "mission from God"—no one will screw with him.

"I want to know exactly what you know about DEA corruption," I said, preparing to write, "because if there are any agents on the take, *I* want to make personally sure they go to jail."

The room was deathly still as I slowly and methodically questioned Wheeler about every bit of knowledge he had—no matter how insignificant. Some of what he said—though it remained to be proven—was startling. In general he claimed that drug-trafficker associates of his were able to buy any information they wanted from DEA agents of the Miami office. He also claimed to having been present when one payoff was made. He gave me detailed descriptions of three agents involved, along with their car. I was happy to be the instrument that would send thieving, drug-dealing agents to jail. I had done it before. To me they were just thieves with badges. *If* Wheeler was telling the truth. And truth with David Wheeler was always a very big *if.*

But I had more ambitious ideas for the report I would eventually write. I would use it to force an investigation that no one wanted. I was going to manipulate the DEA suits into investigating themselves—something they could never do honestly, because to do so was to signal their own demise. *What could be more corrupt than what had been done to Trifecta?* But they would have to do *something* with my report—that is the nature of a bureaucracy—and when they did, I would be watching.

Between three-thirty P.M. and six-thirty P.M. a large planning session was conducted at Customs headquarters. Present again were the expandable group of "supervisors": Hoopel, Soto, Ross, Gerardo, and the undercover team: Urquijo, Wheeler, Pizarro, Sharp, and myself, and a number of others whose role I did not know.

In an aside Hoopel had some interesting news for me. "The AUSA [assistant United States attorney] said that we don't need a Title 3 [legal wiretap]. He said we can record any phone calls made at the undercover house."

"That doesn't sound right to me," I said. I am not an attorney, but I have spent most of my adult life in federal, state, local, and foreign courts. I was sure either the AUSA was wrong or Hoopel didn't get the message straight. It was too important a point to let slide. It meant getting direct evidence against a Mexican general and possibly one of the heads of the Corporation.

It had to be an honest error or a missed communication. Why would an assistant U.S. attorney want to protect a Bolivian cocaine dealer and a Mexican general?

"Just double-check," I told Hoopel. I was conscious of how little time remained. Both the Mexicans and the Bolivians were scheduled to arrive within twenty-four to forty-eight hours. "If we don't apply for the Title 3 now, soon we won't be able to."

I had seen—in emergency situations—the massive paperwork involved in obtaining a court-ordered wiretap completed within twenty-four hours, but it required a team of professionals and a round-trip flight to Washington, D.C., for Department of Justice authorization. But I was beginning to wonder if there was such a thing as an emergency with these people. It would also necessitate the aid and cooperation of the DEA suits. *What chance was there of that?*

Hoopel promised me that he would check with the AUSA right after the meeting.

During the planning session, which lasted until six-thirty P.M., great attention was paid to the logistics of the arrests—who would arrest who, where they would be taken, where interrogations would be held. An incredible amount of time was devoted to the interrogation of the prisoners, down to the most minuscule of details—how each interrogator would be dressed, how each interrogation room would be furnished, where the prisoner would be seated, and which wall he would be facing. In twenty-five years of working undercover for five different federal agencies, I had never seen anything like it.

After about two hours I realized that absolutely no attention was being paid to obtaining recorded evidence against either the Mexican general or Pato Pizarro. Not a word was said about following up the investigation to Panama to trap Remberto the money launderer, or to Bolivia to strike at the Corporation. And when I mentioned a "news blackout" so that we could continue the operation, all I got were blank stares. *The idiocy of the whole thing was overwhelming.*

It was at this meeting I noticed how well entrenched with the Bureau of Customs Wheeler had made himself. He was treated as though he were an agent. The convicted felon, con man, drug-dealing informer, was allowed free access in and out of the Customs squad rooms, use of desks and telephones, and seemed to know and call everyone—right down to the secretaries—by their first names. He could walk through squad rooms, check files and desks, use telephones. *It was incredible!* During the planning session itself he was treated with the deference usually reserved for a supervisor, to the point where he was actually taking part in planning arrests. I marveled at what an undercover job this man had done against a whole government agency.

He was a hell of a lot more formidable an opponent than I had ever imagined.

Late in the meeting I began to push the discussion of how I would manipulate the colonel into making a phone call to his general. Wheeler, once again, was immediately against it. "I think he will smell something," he said.

Ross agreed.

"This colonel is here to pick up a million dollars for his boss, a Mexican general," I said, fighting my anger. "Once I pay him in front of the television cameras and have a little conversation to prove that he knows what the money is for, we can lock him up, right?"

The room was silent except for a couple of nods.

"So what is the point of this whole undercover bullshit exercise, unless we try to make a case against the general—the real boss? If we don't, there's no point in prolonging the thing, we've already got tons of evidence against Girón and Alvarez; as soon as the colonel accepts the money we ought to lock him up and it's case closed."

"Then what about the Bolivians?" asked Ross.

"Hell, we were going to lock them up in Panama, remember? As soon as they get here we can lock their asses up too. We've got more than enough to convict them for conspiracy ten times over. I want to do the same thing with them—that's why I wanted the wiretap of the phones in the house. If they call Pato Pizarro, or whoever else is running the Corporation, I want the conversation on tape.

"If we aren't going to try and follow this whole thing through and do as much damage to the *real* heads of this thing, *and* lock up this guy Remberto in Panama, *and* try to knock off the Corporation's landing fields and labs in Bolivia, then I can't see why we don't just arrest these guys as soon as they cross the border, and stop jerking ourselves off."

For a long moment the big crowded room was silent. Pizarro looked at me, smiled, and looked away. No one said anything to oppose what I had said, so I assumed that the point had finally been made. The discussion continued for another half hour, once again on the theme of coordinating the arrests and interrogations. Finally, as it was about to end, Lydia Soto had something to say.

The newly promoted Customs ASAC* wanted the defendants taken on a pleasure-boat ride on the undercover Customs yacht, with her and Tommy Sharp, because she thought it would be a good idea to "relax them." I looked around the big room in disbelief. No one had a thing to say, all eyes were on me. I caught George Urquijo's eye and he just shook his head sadly.

"These people are coming here to do a drug deal," I said with perhaps a bit too much sarcasm. "After what they went through in Panama, the last thing in the world they want to do is go on a pleasure-boat ride!" *Maybe I should have been more tactful, but my patience had worn very thin.*

Lydia would not get off the idea. After all, she *was* a Customs ASAC. If she wanted to have a boat ride with the defendants in a case that the commissioner himself was being briefed on, up to the minute, *who* would dare try to stop her?

I'm afraid I did.

"Look," I ended up saying, "if the idea of this whole case is to go on a goddamned boat ride, then fine: go ahead. But if you want to make a drug case, it is just plain stupid!"

"I think it's a good idea," chimed in Wheeler. "I think they make a great-looking couple."

"I told you before!" I snapped. "*Agents* make arrest plans, not informers."

Dead silence.

"Look, I want to play a part in this case," said Lydia. "Everyone wants to play a part in this case."

"Then why don't we *invite* everyone? Why don't you post some-

---

* Assistant special agent in charge.

thing in the hallway and invite everyone?" *I thought I was losing my mind.* "I just want to make a dope case."

There was a long silence and the meeting began to break up. One of the senior Customs people pulled me to one side. "I'm really sorry," he said. "I wanted to say something, but she's my boss. I just wanted you to know, I am really embarrassed."

"Believe me," I said. "I *know* how that is."

At about eight-thirty P.M., I was napping in my hotel when a nervous Ross called to tell me that the Mexicans were "definitely coming tomorrow" (January ninth) and the Bolivians "tomorrow night." The whole game plan could be carried off on Sunday, January tenth. I already knew the information came from Wheeler. I just wondered how accurate it was. Ross said that everyone was gathered and waiting for me.

At about nine P.M. Luis and I joined the whole undercover team, along with the expanding group of "supervisors," at the house in La Jolla to continue to rehearse the undercover scenario. Present were Urquijo, Wheeler, Ross, Hoopel, Sharp, Lydia, and some of the technicians who would be working the recording equipment in the attic. As soon as I arrived Hoopel had more "good" news.

"The AUSA said you were right; we can't record any calls made by the defendants," said Hoopel. "He said it would be an illegal wiretap."

"Fantastic," I said, not liking the smile I saw flicker and disappear on Wheeler's face. Hoopel went on to explain that the AUSA had also said it was "too late now" to apply for the Title 3.

How goddamned convenient everything seemed to work out.

"Ask him if we can record the fucking call," I said, my voice straining at the tightness in my throat, "if I can con the colonel into agreeing to have me listening on an extension." I already knew the ploy was legal. I had done it many times before, and was going to do it no matter what the AUSA said. I just wanted to hear what he said anyway. *I no longer trusted anyone.*

More difficulties arose during the rehearsal and planning session. The Mexicans were due to arrive the following morning. The arrival of Méndez and the Bolivians was still doubtful, in spite of Wheeler's assertions that they would arrive that night. Wheeler and

Ross were against my meeting with the Mexicans until the Bolivians were already in town. I wanted to meet with Colonel Carranza immediately.

"I'm the guy who he's expecting to get a million bucks cash from, right? Then I'm the guy he's going to want to impress. The more time I have with the man, the easier it is going to be for me to say, 'Look, Colonel. I really like you and trust you and all, but a million dollars is a lot of money. I don't want you to be offended or anything, but would you mind calling the general while I listen on the extension? I just want to make sure there is no problem with our arrangements.' "

"But he's going to get hinky," said Wheeler.

"I agree," said Ross. "I think he'll get hinky."

"And what fucking difference does that make?" I said, and we were back into the same argument we had had twice since yesterday. Finally, Ross, charged with the running of the case by Customs, stepped in and exercised his power as "case agent," in backing Wheeler's wishes. I looked at Hoopel, the DEA "case agent," and he said nothing. *It was at that moment that David Wheeler took complete control of Operation Trifecta.*

Wheeler's idea was to get the Mexicans relaxed, take them to dinner and a few drinks. "Maybe you could meet with them later in the evening," he said. "You can only get the general at home during the evening, anyway."

I sensed from the looks they shared, and the tone of the conversation, that there was no way they intended me to meet the Mexicans until the last possible moment. I could not imagine why they would *not* want the call to the general recorded.

The final plan was that Urquijo and Wheeler would pick the Mexicans up at the border and bring them back to the undercover house where Lydia and Sharp—according to Lydia's wishes, to which Ross had acquiesced—would be waiting as part of my mythical organization, to help "entertain" them. The Mexicans would be told, "Luis is not in town yet."

"And Tommy and I can take them out on the boat," said Lydia.

I glanced at Pizarro, who was intentionally looking the other way, and really flipped my lid. "Why don't you take them to fucking

Disneyland, too, while you're at it, and get them a bunch of stuffed animals they can play with while they're in jail?" Once again the whole object of Operation Trifecta had become a *boat ride.*

"I don't know," said Wheeler, grinning like a devil, "I think Lydia and Tommy make a great-looking couple."

Another argument began. Either these people were losing their minds or I was. Around and around we went. Finally I said, "You people are acting like you have to beg these bastards to *accept* my million fucking dollars. That's bullshit. We can have enough evidence to hang the colonel in five minutes." Once again I found myself repeating, "If we aren't going to try and hook the general in, and follow this whole operation up as far as it will go, then just let me give the guy the money the minute he gets here and lock his ass up."

"Then what about the Bolivians?" asked Wheeler.

I felt like I was in some sort of idiot's Ping-Pong game between Lydia, Ross, and Wheeler, and I was the ball. Nothing they were saying made sense, yet I had no referee to call a halt to the lunacy. I finally agreed to a plan whereby they would tell the Mexicans that Luis was in town but very busy. I would meet the Mexicans in the evening, *after* they had been sufficiently "entertained." I would then ask the colonel to telephone the general.

The phone rang and Wheeler answered it. I looked at my watch. It was already two A.M. *How time flies when you're having fun.*

It was Méndez reporting that he was in "Rio" (according to Wheeler). It was Saturday morning and they would have to wait until Monday for the American consul to open to get their visas. When Wheeler hung up the phone the room was in shocked silence. Méndez and the Bolivians would not be able to arrive in the U.S. earlier than late Monday night or Tuesday, a two- to three-day delay.

Ross and Wheeler were in a panic. What if the Mexicans got burned? What if they suspected something? According to the Mexicans, General Silva had set a deadline—they had to have the money and be on the way back to Mexico by no later than Monday Now what do we do?

"This is the best break we could have had," I said, picking up the phone. "Now we can really get the general." It was the weekend; there would be no time to get the legal wiretap, and I was sure the DEA suits in Washington would intentionally screw it up, anyway. But I would have plenty of time to manipulate the colonel into calling the general with me listening in on an extension. I telephoned a friend of mine, John Hughes, the DEA country attaché to Brazil, at his home in Brasilia and told him about our situation.

"No problem," said the ex–Dallas Cowboy. "I'll make sure your boys get their visas." John was going to leave for Rio immediately.

After I hung up I resisted the temptation to ask Ross who had told him the Bolivians would be arriving Saturday night and ask Wheeler who had told him that Méndez was going to São Paolo. I would play their game. They had their secret agendas; I had mine— to document them.

Ross was in a real panic about stalling the Mexicans for the weekend. "If they even make a move like they are going to split," he said, "we'll just lock them up on the spot."

"There's no reason to panic," I insisted, picturing my chance at the general being destroyed by a panic arrest. Ross swung like a pendulum, from one extreme to the other. One minute he wanted to take the Mexicans joyriding on a yacht, the next he was going to arrest them if they even so much as faced south. "They are here to pick up a million bucks," I said, trying to calm him. "If I just tell them that the Bolivians are delayed and I am not paying them until I am sure there is a deal, they will understand."

Ross looked at me as though I were speaking another language.

By three A.M., we finally agreed that the Mexicans, who were to arrive at ten A.M., would be wined, dined, and entertained during the day—with no boat ride (a nervous Ross was suddenly siding with me on this one)—after which they would be brought to the house in La Jolla, where I would arrive as Luis the Magnificent, to tell them of the delay and to begin manipulating Colonel Carranza into calling the general.

On Saturday morning, January ninth, at about seven-thirty

A.M., Hoopel called me at the hotel. We discussed what had happened during the evening.

"You know," I said, "it sounds to me like Customs is getting ready to arrest the Mexicans no matter what."

"Well, I had a talk with [Ross] a little bit about that this morning. I think they were just excited last night. I think now he realizes they can't just arrest the Mexicans when we got [the Bolivians] en route. I think you made the perfect point last night when you said it would be a perfect opportunity to get [the general] on the telephone."

"Yeah." I wanted to shout hallelujah. That was the first time anyone had said my plan was a good idea. I just wished that Hoopel had stood up for me the night before—when it counted. There was another thing that was puzzling me about the night before.

"What's Lydia's position in this?" I asked, remembering how she had suddenly included herself and Sharp in the undercover scenario, and the boat ride. "Is she running this thing now?"

"I don't know," said Hoopel. "She phases in and she phases out. I won't see her for weeks and she pops up again, and she's in charge."

"When she told me again last night that she was going on a boat ride, I flipped. All of a sudden it was like we were doing this whole operation so that she could go on a boat ride."

We discussed the strange relationship between all the Customs supervisors and Wheeler. I was relieved to find that Hoopel found it as bizarre as I did. I was looking for some key to understand what might be the basis of such an "unholy union."

"It's the weirdest thing I've ever seen in my life," I said.

"Yeah," Hoopel agreed. He had told me all he knew.

"This thing is a nightmare for me," said Hoopel suddenly. "Having to stroke this thing with Customs. . . . You know," he said, his voice, for the first time, almost cracking from the strain he was under.

I did know. I suddenly felt sorry for him. He was just a young agent put into something that was way over his head. He was as much a victim of the suits as I was. Hoopel had been named case agent because it was a position no one else wanted, particularly in a joint investigation between two archrivals vying for power and turf supremacy in the drug war.

President Nixon had actually created DEA in 1973 to avoid a war between DEA's predecessor, the Bureau of Narcotics and Dangerous Drugs (BNDD), and the Bureau of Customs. BNDD was abolished and all its agents transferred to the newly created DEA, along with 750 Customs agents—all the agents working narcotics investigations, of which I was one. The war, however, was not avoided, only delayed.

By 1987 the two archrivals clawing at each other's throats—of course, telling the public how well they worked together—were now Customs and DEA. But the years had made the suits on each side a lot smarter. They realized that if a media war did break out, it would be the bureaucratic equivalent of a thermonuclear war, ending in the destruction of both. Each agency could easily prove the other frauds and incompetents. But it was much more advantageous to snow the public into believing that all was well and continue to snipe at each other on a case-by-case basis.

It was poor Hubert "Helmet Head" Hoopel's primary duty to "stroke" Customs—get along with them at all costs. The media and appearances were everything; drug investigations and the lives of agents meant nothing—there was an inexhaustible supply of each, a dime a dozen.

"The politics involved," said a suddenly bitter Hoopel, "are unbelievable—un-fucking-believable. I was talking to Bill Brown this morning and he said that it was a good thing we've got guys with a strong personality like you in this thing, otherwise Customs would be fucking running away with it. . . . It would be a disaster."

I listened to Hoopel talk and realized that I was no better than he, or any of the other DEA agents who realize that the whole drug war is nothing more than a game—a dangerous game, but a game nonetheless—and continue to play, risking their lives but afraid to risk their jobs. I was as afraid as any of them—afraid of a truth I had refused to see ever since the nightmare of the Roberto Suárez case.

"Listen," I said to Hoopel, remembering something important. "Last night Wheeler said the old man was in São Paolo. The other day he said Rio. I don't know what his game is, but I have John Hughes running to Rio, and it might be for nothing."

Hoopel had also heard the contradiction and said he would ask Ross to check the tape recordings of the conversations. My heart sank. I was suddenly sure that I had sent my friend on a wild goose chase across Brazil. Wheeler had done it again. But for what reason?

"Why don't you go get breakfast or something," said Hoopel. "They aren't going to arrive until maybe in the afternoon."

"Wheeler said ten o'clock, yesterday."

"I don't understand. Jim [Ross] said they were first leaving where they are in Mexico at ten."

There was no sense discussing it any further. Wheeler, Ross, and company, at that moment, were running their own show and there was no making sense of it.

Right after Hoopel hung up I got a panic phone call from Scuzzo. "Do you have John Hughes's phone number in Brazil?" he asked. "Just in case we have to have them arrested down there." Then he said something that tipped me off to what was behind the sudden call: "Is there any chance of you getting the Bolivians to come back to Panama?"

I took a deep breath and said, "After what we went through? Not a fucking chance." Since my arrival in San Diego he had completely distanced himself from the case, but now the DEA suits were in a frenzy and coming down on his head. Customs, I reasoned, must be a lot closer to arresting the Mexicans than I had thought, and the DEA suits were suspecting the Customs suits of getting ready to "steal" the media show—the *real* drug war.

"The only reason I ask," continued Scuzzo, "is that we have a lot more people there [in Panama]. I talked to the [Panamanian] police and they're in pocket to help with the other guy [Remberto]." Then the big droning Californian slipped into his hopeless telephone code. "Well . . . the people that I've been talking to; they'll jump. . . . They'll help us. We have to have money and jump on their plane . . . and wire out the plan."

"The big problem you have," I said, deciding to cut the bullshit off, "is that Customs is getting ready to lock these guys up any minute," I guessed.

"I know," he said, confirming my suspicions. "Did Hubert tell you about that?"

"Yes," I lied.

Scuzzo again launched into a coded babble that I deciphered to mean that the DEA had suddenly become concerned because no one in DEA had any idea where any of the "defendants," Wheeler, or the Customs agents were, or what they were doing. *I would not have been surprised if they had already arrested the Mexicans. But why?* Their sudden rush to make an arrest still made no sense to me. I sat there listening to his voice drone on, not hearing a word. Then he said something that registered.

"What they [Customs] have done is . . . they've got a whole national press release ready for Operation Saber."*

So that was Ross's game. He wanted to make sure our Mexican defendants would be part of a press release that was probably scheduled for either Sunday or Monday. Of course. The grandson of an ex-president of Mexico was a great trophy for von Raab. It was Customs's turn to enhance the image of the commissioner.

"Hey," I said, an idea hitting me. The only chance I had to save what was left of the operation was to set a fire under Scuzzo's ass—a seemingly impossible task. "We could have fucked Operation Saber by arresting the Bolivians in Panama, right?"

"Right."

"And we didn't, right?"

"Hey," said Scuzzo. "I'm glad you said that. You just gave me an idea." Suddenly Scuzzo couldn't wait to get off the phone. He was going to take the matter up with his boss, Charlie Hill. I wished him luck. *The poor boob was no worse than Hoopel or me.*

By ten A.M. I still had no idea of what was going on. I grabbed my witness, Pizarro, and headed for the undercover house. Hoopel was there with a couple of technicians working on the wiring. The phone rang. It was Wheeler. I surprised him; he was looking for Ross.

---

* Operation Saber was the Customs probe into Mexican corruption that had actually led to Trifecta. Customs had numerous other corrupt, low-level Mexican officials that they wanted to arrest at one time.

"What the fuck is going on?" I said.

"We are on the way to the border to pick them up," he said enigmatically. "And the game plan is different."

"What do you mean?"

"Well, we are going to tell them that Luis hasn't arrived in town yet and that he doesn't have the money yet."

"You slimy motherfucker," I said, all vestiges of control out the window. *If I'd had him in front of me I'd have probably punched his lights out.* "When this is over, you better get far the fuck away from me. You follow the fucking game plan we agreed on!" I shouted into the phone.

"Inglesby changed it," said Wheeler, referring to the special agent in charge of the San Diego Customs office, the highest authority he could possibly invoke.

"I don't give a fuck!" I shouted. "You follow my fucking game plan!" I slammed the phone down and turned to see a smiling Pizarro and a slack-jawed Hoopel watching me. "Excuse me," I said, heading for the door. "I need some exercise." I went straight to a local gym and tried to straighten out my twisting guts in a furious two-hour workout.

I no sooner reached my hotel room than my phone rang. It was Hoopel to tell me that Wheeler and Urquijo would be picking up the Mexicans shortly and that they were back on the agreed game plan. I asked him if he had heard anything from John Hughes or the Bolivians. "Albert is taking care of that," he said. "I'll call you as soon as there's anything new."

About an hour later Hoopel called to say, "They're at the border." He would call to let me know what progress was being made.

The next call from Hoopel was late in the afternoon. He said that Customs was now assuring DEA that they would not make the arrests until the Bolivians arrived. *There was a temporary truce in the media war so that the drug war could continue.*

Everything was apparently going well with the Mexicans too. Hoopel reported that they were "very relaxed" and not at all nervous. They were being wined and dined by Urquijo and Wheeler, and then he added: "It has been decided that you should not meet with them until tomorrow."

I did not have to ask who had made the decision.

Day one of my opportunity to catch the general was lost.

At eight-thirty P.M. the phone rang. It was George Urquijo, calling me from a phone booth in the restaurant. He reported that everything was going well; that the Mexicans were relaxed and enjoying themselves. He laughed and said, "Hector [Álvarez] really has a thing for you, man. You better watch out, that sucker is in love."

I thanked him for the compliment. I really liked George. He seemed to be the only agent assigned to the case—from either side—who was above the politics and just wanted to do the job. I asked him to try and determine whether or not the Mexicans and Bolivians were still in contact with each other. He said he would and that he would call me as soon as they got back to the undercover house.

At ten-thirty P.M. I received another call from Hoopel, who reported that the hidden microphones at the undercover house had picked up the three Mexicans discussing a general by the name of Salvador de la Vega who was supposed to get three hundred thousand of the million dollars. Girón and Álvarez were also going to request twelve VCRs apiece, as additional booty.

Twelve VCRs? Big-time drug dealers?—No way! It just didn't fit. The only thing that fit perfectly were Girón and Wheeler.

"Hubert," I said, "it's now more important than ever that I get a shot at conning the colonel into calling his general. Two different generals have been mentioned. How the hell are we going to know which one to indict, unless we get him on the phone?"

"Uh-huh," said Hoopel. *Long silence. What the hell, I was beating a dead horse. There was nothing he could do either.*

"The colonel is all excited about meeting you," said Hoopel finally.

"Yeah, when is that going to be?"

"They want you to come over early tomorrow morning, *before* they go on their boat ride." *Yes, the boat ride was back on.* Hoopel was quiet for a long moment—waiting for me to explode, I suppose. But I just felt too weary and beaten. "The surveillance team is following them back to the hotel now," said Hoopel. "Wheeler's probably drunk by now."

"Great," I said. "What's next?"

"As soon as the Mexicans are dropped off, Wheeler and Urquijo are going to return to the Catamaran, room ten fifty-six—Customs set up a little command center there—to brief us on everything that happened. Are you gonna come?

"You think I should?"

Pizarro and I arrived at the room at about eleven-thirty P.M. Ross and Hoopel were already there awaiting the arrival of Urquijo and Wheeler. The Mexicans had been safely tucked away in a Bay Area hotel with an army of Customs *and* DEA agents watching them. *The DEA suits were no longer taking any chances in losing the media war. What they didn't know was that it was too late already.*

Hoopel informed me that the AUSA had given his okay to record Colonel Carranza's call to the general (if I succeeded in getting him to make the call). "But he said you've got to be on the extension listening, and the colonel *must* give his consent for you to be there."

"Yes, I know," I said, wondering if I would even get the chance.

When Urquijo and Wheeler arrived, Wheeler acted drunk and sick. He did not want to talk. He wanted to just go to bed. Urquijo in an aside said that Wheeler had wanted to go home to bed in the middle of dinner.

"I just don't know about that guy," I said.

"Neither do I," said Urquijo, "and I've been living with him."

Wheeler's "sickness" notwithstanding, he stayed and we discussed the events of the day. Carranza, or "the little colonel," as he came to be known, had brought his full-dress army uniform to impress me. Incredibly, he had also brought his officers'-school yearbook, as further proof of who he was. He was speaking very freely, according to Urquijo. In fact, he had even bragged, among other things, about helping to train Nicaraguan Contra guerrillas. *This last should have immediately alerted me as to the depths of the special interests Trifecta was up against.*

"That's exactly the frame of mind I want him in," I said. "He has it in mind to prove to me that he is the real thing. I *know* he will bite when I ask him to call the general."

Once again, a suddenly "well" Wheeler was arguing against the phone call. "Pablo [Girón] is acting funny," he said. "I think he smells something."

"What the fuck is the difference?" I said, wishing I were sixteen again and back on the streets of The Bronx with the slime-ball stool-pigeon.

I suddenly remembered something a police sergeant, Sal Forzano, who had worked with me in the New York Task Force a few years before, had said by way of an explanation of why I did so well working undercover: "You know, Levine, the bad guys all think you're bad, because you're one of these guys that *should* have gone wrong, but somehow wound up on the right side of the law."

What is the right side? I wondered.

"Maybe Dave is right," said Ross. "There's no rush."

Once again I found myself alone in a battle that somehow had become routine. It was late and I was too tired to continue. We reached a tentative agreement that Luis "might" be allowed to meet the Mexicans the next day *after* they had their "boat ride" with Lydia and Sharp.

SEVEN

THE ODYSSEY

On Sunday morning, January tenth, *real* panic struck. At eight forty-five A.M. Hoopel called to tell me that Wheeler had reported that the Mexicans were nervous and suspicious; that they were demanding to see the money. They also wanted women and drugs. Hector Álvarez had said, "If Luis won't give us women and dope, we'll go over to T.J. [Tijuana, Mexico]"

Álvarez had no idea how close he had come to getting himself arrested on the spot. The entire Bureau of Customs was thrown into a panic every time the Mexicans even mentioned leaving. Arnie Gerardo suggested that to entertain them and occupy their minds, we send them on a trip to Las Vegas until the Bolivians arrived. In any event, it was time for me (as Luis) to make my entrance.

"Wheeler is going to call you and put you up-to-date himself," said Hoopel. "He did say that he wanted you to really relate to Hector [Álvarez], in explaining the delay. He thinks Hector will have a lot of influence on the others." *Now Wheeler wanted me to flirt with Álvarez; what next?*

As soon as I hung up the phone it rang again. It was Wheeler. "Good morning, Michael."

"I heard already," I said. "They want women and dope."

"Yeah, I gave them my gun, and that wasn't enough."

"You gave them your gun?" I was stunned. In twenty-five years as a federal agent I had never heard of an informant being allowed to carry a gun, much less a man on bail for selling drugs. And to allow him to give his gun to a drug dealer we were about to arrest . . .

"I said," continued Wheeler, " 'All I've got is my baby [gun]. . . . Here it is.' " Wheeler wanted me to come right over to the undercover house.

"Are the Mexicans there yet?" I asked.

"No! We were kind of thinking you would come over and we would talk it out . . . find out what *you* were going to do."

"Yeah," I said carefully. He was trying to find out if I would attempt the phone call to the general—I wasn't going to. The information we had was that the general would not be at home in Mexico until the evening and I wanted to make sure we got him on the first try. But I did not want Wheeler to know what I was planning; I was sure he would do something to screw it up. I changed the subject and said, "One of the things that was mentioned was a trip to Vegas." I was still trying to figure out what secret moves he and Ross had up their sleeves.

"Yeah," said Wheeler. He wasn't biting, though. He was too smart to talk too much on a telephone—much smarter than the agents controlling him. He must have suspected that I might be recording the conversation. "Why don't you come on over?"

It was about nine-thirty A.M. when Luis and I arrived at the undercover house. Hoopel, Ross, Gerardo, Wheeler, Lydia Soto, Tommy Sharp, and some of the technicians working the attic were there. During the meeting that ensued, others were in and out, including Arnie Gerardo.

In the twenty minutes since my phone call Wheeler had been able to whip Ross and the others into another panic. He had them all *again* convinced that the Mexicans were on the verge of splitting at the drop of a tortilla. Fueling the fires was a surveillance report that they had been up and walking around their hotel until the wee hours of the morning.

Hoopel told me that I was now going to be authorized to front the Mexicans up to fifty thousand dollars. Arnie Gerardo said that Customs was going to authorize giving them ten thousand dollars for a fun-filled weekend in Vegas.

Man, *that* is panic, I thought.

It was only Sunday morning and the Bolivians, at best—according to all available plane schedules from Rio—would not arrive until early Tuesday. And it still was not even certain that they *were* in Rio.

I looked at the faces of the agents around me—with the exception of Lydia Soto, who was still wondering out loud about the boat ride, and Pizarro, who just smiled—and realized that they reminded me of passengers on an airplane who have just been told that an engine has failed.

"Just leave it up to me," I pleaded with anyone who would listen. "They've come here to get a million bucks from me. I control them. Just leave the whole fucking thing in my hands."

"What are you going to tell them?" asked Ross suspiciously.

"Simple, the fucking truth. I want to give them the money, but until the Bolivians arrive I don't even know if there is a deal. Then I'll politely ask the colonel to call his general so that I can be sure his end is still okay."

"No good," said Wheeler. *I fought the urge to kill him.* "They are so hinked up already, they're liable to just fucking leave. You know what Girón told me last night? He said, 'I know you a long time, David. You are not acting like yourself.' "

I wondered which "self" he was talking about. Once again the familiar battle raged. I wanted to push for the call to the general. Ross and Wheeler didn't want me to. *Lydia wanted the boat-ride option.*

We finally agreed that Luis the Mafia boss would have to make his appearance to get the situation under control. I was going to be allowed to either send the Mexicans to Vegas or front them fifty thousand dollars, but I had to promise *not* to try for the phone call.

At twelve noon, dressed in solid white like a Puerto Rican *santero* from New York, diamonds on both hands, heavy gold chains on my neck, and a solid gold watch on my wrist, I parked my

Mercedes 450SL sports coupe in the driveway of the undercover house. Inside, the videotapes had been rolling for almost an hour as the Mexicans nervously awaited my arrival. Luis García-López, sometimes known as Mike Levine, was about to make his grand entrance. It was precisely the psychological setup I wanted. There was no doubt as to who was in charge.

When I first saw Colonel Jorge Carranza-Peniche I almost choked fighting back my laughter. The solidly built little man in full-dress Mexican army uniform, decked out with a chestful of medals, stood at full attention as I came in the door. He had on eyeglasses with lenses so thick, I thought he had bought them in one of those cheap joke stores. I looked at Urquijo, who had to turn and look out the window.

The hour-long meeting went incredibly well. The three Mexicans addressed me as though I were visiting royalty. It was exactly as I had predicted—they wanted to please me. The colonel had brought his military-school yearbook and pointed out the photos of the officers who would "work" with my organization. It seemed that the whole Mexican army was for sale. The colonel spoke freely, making it very clear that he was not on his own; his boss was General Poblano Silva.

Three feet in front of a camera disguised as a lamp, the colonel and I laid out maps and photos of landing sites where my cocaine-laden plane would land. Meanwhile, four feet above our heads, in the attic, video and sound recorders whirred softly. He pointed out where his troops would be and how they would protect and refuel the plane. We went on to discuss future, much larger cocaine shipments.

The little colonel and I really got on well. Within a short time he was speaking freely on almost any subject I probed, and volunteering information I had not asked or bargained for. He even pointed out an area on the maps, stating that they were bases for the training of Contras. Once again, this information had no significance or importance to me.

The colonel was so relaxed and seemingly eager to please that I had to fight the urge to ask him to make the phone call. I was sure he would have done anything I asked. But I couldn't do it. I decided

that if I was going to break my promise not to press for the phone
call, it would be in the evening when the general was supposed to be
home. It was still too early in the game for me to alienate Ross. With
the Bolivians delayed I was sure I would get plenty of opportunities
for the phone call.

It would be a decision I would regret.

When I explained that I could not give them the money until
Méndez and the Bolivians arrived, and I knew for a certainty that
there *was* a deal, the colonel reacted just as I thought he would. He
would have no problem waiting for their arrival. He would call the
general and inform him of the delay.

An hour into the meeting my "nephew" Luis Pizarro appeared
with a satchel full of money—the million dollars that had finally
arrived from Miami.

"My nephew has been picking up some money for me," I said,
casually removing a packet containing ten thousand dollars and
tossing it to Wheeler, making sure that the camera never lost sight of
the money's trajectory.

"Take these gentlemen to Las Vegas as my guests," I said in a
show of casual disdain for money, an impression that I hoped would
stay with the Mexicans until we had squeezed them dry of all the
intelligence and evidence we needed—especially the recorded phone
call to their leader.

After the meeting I went back to my room and lay down with a
wet rag over my face and fell asleep that way. The phone woke me
up at about seven in the evening. It was Hoopel to tell me how well
everyone thought the meeting had gone and that Wheeler, George,
and the Mexicans, with an army of agents following them, were well
on their way to Vegas by car.

I went back to sleep.

On Monday, January eleventh, at nine A.M., I called Hoopel at
the office to find out what was going on. I particularly wanted to
know if the colonel had telephoned the general from our undercover
house as I had thought he would.

"I think he did," said Hoopel. The casual way the man accepted being manipulated out of the most important evidence, in a

case that would probably be the highlight of his career as a narcotics agent, drove me wild. "Well, uh, they may be trying to indict the general anyway," he added.

"Could you imagine what we would have had if we had the phone tapped?" I said.

"I know," said Hoopel dully.

"Well, at least you're learning," I said, thinking: *At the expense of the American taxpayers.*

"Everything is going well in Brazil," said Hoopel, changing the subject. "They are going to have their visas the first thing tomorrow morning."

"Tomorrow morning?"

"Yes, in fact, Albert is sending John [Hughes] travel authorization to follow them to the States."

"Great." At least that side seemed to be coming together, thanks to John Hughes.

"You want to hear a funny story?" Hoopel had already heard the first account of the Mexicans' adventures in Las Vegas. "The little colonel asked Wheeler how to get laid," said Hoopel, already laughing. "So Wheeler points out a line of hookers and says, 'You take out a hundred-dollar bill and just show it to one of them.' So the colonel goes over to one of the girls, takes out the hundred, and shows it to her. The girl takes the money, sticks it in her bra, and walks away." Hoopel exploded in laughter.

I laughed with him. *This was the man they said was going to get suspicious if I asked him to call his general.* I hung up the phone thinking that I would finally have twenty-four hours to relax and enjoy San Diego.

But it was not to be.

On Tuesday, January twelfth, at about nine A.M., I received an incredible phone call from Hoopel. With an idiotic laugh he told me that Méndez had telephoned the house in La Jolla, from Rio, to report that he and the Bolivians were now on their way to Mexico City.

"How come Mexico, all of a sudden?" My head swam with all the changes.

"Well, what happened was that while they were in São Paolo, they got turned down for visas from both the United States and Mexico." Hoopel laughed again, he really thought all this was funny.

I was furious. The idiot didn't have enough sense to see that we had come within a hair's breadth of losing the whole case. John Hughes, thanks to Wheeler's misdirection, had gone to Rio. What had saved the day was Méndez having his *own* connections at the Mexican embassy, where he finally got the Bolivians their visas.

They were *now*—according to Hoopel, which offered me no great assurance—on their way to Mexico City, where they would connect to a flight to Tijuana, from there we would "smuggle" them across the border.

"Maybe they didn't even apply for the American visa and just applied for just the Mexican one," said Hoopel, still laughing.

"We should know that!" I said, once again so angry that there were tears in my eyes. "We should already know that. We're a fucking hot-shit, international enforcement agency. We should already know everything they did. Fuck it! I shouldn't be telling you what to do. I'm trying to just do the undercover job." I knew that if I didn't get off the phone quickly I would say a lot of things I might regret.

"Okay," he said finally. "They're coming, anyway. Just thought I'd let you know."

When I got off the phone I calculated that with luck the Bolivians might be delayed an extra day. I would then have tomorrow to catch the general at home.

At one P.M. I received another call from Hoopel. He had found out that the Bolivians had, in fact, gotten Mexican visas in Rio and were still there. They had called Lydia at the undercover house and left a message: "Tell Luis everything is fine, and we'll see him tomorrow." They told Lydia that they would be leaving for Mexico City in the afternoon.

Hoopel thought that they would arrive in Tijuana by ten in the morning. I figured he was at least twenty-four hours off. He said that everything had been rigged with Customs and Immigration for Wheeler to "walk" them across the border as though he owned it.

"Well, it seems that everything is going like clockwork now," said Hoopel hopefully.

I felt my insides cringe. "So [the colonel] had no trouble with the general about missing the deadline, after all," I said.

"Hell, they are having so much fun"—he laughed—"they aren't talking or thinking about coming back, now." Then he told me another little-colonel story. "The little colonel," he said, already laughing, "broke his glasses. And you know those thick Coke-bottle glasses he has. Well, they only had women's glasses—the big, curly, sequined kind. Well, he's wearing these things around the casino trying to pick up women . . ."

The image of the little macho guy in the Mexican army uniform with all the medals, wearing sequined women's eyeglasses threw me into uncontrolled, chest-aching laughter. My insides were molten with rage and frustration, but there I was laughing.

"They say he's hilarious," wheezed Hoopel, trying to catch his breath. "These [Mexicans] are going to be fucking devastated."

I stopped laughing.

"No wonder Mexico's in such bad shape," he said, trying for another laugh.

"What's the next move?" I asked.

"Well, the Mexicans are leaving Vegas this afternoon. Jim [Ross] is flying back to begin planning the arrests and everything. Oh, and the jet to take you and George [Urquijo] to Panama is all set . . . And I got a note from Duncan that he's all set [in Panama]. They're just waiting for our word to do it. You can have access to everything."

With the mention of Duncan's name I had sudden visions of Noriega and big problems. "You've got to tell Duncan to get that guy [Remberto] under surveillance now, so we know he's there."

"Yeah. Okay."

"Because if we don't, we're going to drive up with Duncan, knock on his door, and he might not be home. Then we'll never get him."

"Yeah, that's a good idea, to get ready."

"And let him do all the background on the guy now—who is he, et cetera."

"They have that," said Hoopel. "I don't know who he is, but they've got it already."

"Okay, excellent," I said, not liking the vibrations I felt about going back to Panama. Duncan's strange behavior combined with the possible ties to Noriega really frightened me. I had heard much talk over the years about how "dirty" the military strongman was. And that was *his* country, not mine.

I asked Hoopel if there would be room to take Luis Pizarro with us. He said that Wheeler, Bill Brown, Jake (the CIA pilot), and another Customs agent would also be on board for the second leg of the flight to Bolivia; there would not be room for him. I was really going to miss my witness, but at least it would be for a worthy purpose.

After hanging up I figured that, since the Mexicans were returning that evening, I had better begin laying the groundwork for the call. The first thing I had to make sure of was that the recording equipment was working. With this bunch I could take nothing for granted. I waited until two P.M. and called Hoopel back to tell him that I had a plan.

"I don't want you to say anything to Wheeler or George," I said. "It's important that when I spring it, they react naturally."

"Okay," said Hoopel cautiously.

"It's important that Bill [Bill Brown, working in the attic] listen closely to me so that when the colonel and I get on the phone, he records the call."

"Okay."

"Tell him to double-check those phones, to see that they're working, because I'm gonna have that sucker on the phone."

"Sounds good," said Hoopel.

At six P.M. Scuzzo paged me at dinner. When I got him on the phone he told me that Gospadarik in headquarters was already preparing the press release for the case and it was going to be "a big one."

"Albert," I said, "if they put out the news release before we get to South America, they'll screw up Remberto's arrest and any chance to get anything in Bolivia. Not to mention the danger they'll be putting us in."

"I'll tell him," said Fast Albert.

I went back to dinner.

At seven P.M. I received a call from Hoopel. He was in the hotel command center waiting for Ross, Gerardo, and others, to begin planning the arrest scenarios. He laughed and said there was no rush. "The Mexicans haven't even left Las Vegas yet."

"They haven't left yet?" All I could think of was losing my chance at the general.

"Girón and Álvarez have locked themselves in a room with two girls and will not come out."

At eight P.M. Luis and I arrived at the command center and met with Gerardo, Ross, and Hoopel. Ross lay on the bed and spent most of the time speaking on the phone, in very cryptic terms, about what sounded like press arrangements and the effect the case would have on his career.* He was grinning and purring like a Cheshire cat. "So they're all *really* excited?" I heard him say.

I took advantage of the opportunity to question Arnie Gerardo, an ex-FBI agent, about the unusual latitude Customs had given their informer. He just seemed much too professional to allow what I had seen.

"Arnie," I said, "I have never seen more of the rules on handling informants violated with one man, in my twenty-five-year career."

To my great and happy surprise Gerardo agreed with me. "I inherited this case," he explained, shrugging his shoulders. "That guy was spoiled long before I got here."

When Ross got off the phone, I again broached my plan for the call to the general. The arrest plans were being made for January fourteenth, two days hence. The Mexicans were due to arrive late that night, so I would have Wednesday evening, the thirteenth, to make the attempt. "Wheeler said we have to call in the evening to catch the general at home," I reminded him.

"Well, we'll see," said Ross.

---

* Ross was subsequently promoted to a group-supervisor position.

Ross was barely paying attention to me. He could not have cared less about the three stooges in Vegas, the Bolivians, or anything else. His concern was the media coverage of the arrests and how it would affect his career—he was a perfect suit. I found, however, that without Wheeler there, he did not put up much of an argument. I finally got a halfhearted agreement that I would make the attempt Wednesday evening.

January thirteenth, at six-fifteen A.M., my hotel-room phone woke me up; it was Hoopel. "We've got some problems."

"What?"

"While they were in Vegas, the little colonel had to make a prearranged phone call to the general. He made the call and then came back real nervous and upset."

"Yeah. . . ."

"You know why?"

"Why?" I was beginning to wonder if this was another little-colonel story.

"The general is accusing him of squandering his money. He's saying, 'What the fuck are you doing in Las Vegas? I know what you did. You fucking ran that plane and kept the money yourself, you sonofabitch.' " Hoopel laughed. Once again our senses of humor went in opposite directions.

"No kidding," I said, an idea exploding in my mind.

If we could catch the general at home tonight, the scene was set for an incredibly damaging conversation. I had visions of the media replaying an argument between a Mexican colonel and general over the squandering of drug money in Las Vegas. The Mexican government would be getting just what it deserved.

"We've got to get him on the phone," I said.

Hoopel—as he usually did on the telephone—agreed with me. "That's it. This is the perfect opportunity. . . . You got it now."

"That's excellent," I said. There was no way Colonel Carranza could refuse to make the call. I now had good reason to have doubts about the whole deal. I would demand the call. "Are they all back now?" I asked.

"Yeah, they are all back now. They got in at about four [A.M.]."

"The only thing missing now is the Bolivians."

"If they're on the flight we think they are, it left on time this morning. Wheeler is reaching out for whatever intelligence he can get," said Hoopel.

"You mean from Mexico City to Tijuana?" Once again we had to depend on Wheeler's words.

"Yeah. I think he's calling Choo Choo [Chuy]. Choo Choo, in fact, called a couple of times to give him updates."

"But they made it to Mexico City?"

"I don't know," said the man called Helmet Head.

At nine A.M. Pizarro and I went to the hotel-room command center. Jake the pilot, just arrived from Miami, was there ready to work the undercover meeting with the Bolivian pilot and then continue his mission to Bolivia to try and locate the landing strips and cocaine labs he and Wheeler had been shown.

Hoopel and Ross were also there. A planning session was set for the undercover house later that evening. Hoopel told me that Méndez and the Bolivians had missed their flight and would not be in until the next day.

"That's great," I said. "That'll give me today to get the call in."

Ross looked at me and said nothing. I knew I was in for big problems.

At eleven-thirty A.M., most of the cast was once again gathered in the undercover house—Jake the pilot, Lydia, Sharp, Ross, Wheeler, Urquijo, Pizarro, and two customs agents assigned to work the attic. Wheeler and Urquijo were recounting the events of the Las Vegas trip. "I'll tell you," said George. "The little colonel had to call Mexico to talk the general and explain the delay—you know, explain why he was in Vegas spending the general's money." George laughed. "I don't know what the general told him, but when he got back he was scared shitless. I mean he was pale."

It was my cue.

"The timing couldn't be better," I said. "As Luis, I would justifiably be nervous about my deal in Mexico. We've got to drag the little colonel's ass right over here to prove to Luis that the million bucks is not going for nothing."

"But we're not supposed to tell you about the phone call," said Wheeler.

"Are you nuts?" I exploded. "You work for Luis. Of course you would tell me. And the Mexicans will understand that. But let's forget Luis. As a DEA agent *I'm* telling you, 'What the fuck difference does it make anyway?' They're finished as of tomorrow. Today is our last chance to make the call."

"Well, Girón is very suspicious," continued Wheeler, as though I hadn't said a word. "I kind of thought if we took them on a boat ride with Lydia and Tommy [Sharp], it might calm them down a bit." Ross and Lydia nodded their enthusiastic agreement. Hoopel's face flushed, but his mouth stayed shut.

"Bullshit!" I was on my feet and glaring up into his face—a face that for a dangerous moment was the face of every slime-ball informant I had worked with for twenty-five years. "I'm going to tell you something, mister. Luis, right at this moment, is as fucking enraged as Mike Levine really is. I want that fucking colonel over here, front and center, to assure Luis that his general is still part of the deal. Do you understand?"

For a moment it seemed that I had frightened the room into agreeing with me. But I hadn't counted on Lydia. "I don't know," she said. "I think taking them on a boat ride *would* relax them."

"I am fucking sure it will," I snapped. "But I don't want the man relaxed! And tonight is liable to be my last fucking chance!" Once again the boat battle raged, with Wheeler, Ross, and Lydia on one side, and me on the other. They finally agreed—I'm sure because I looked like I could get violent—that I would attempt to get the recorded conversation with the general that evening.

The planning then turned to the actual arrest scenarios, to take place on the following day, January fourteenth. Wheeler once again was doing the planning for Customs. I finally said, "Planning arrests is a federal agent's job."

"Well, I'll tell you this," said Wheeler. "George [Urquijo] and I don't want to be there for the arrests. Maybe you enjoy looking into the faces of these guys when you do them. But we've been living with them."

I looked at Urquijo; he said nothing and looked away. I looked at the two Customs supervisors, Ross and Lydia; they remained silent. The slime ball had turned on friends that had trusted him for a decade, and he was suddenly having a conscience attack?

"I just want to tell you something, mister," I said, already wishing I hadn't opened my mouth at all. "I get paid for what I do." *I almost said, "And I'm proud of it," only I was no longer so sure of that.* "If they [Customs] don't mind, I couldn't care less."

I suddenly felt the need to get as far away from these people as I could. The agreement had been reached, there was no longer a need for me to stay there. It was almost twelve-thirty P.M. when I got to my feet. I had plenty of time to go to the gym and get a much-needed workout. They all knew that the call had to be made in the evening. I calculated that I had at least three or four hours.

"I'm going to take off for a while," I said, turning toward Wheeler. "Just tell the colonel that Luis is very concerned about something and bring him over here. Then call me on the pager or in my hotel room."

Wheeler, with a sly look at Ross, said that he would.

At four-thirty P.M., I received a phone call in my hotel room from Hubert Hoopel. The tight sound of his voice told me that he was wishing desperately that someone else had made the call. Something was wrong.

"What's going on now?" I said, my heart already hammering in my chest.

"Uh, they [the Mexicans] went in there . . . to the house. . . ."

"Yeah," I said impatiently. He was talking at Fast Albert speed.

"Uh . . . they're real low-key."

"Yeah."

"Real low-key."

"Yeah."

"Wheeler told them that Efrén's not going to be in until tomorrow. . . ." Then he mumbled unintelligibly and said, "They were just kind of laid-back. I guess the colonel's wiped out. . . . And Hector [Álvarez] says, 'I guess there's time to . . . Maybe I'll go down to T.J. [Tijuana] and look up some friends.' And Pablo says, 'No, you're not! We are staying right here until this deal is over.' " Hoopel laughed a very nervous laugh.

"Did Wheeler tell him that Luis is upset and wanted to have a meeting?"

"Uh . . . he just said that Luis . . . uh, has got somethin' to talk. . . . Uh, what it bottomed out to . . . what it boiled down to was . . . the fact that . . ."

"In other words he just did what he wanted to!"

"No, not that. . . . It's just that they weren't interested in having a meeting."

"Yeah, but *Luis* wants a meeting."

"Yeah, I know, but . . . Mike, listen to me for a second. . . ."

"Yeah."

"They were afraid . . . and I could see their point. . . . They want to get the money. That's what they are interested in. And I think that if we had the meeting tonight we wouldn't be in a better position than we would be tomorrow when we've got the money sittin' in front of them ready for them to go out the door with it. . . . Don't you think?"

"Like Wheeler said, 'You can't get the general during the day.' At night you gotta get him."

"Well, we could get him in the morning. . . . If . . . uh . . ."

"You are going to lose it. . . ."

"The bottom line," said Hoopel, "is they did what they did."

"In other words there's no meeting."

"Yeah."

"Okay."

"That's the bottom line, they—the Mexicans—wanted to go to Sea World."

"Oh, man." *Sea World.* This was too bizarre for even Hollywood. "Is that where they've gone already?"

"Yeah."

"In other words they are already gone."

"Yeah."

"You let the informer talk you out of the general," I accused, and immediately felt ridiculous. Hoopel had about as much control of this case as Oliver North had of the Ayatollah Khomeini.

"I mean, I wasn't there. This is what I was told when I was back in Customs. . . . That's what they did."

"In other words Customs just told you."

"I guess so, I mean Jim [Ross] and I left the house when you did. We were down at the U.S. attorney's office. We went to Customs and got a call, and that's what the call was about."

"Wheeler is doing exactly what he wants to do. He is doing anything he wants."

"Arnie [Gerardo] said the exact same thing."

"You just lost the general. And Wheeler knows you can't call the general until . . . He said so himself. So he just—right in front of you and Ross—maneuvered us out of a call to the general," I said, trying not to scream, which at that moment was something akin to a car with a four-hundred-horsepower engine racing and its emergency brake on. "And you are going to see tomorrow, there will be no way of getting the general. . . . I saw it coming. It's incredible. I saw him choreographing arrests, right in front of you and Ross."

I babbled on for a while, out of control, rehashing and re-rehashing what Wheeler had accomplished. I had been outmaneuvered by a scummer—a stool pigeon. But why? How? After all these years. And it wasn't just me he had whipped—the con-man drug-dealer had beat the whole fucking system. *And at that point I had no idea just how badly.*

"Well, there ain't nothing I can do about it," said Hoopel.

"I don't know about that," I said. "If I were you, I would get hold of these guys and say, 'Luis is very upset. . . .' But I'm going to leave that up to you."

Hoopel said, "Okay," but I knew it was over.

After an hour of pacing the floor of my hotel room I called Hoopel back and asked that he take me off the mission to capture Remberto. "I don't even want to get on a plane with this guy," I said. "I don't think you can blame me, not wanting to go from this mess into Duncan country. If George has a hard time identifying Remberto, I'll fly to Panama from New York."

Hoopel agreed to express my wishes to the powers that be and hung up.

Among Wheeler's many claims about his background was his statement of having "big connections" in the Cayman Islands. He said he had lived there for several years and co-owned a restaurant and some condominiums and had "high level" connections with all the banks there. He, at one point in the planning of Trifecta, suggested we have the undercover meetings there.

I had my own connections in the Cayman Islands, not the least of which was the man Wheeler had claimed was his partner in the restaurant. I had saved my own investigation of his background story as a last resort. Doing a background check on your own informer in the middle of an undercover investigation was unheard of. It was something a professional narcotics agent always did well in advance of the case. I had never had occasion to do anything like it in twenty-five years. But if ever I had lived through unusual times, this was it. I had to see just how much of Wheeler's claims Customs had verified.

I spent the next several hours on the phone with Miami, New York, and the Cayman Islands, and learned that Wheeler was *very* well known to my sources; however, not in the way he had alleged. He was known as a con man and braggart who had been living as the guest of a wealthy island resident—who, for some mysterious reasons, was giving Wheeler an "allowance." He had no ownership interest in the restaurant, or any other business that my sources could determine.

Late in the evening I considered checking on his alleged CIA involvement, but decided that I had gone far enough. I still had no idea of how many hidden feet I had already stepped on, and once again my experiences in Argentina and Bolivia, loomed over my shoulder to warn me, *Back off!*

What the hell was I doing? It would all be over tomorrow for me. All the players would show up like good little lambs for their sacrifice. We'd chop off their heads. The suits would be happy with their victory and a little more secure in their empires. The media would be happy with a story that would sell their papers and pump their ratings. The politicians would decry the evil foreign drug barons, and arm in arm with the suits assure the public that once again good had triumphed over evil. And Mr. and Mrs. Public would just shake their heads in wonder, cluck their tongues, and keep paying their taxes. It would be a replay of a thousand other "victories" I had given them.

I fell into a deep sleep. I rarely remember my dreams, but when I woke up later that night, I did. I was inside an old western-style shack, staring out at a golden desert sunset. Outside, the figure of a man sat on a wooden porch railing, his back to me. He was motionless, also staring at the sunset. I started toward him, but no matter how much I walked I could not get closer. At first he looked familiar. I soon recognized him; it was my brother David. I called his name, but he wouldn't turn toward me. I started to cry. "I haven't seen you since you died," I said. "Please turn around. Let me see you." He would not turn. I wanted to see my baby brother's face so badly that I felt like I was on fire. All I could do was cry.

I woke up crying and kept crying long into the night. It was the first time I had dreamt of my brother since his drug-related suicide eleven years before, and I'll never forget its images.

In 1959 a man put a gun to my stomach and pulled the trigger and it misfired. The gun was test-fired after that, and worked every time. From that moment on I believed that there is some kind of grand design to this life. Nothing happens without meaning.

I'm not sure what the dream meant, or why it happened that night. Maybe someday I'll understand it. The only thing I am sure of is that it was an important part of everything that happened.

Thursday, January fourteenth, the day of the arrests, began with an eight-fifteen A.M. phone call from Ross.

"Let me fill you in on what's going on," he said, in a very clipped, businesslike voice. "Méndez and the Bolivians are going to be at the border at about ten. Wheeler is going to be there to pick them up. There's going to be a surveillance team close behind him." He went on to describe the arrangements that had been made to "grease" them into the United States. He said that while Wheeler was at the border, Tommy Sharp and George Urquijo were going to "hang out" with the Mexicans to "sort of keep them in pocket."

"Yes," I said, thinking about the general, and when he was going to get around to the missed phone call. His cool, measured tones told me it was very much on his mind.

"That way," continued Ross, "if Wheeler has a problem getting Méndez and the Bolivians to come across the border, he can let them call the Mexicans at the hotel and they can reassure each other. The Bolivians can assure the Mexicans that they are here and everything is all right. The Mexicans can reassure the Bolivians that everything is safe to come across."

Wheeler, he said, was going to try and get as many of the Bolivians to cross the border as he could. As the man spoke I could not believe the paranoia I heard in his voice. Wheeler had really done a job on him. These poor bastards had spent a week traveling back and forth across the continent on an odyssey of seven thousand miles, just trying to get visas to get here, and Ross was worried that they wouldn't cross the border. I hoped that it wouldn't turn out to be a self-fulfilling prediction.

And then for a moment, I hoped that it would.

"What happened last night . . ." he said, starting to talk about the missed opportunity, then quickly changing his mind. "Let me finish with the scenario." Ross said that Wheeler was going to check the Bolivians into a nearby hotel, at which point Urquijo and Sharp were to bring the Mexicans to the house for the meeting that would end in their arrests.

"Right now," said Ross, "I think you ought to know, those Mexicans were ready to deadline it at six o'clock this morning. The guys drank with them late into the night. And the guys offered them each—Wheeler did, on his own—an extra ten thousand dollars apiece to wait . . . if they would just bear with us and stick it out—"*

"Oh, my God," I said.

"I don't see any problems with that."

---

* Wheeler later denied this under oath during the trial.

"It should have been the shoe on the other foot," I said, really wanting to ask the man whose side he was on.

"What do you mean?"

"I think Wheeler managed to get us to miss the call to the general," I said, my body trembling with rage. The idea that this informant had managed to convince U.S. government agents to blow an opportunity—probably the final one—to get a tape recording of a member of the Mexican high command doing a drug deal, for a trip to Sea World, was too bizarre for words.

"No," he began slowly, "Hoopel and I—"

"The other thing, by the way, is . . . You know the things Wheeler told you about the Cayman Islands?"

"About the Caymans?"

"Yes. Everything was a lie. Every last detail was a lie."

"What do you mean?"

I ran down the results of my Cayman Islands investigation and finished with "I am telling you this, because *you* are handling him."

Ross was quiet for a long moment, then he said, "Are you a hundred percent sure?"

I'm a hundred percent sure. Every detail was a lie."

"How about the guy that he knows out there?"

"Absolutely bullshit!" *The "guy" he was referring to was my friend.*

"He doesn't know him?"

"No, he *does* know him," I said, and again repeated what I had learned.

"Well, he was there," said Ross, as if just the fact that Wheeler had *been* in the Caymans was close enough to consider the whole story truth.

"He's your stool," I said.

"Well, that goes with the territory with stools, right?"

"I don't know about that." *It sure doesn't, man! And if I have to tell you that, you shouldn't be carrying a badge.*

"Well, I appreciate the information," said Ross, his throat now as tight as mine. "Well . . . anyway. He [Wheeler] offered them ten each. . . . We can give it to them out of the flash roll. . . . And he got them off the six o'clock deadline. They said they would stay until twelve—not twelve oh one. Not twelve oh two. But twelve o'clock. If the shit's not done by then, they are leaving. . . . So, we have to stroke those guys.

"Now, as far as that call last night, he went on. "That was Hubert's and my decision. That was not Wheeler's decision. . . ."

"Which call?" *He should have checked with Hubert first before lying to me.*

"Can I finish?"

"I'm not sure what call you're talking about," I lied.

"The call to the general."

"Yeah."

"The one we missed. That was Hubert's and my decision. We didn't want to have any meetings last night because we didn't want to upset the apple cart. We want at least status quo . . . as long as things are going smooth, let 'em go smooth . . ."

"All right," I said.

"We had the option," he continued, for some reason unable to let the topic drop. "Wheeler did not shut the option off. He took them to Sea World and then we decided against it. . . ."

I was silent. The worried little bureaucrat was trying to include the poor hapless Hoopel as his partner in the "decision."

"Well, that's all the information I have," he said finally.

"Okay," I said.

"Any questions?"

"No, not a one." I said. The questions I had could never be answered by him.

"Okay, so, uh, when do we see you up here?" He was calling from the command center in room 1059.

"Do you need me up there?"

"No, I guess not," he said. Then for some reason he did not want to let me go. "Are you going to be in your room?"

"I'll be in my room, or on the beeper. Just call me and let me know when my next act is, and I'll do it."

"Well, your next act would be at about eleven o'clock, roughly. I, uh . . . I'd like to have your input on how you think it should go down. . . . I mean, who enters first, which person comes on the stage first. Do you want to be present at the house when the Mexicans arrive, do you want to walk in later?"

We discussed a couple of different scenarios. I tried to listen, fighting for that cool, calculating part of me that had protected me for all these years—the part of me that was documenting everything that had happened as though I were not a part of it. But I just couldn't manage it; anger clouded my mind. "Look," I said, wanting just to get off the phone, "I think I've gone much too far in giving input in this case already."

"I don't think so," said Ross.

"I do," I said, childishly, and was immediately angry with myself.

"Your input's been very helpful," he said, choking slightly on the words. His trying to con me snapped me out of it. I was suddenly back in control again.

"Gee, thanks," I said, and managed a laugh. His answering one was little more than a nervous cough, but it was good enough. I didn't want the rift between us wide enough to stop him from talking.

"I disagree with you," he said.

"Well, I just want this thing to come off as good as possible," I said in as friendly a tone as I could muster. "But in all honesty, had this Luis character been real . . . he would have really been pissed and would have made the guy call the general."

"Can you take a shot at it at this meeting?"

"Okay," I said, "but do me a favor. Don't tell Wheeler what I'm going to do. For some reason he's against the call, and I don't want him to mess it up again."

"Fine," said Ross, and I had won my first small victory in this little mini–drug war I had named "Trifecta."

■

At about ten-thirty A.M., I went to the hotel-room command-center to see if there were any changes. I had an ulterior motive. I wanted to revolunteer myself to go to Panama with George. I had made a vow to myself that I would document every dirty step of this case, and it was too close to the finale for me to back out now.

As it turned out, I didn't have to say a word. George had already told Hoopel that he wanted me along with him. I quickly agreed. Hoopel said that all the preparations had been made and that immediately after the arrests I was to grab my bags and head to the airport, where he would meet me with tickets, money, and instructions.

At ten forty-five A.M., I headed the Mercedes north, on Mission Boulevard toward La Jolla. I switched on a cassette featuring *El Gran Combo de Puerto Rico,* one of my favorite Latin groups, playing some hot, driving salsa rhythms, and let the music drift me into my role of Luis.

With Wheeler off picking up Méndez and the Bolivians, the meeting with the Mexicans went perfectly. Tommy Sharp and Luis arrived on schedule with the million dollars. Luis placed the suitcase on the table in front of them and opened it. As they eyed the stacks of hundred-dollar bills hungrily, I went into my act.

"My colonel," I said, "I do not want you to be offended, but my investors in New York have made a request of me. They said that with all the delays—I understand you have had some difficulty with the general—they want me to verify that there will be no problems in Mexico, before I release the money."

"Of course," said the little colonel, "by all means."

"Would you mind calling the general, with me on the extension, so that I might assure my people that there will be no problem?"

"But of course, Luis," he said immediately. "And I am not offended. I understand your position perfectly."

"If there is a problem with the general, you may tell him that I am going to advance you an additional million dollars for the next shipment."

The colonel astounded me by refusing to take the extra million, saying that it was not necessary. He only expected payment when services were needed. Whatever doubts I might have had before about the man's veracity were dispelled at that moment. Girón stared at the colonel, jaws agape, as if his heart had stopped.

A short while later I sat in a side bedroom, my heart pounding, listening on an extension telephone to a noisy connection. Carranza had dialed from the master bedroom at the other side of the house. The static was suddenly broken by an intermittent *beep* as about a thousand miles south of us a phone rang.

A man answered. My heart beat loudly in my ears. God, how obsessed I was.

"The general will not be home all day," said the voice.

"This is Colonel Carranza."

"Yes," said the voice guardedly.

"I am just calling to make sure that everything is all right. You know, the arrangements we made for the road."

"Yes, everything is set."

"Fine. Tell him that I am leaving for there shortly."

"That was Pablo, the general's brother," said the colonel after hanging up the phone. "It is unusual to get the general home during the day."

The words *I know* were on my lips. "That is fine," I said, wanting to find Wheeler and rearrange his features.

The phone call, as evidence against the general, would be worthless. Wheeler had known he would not be there. He had won. He had managed to play government agents against each other right to the end, and won. I suddenly had some new insight into the con man's game:

When we returned from the aborted Panama trip, the Mexicans had wanted me to come to Mexico and personally check out the arrangements—landing field, refueling sites, et cetera. Customs decided to send Wheeler—alone—in his role as my employee. On his return he claimed he had met General Poblano Silva, in person (among others), and had discussed the whole transaction with him. If this could be proven, we had a great conspiracy case against a member of the Mexican high command. The tape recording also would have done exactly that.

But on the other hand—from Wheeler's possible point of view —if we got the tape recording (the possibility of which Wheeler had never contemplated until the moment I suggested the plan), and something was said between General Silva and Colonel Carranza that proved Mr. Wheeler a liar, not only would all his veracity as a witness be destroyed, but he might well have bought himself a ticket back to where he had started his odyssey from—the Oklahoma City jail.

This was one of several theories I had as to why David Laird Wheeler had destroyed our chances at getting that crucial piece of evidence. The others ranged from psychological reasons, to the self-proclaimed screenwriter wanting to be the "Lone Star" of the whole operation so that he could later sell the screen rights to his own semifictional creation of derring-do, to the somewhat unlikely possibility that he really *did* have CIA connections (remember Colonel Carranza's connection to the Contras) and was protecting General Silva.

Whatever Wheeler's reasons were, the fact remained that with his lone testimony, General Poblano Silva might be indicted, but the Mexican government would laugh at the proof.

I watched Girón and Álvarez, still full of themselves from their trip to Las Vegas and the high life, their greedy little eyes unblinking as they eyed the suitcase full of stacks of hundreds—six hundred thousand dollars. I told myself that they, like the thousands of others I had destroyed while watching their eyes, were getting what they deserved. I told them to count the money. Girón and Álvarez began to, but the colonel—too proud—stopped them. He trusted me; to count my money would have been impolite.

As we started to leave, George Urquijo pulled me aside to remind me that I was to give Girón and Álvarez a "finder's fee" of twenty-five thousand dollars each, and that they did not want the colonel to know about it. The two men were eyeing me hungrily. I nodded for them to follow me into the bedroom with Pizarro, who had the suitcase with the remaining four hundred thousand. The two collided trying to go through the bedroom door at one time. I gave them the money and watched them frantically shoving it into hiding places under their clothing. I thought for a moment that Girón—Wheeler's lone "high level" drug contact—was going to kiss my hand.

Moments later, after a lot of hugging and handshakes, I sent the three Mexican stooges off to their arrests, which, without a doubt, were going to win Ross and some others awards and promotions, and the suits another drug-war "victory."

I sat down wearily to await the Bolivians' arrival. Mentally, I added General Poblano Silva's name to a growing list of top international violators who would never spend a minute in a jail. I thought of all the faceless drug-dealing Mexican generals, murdering policemen, and corrupt politicians whom I might have met face-to-face and destroyed, had DEA permitted the five-million-dollar buy. I thought of Kiki Camarena, tortured to death by the same people we were protecting, and I wanted to cry.

■

"Oh, Luis," said Méndez, smiling as he led Román, Vargas, and a dark, young, cocky-looking Bolivian, who had to be the pilot, across the threshold into the eyes of two hidden camera lenses, a slyly grinning Wheeler just behind them. The old man hugged me. I shook hands with the others. A weary-looking Méndez shook his head and said words I would never forget: "Luis, it has been an *odyssey.*"

"I know, my brother," I said. "But it will soon be over."

"*Ojalá!*" he said.*

The meeting went as smoothly as that of the Mexicans'. I jockeyed Méndez and the Bolivians into good camera positions and discussed every minute detail of the negotiations—as I had done thousands of times before—as though there weren't the slightest doubt in my mind that this was the first of many, many deals to come. I spoke of the possibility of sending two planes for ten thousand kilos of cocaine on the next trip, and they believed me. They had spent a hellish week traveling back and forth across South America *because* they believed me. And now it no longer really mattered.

After all the details of our negotiations were finished, I relaxed

---

* Let it be God's will.

with Méndez, Vargas, and Román in the living room and watched them sipping their final drinks as free men. I monitored their eyes and facial expressions for some sign that they "smelled" something wrong. They seemed perfectly relaxed, yet there was something—some sad, terrible feeling in the air, and we all felt it.

Meanwhile, in the dining room, Jake the pilot was doing the same with the Corporation's pilot, a young hotshot named Rolando Ayala, who thought he had traveled all those miles to guide our plane into a jungle landing strip completely invisible from the air. Ayala, like many young Bolivians who grew up in the Beni, had been flying almost as long as he had been walking. The little he had seen of the United States during the short ride from the border hadn't made him the least bit curious about the giant country to the north that supported him and his countrymen with its voracious appetite for cocaine. He could not wait to get to the plane and be on his way home.

For a moment a strange, sad feeling came over me, that I have heard other undercovers speak of. I could see the members of each of these men's families, wives, mothers, children, brothers, and how their lives were about to change. Nothing would ever be the same for them. I was sure that if given a choice, some of these men might prefer death. The feeling is not a pleasant one. I shuddered and pushed it from my consciousness.

Right on schedule Tommy Sharp and my "nephew," Luis Pizarro, arrived with the million dollars so rudely removed from the Mexicans' greedy hands, and laid it out for the Bolivians to count. The whole cast was in the room now, playing their roles as members of the Luis García organization to perfection. If there were such a thing as Academy Award presentations for "best performance of undercover agents," it was won that day.

"The rest of the money is on the plane," I said. "This was the last million. Perhaps you had better count it now, to save time. Then we can go to the airport. I'm anxious to begin."

Count is exactly what they did—and very carefully. After they had finished, Román looked at me, smiled, and asked permission to use the telephone. He had to call Bolivia, he said. There were people waiting for the phone call. Within minutes he was on the line with Pato Pizarro, perhaps the most powerful cocaine dealer alive. It was just as I had predicted. In a short coded conversation he signaled Pizarro that everything was okay and that the plane would be leaving shortly for Bolivia.

"Now everything will be made ready," he said when he had hung up. "I had to call to get authorization before I could leave for Bolivia."

Thanks to the San Diego United States attorney's office decision of not obtaining the Title 3 intercept order, the call was not recorded. It reminded me of another strange decision made ten years before by the United States attorney in southern Florida, after the arrests in the Roberto Suárez case, freeing one of the biggest drug dealers of that decade.*

The happy Bolivians then headed out to my fleet of cars to be taken to a plane that did not exist. I told them that I had a quick stop to make and that I would meet them there. With a sick feeling in my gut, that I still have today, I watched them drive off toward their arrests.

---

* Pato Pizarro was later cut down by a hail of machine-gun fire. His murder is alleged to have been carried out by Colombians, slighted that the Corporation had agreed to deal with me, with the stated intent of "cutting out the Colombians."

EIGHT

PANAMA
VANISHING ACT

I followed the cars carrying the Bolivians a short distance, driving the Mercedes. It was hard for me to look at them taking their last ride. Jake the pilot was with me. I slowed as a dozen nondescript cars, carrying two and three men each, suddenly swung into traffic behind them, from side streets, driveways, and parking lots, and a helicopter chugged the air above them. I watched the entourage disappear over the crest of a hill. Méndez and Román, still chatting in the rear of their car, hadn't noticed a thing.

I swung the Mercedes into a quick turn and pushed the accelerator pedal to the floor and Méndez and the Bolivians from my mind. Another quick turn and I was on Mission, heading toward the Catamaran Hotel. Phase one of Trifecta was a closed book. My total concentration was now mercifully focused on Panama and Remberto the money launderer. Lately all the "experts" had been making public statements that the way to win the drug war was to attack the easy flow of money, and we were about to arrest the biggest money launderer of all time. If there was any facet of Trifecta left that seemed to make the whole effort worthwhile, it would be the arrest of Remberto. I had a feeling—which I had mentioned to no one—that the arrest of Remberto might result in the seizure of hundreds of millions, perhaps billions, of dollars. Noriega himself might be implicated. There was no way that Remberto could have handled all the Corporation's money passing through Panama, without Noriega knowing.

It was almost five P.M. and we had to catch a six P.M. flight to Dallas, where a Customs undercover execu-jet was waiting to carry us—Jake, Wheeler, George, and I—back to South America, for the final two acts of Trifecta.

Success now depended on secrecy. We had to keep the arrests from the press for forty-eight hours. With any luck we would snare Remberto in Panama, and a couple of thousand kilos of cocaine in Bolivia, where an unsuspecting Pato Pizarro was awaiting our arrival. Some of the top members of the Corporation might also be there. If any of the people we caught cooperated, it could open investigative doors that no one had imagined. Jake felt certain he could guide our plane right to the places he had visited earlier. He had many years' experience jungle flying in South America and I had all the confidence in the world in him.

For a moment I was giddy with adrenaline and forgot everything that had happened. Everything seemed promising.

I raced the Mercedes through the hotel parking lot, people gawking at us, and came to a screeching stop in front of my room. Luis was already there waiting for me. Jake ran for his room and I tore into mine and began throwing clothes into my two-suiter. Pizarro followed me, shaking his head in wonder and describing the arrests. Customs had directed him to drive each group—the Mexicans and then the Bolivians—to a shopping center, using the pretext of making a small purchase. The moment the cars stopped they were converged on by an army of agents, followed by a much larger army of newsmen and photographers.

"Jesus," said Pizarro. "There had to be fifty photographers out there. And there were television camera crews. They were all set up waiting for us."

"Did they get your picture?" I asked. The young agent was

involved in a lot of undercover cases in New York and had a long career ahead of him. His picture in the press would do him no good.

"Hell, they got everyone." He laughed.

"What about the news blackout?" It did not make sense. If the news were released, Trifecta was over. Not only was there no sense in us leaving the country, but in Panama and Bolivia, nations run by drug dealers, we would be in extreme danger. Trifecta was touching at the top of both governments.

"What can I tell you." Luis shrugged his shoulders. "The DEA guys were as surprised as the bad guys. Customs had it all set up."

The media war was on and Customs had fired the first shot.

Moments later Jake and I were back in the Mercedes and racing toward the airport. Jake shook his head sadly and told me that in all his years of doing missions for both the CIA and DEA, in the Far East and South America, he had never seen anything that could compare with what he had witnessed in Trifecta. "If I ever had any doubts about what a load of bullshit this whole thing is," he said, "I sure ain't got 'em now."

They were my sentiments exactly. But old habits die hard and if there was even the slightest chance, I was going after it. Remberto was waiting.

We arrived at the San Diego airport just in time to catch a six P.M. flight to Dallas. Scuzzo and Hoopel were waiting for us with tickets and money. Wheeler and Urquijo were already on board the plane. Arrangements had already been made to rush us through boarding and around security (I was carrying a nine-millimeter automatic strapped to my ankle).

"What's the sense of us rushing, if they're putting out a news release?" I asked angrily.

"They promised they would hold it for forty-eight hours," said Scuzzo. "I was pissed. I told Washington and they promised me."

"If they don't," I said, "we're not only going to lose all the main violators, but they'll be putting us all in one dangerous spot. You're going to have all the undercovers—the whole case—on board one plane."

"They promised," repeated Scuzzo. "Lawn [John Lawn, administrator, Drug Enforcement Administration] and von Raab [William von Raab, commissioner of Customs] have promised to hold up the news conference for forty-eight hours. The newspeople are going to hold up the story."

"Customs really screwed us," confided Hoopel. "They not only had the newspeople set up. Last week, while no one was there, they sneaked NBC cameramen into the attic and filmed the control room."

"You mean while we were still working undercover?" I asked, not wanting to believe the words.

"That's right," said Hoopel.

"I wonder, did they do a background check on the camera crew?" I asked sarcastically.

"Nope," said Hoopel, seriously. "They never even told *us* about it."

"I don't believe anything that's happened in this case," I said, for the first time understanding Ross's actions. He had his mind on one thing: the media show. If he had brought a camera crew up into the attic a week before the arrests, every minute of delay had to be like years for the frightened little bureaucrat.

"Yup! Customs really screwed us," added Scuzzo.

No, I thought as I moved down the jetway to board Delta flight 265YN, *it was the American people who got screwed.*

■

On the morning of January fifteenth a small private jet piloted by Customs pilots Randy Yates and Dave Koontz streaked skyward over Dallas, Texas, angled sharply, and headed south toward Panama. On board was the entire Trifecta undercover team. If the plane had fallen into the sea, four corrupt, murdering Mexicans and three drug-dealing Bolivians would have been free men within a day, and —I believe—many shadowy figures cashing the same green paychecks that I did would have breathed a sigh of relief.

Also on board was Customs Special Agent Jack Bright, who had joined us from Customs headquarters in Washington. He was to accompany Wheeler into Bolivia. (I later learned that his true mission was to "protect Wheeler from DEA.") Before leaving, Wheeler had insisted on bringing his gun with him. "There is no way," he said, "that I am going back into Bolivia, counting on DEA to protect me." Not even government agents were allowed to bring a gun into a foreign country without that country's prior approval. Customs circumvented the law by having Bright carry Wheeler's gun for him. They also helped him violate the Gun Control Act of 1968, under which a convicted felon transporting a firearm interstate was guilty of a felony. And the truth seemed to be that he was more fearful of DEA than anything else.

It was just a few minutes before landing to refuel in Cozumel, Mexico, that Bright looked at his watch and informed us that the news conference was being held at that moment.

Dear reader, bureaucrats in a media war are like teenage boys making love—no self-control and no regard for the safety of others.

Our stop in Mexico was a short, terrifying one. As the Mexican airport officials wrote our names down and checked our identification, I wondered whether the news had reached Mexico yet, and if our names had been made public. Enrique Camarena had been arrested and killed by Mexican cops in Mexico's second-largest city for doing exactly what we were doing—embarrassing the Mexican government. If something did happen to us as a result of this premature ejaculation of a news release, I wondered how Customs, DEA, and the attorney general (also part of the news release) would cover up their idiotic roles in our disappearances. Maybe they would name a building in Washington after me; or a water fountain. I figured a public rest-room in the Department of Justice would do Wheeler's memory "justice."

An hour—that seemed like half a lifetime—later, we were once again winging our way toward Panama.

Nothing could go wrong in Panama, I told myself. DEA and the Panamanian police, according to Scuzzo and Hoopel, had Remberto under surveillance. If the news broke they would simply arrest him. If there was some other sensitive problem—like Noriega interceding—Duncan would have warned us.

DEA Special Agent Michael Todd, a young special agent on temporary duty in Panama, was waiting for us when we landed at Howard Air Force Base, at five-thirty P.M. Another nightmare was about to begin.

"What is the status?" I asked after he introduced himself.

Todd looked at me blankly. "Status?"

"Don't you know why we are here?" I asked incredulously.

He did not. DEA's Panama country attaché, Alfredo Duncan, had merely requested that he pick us up at the airport. Todd had not the slightest idea about the case.

I threw a public fit right there on the tarmac. I wanted to make sure that not only George, but both customs pilots, heard everything.

"Where is Duncan?"

"I really don't know, there's a party over at the Marine house."

"Aren't the Panamanian police sitting* on someone at the Las Vegas Hotel?"

He shrugged his shoulders nervously. "Not that I know of. I'm only TDY here. . . . I really don't know what's going on."

After Todd dropped us off at our hotel—the Marriott—I said, "Tell Mr. Duncan that I am going to my hotel room now, and if he doesn't get hold of me right away, I am going to start making phone calls. I'm going to call John Lawn and if he's not home I'm going to call some-fucking-body else, maybe Ed Meese."

The news of the Trifecta sting was now all over South America. From the time George Urquijo and I had first met him, two months earlier in November, we had been told that the Panama money launderer was under surveillance, his phone tapped, and that he was a "key figure" in the movement of not only the Bolivian Corporation's drug money but the Colombian cartel's as well. Just before we left the U.S. we had been told that Duncan had him under twenty-four-hour surveillance and was awaiting our arrival to arrest him. At that moment, if they did not have him under surveillance or under arrest, not only would he be long gone but Urquijo and I—the only two

---

* Keeping under surveillance.

living witnesses against a man with almost certain ties to Noriega—
were in serious danger.

At about nine P.M. Alfredo Duncan finally telephoned my
room. He had been at a party at the Marine house and was a little
miffed about the interruption. He had absolutely no idea where the
Panamanian money launderer was. The only thing he knew for sure
was that the "guy's not there."

"Was he just out, or has he moved?" I asked.

"I asked some cop to put in a call to him, and he wasn't there,"
said Duncan with finality.

"Who made the call?"

"Am I on the witness stand?"

"Hey, that's what somebody is sure going to ask me," I said,
wishing it so.

"Look, I work with about five hundred guys," he snapped impatiently. "How am I supposed to remember *who* made the call?"

I fought to control my temper, reminding myself that I was
talking to the man in charge of all DEA operations in Panama and
in my present circumstances was in no position to fly off the handle.
I asked Duncan just what he *did* know about Remberto.

My worst fears were confirmed. Duncan claimed that, since our
departure in November, he had conducted no investigation whatsoever into the identity of the Corporation's principal money launderer
in Panama.

My mind reeled with contradictions. Duncan himself had told
me, when we spoke in Scuzzo's room in the Marriott in December,
that he was going to put a tap on Remberto's phone. And Scuzzo
had all that information—such as the Corporation's blaming Román
for the screwup—that *had* to have come from a wiretap. *"Calls at
the highest level,"* Bill Brown had said. *"The CIA is in it. . . ." "The
top of three countries. . . ."*

"They already know who he is," Hoopel had said. *"He's a key
player. . . . They have him under surveillance; they're just waiting
for you to get there."*

I could *not* be the one to confront Duncan with the conflicting
stories; he was *not* on a witness stand, and putting him there would
be up to DEA—although I doubted that they would do a thing.

Duncan was not the kind of man to do anything as serious as this, without the blessings of the suits.

"Well, we're here now," I said. "Let's see if we can find him."

Duncan reluctantly agreed to contact some Panamanian police and then meet us at our hotel. After I hung the phone up, Urquijo, who had heard enough to get the gist of the conversation, had a concerned look on his face. "Do you think we could be in any danger?" he asked.

"I really don't know," I said. "I guess we probably are."

Before Duncan's arrival Urquijo received a call from some of the Customs people in the States. The case had made big headlines, they said, but the Mexican government was claiming that Colonel Carranza was not on active duty and had no connection to the general. According to the Mexican authorities, that final call to "Pablo" had gone to a "nonworking telephone number."

Wheeler, with the unwitting and unconscious help of Ross, had done his job well.

When Duncan finally arrived at my hotel room, about an hour later, he said, "Look, I did everything requested of me."

"You're saying that no one requested anything of you?"

"That's right."

I immediately telephoned the States and got Albert Scuzzo on the line. "I have Fred Duncan here," I said. "He says that everything you said about Remberto being under investigation and a key man to the Panamanian police is not true. He said that he did everything you asked him to do, which was nothing."

Scuzzo had not been able to get his first word out when I handed the phone to Duncan. He spoke with Scuzzo for a few moments, then listened. After a minute or two, with a pained expression on his face, he held the phone away from his ear. In the quiet of the room I could hear Scuzzo's voice droning away in his maddening code. Duncan, shaking his head in disgust, handed the phone back to me.

"I guess he's got us there," said Scuzzo. "I thought I sent a cable asking him to find out who the guy was. . . . I'm going to have to check the cables."* Scuzzo, plainly frightened of confronting Duncan, began babbling more incoherently than usual.

The call to Scuzzo had been a mistake. I was in Panama, Duncan's country, trying to get his help in arresting the biggest drug-money launderer in history. What would I gain by proving him a liar? Scuzzo and Hoopel had been in constant contact with Duncan for the past two months, reporting that the money launderer had been identified and that he was a under heavy police surveillance waiting for George and me to get there to make the arrest. *What had happened in the interim? I was in no position at that moment to find out.*

Duncan himself was no fool. He had been aware of the importance of Remberto, right from our arrival in Panama in November. In December he had told me he was going to have the Panamanian police tap his phone. As the DEA agent in charge of the Panama country office, *not* to have made Remberto a primary concern of his office was beyond incompetent—which Duncan was not.

There was no legitimate reason for what was happening. There were other forces at work here. Someone wanted Remberto out of the picture. He was a man who handled billions of dollars in drug money—the kind of cash that bought a lot more power and influence than Urquijo and I had at the moment. He had to have Noriega's protection. What the hell could two lone, frightened Americans do in Panama?

I was already sure that we would not find Remberto. But I had to make Duncan go through the charade of looking for him. Every detail, every statement, had to be documented. As we headed for Duncan's car in front of the hotel, I looked at George. He didn't know it yet, but he was my new witness.

A half hour later Duncan, Urquijo, and I were joined by a Panamanian police captain named "Gómez." From the darkness outside the Las Vegas Hotel we had a good view of the uniformed security guard through the window. He was the same man who had been there when we met Remberto in November, and again in De-

---

* Scuzzo and Hoopel later verified that they had sent several cables requesting that Duncan investigate Remberto.

cember. All the other times I had been there, there was a sense of secrecy and heavy protection about the place. There were always two or three plainclothes security men in the lobby with the security guard. This time he was alone.

While Duncan and Captain Gómez went inside to speak to the guard, Urquijo and I waited nervously in the darkness. As they spoke, the guard turned to peer out at us. Instinctively, we turned our backs and moved farther into the covering darkness of the street.

"I don't like this whole fucking thing," said George. "It really stinks."

I felt the same fear that I saw on his face. We were two American undercover agents in a foreign land, trusting our own side in the drug war less than the enemy. It really did stink. If George and I were eliminated, there wasn't another American witness that Remberto had to worry about. With us alive he would have to worry about an American drug-trafficking indictment against him for the rest of his life.

Duncan and the captain came out of the hotel with a list of the current guests. "Which one is he?" asked Duncan, showing me the list.

"Christ, you don't even know what rooms he was renting?" *In my first telephone conversation with Duncan he had said, "I asked some cop to put in a call to him, and he wasn't there." If Duncan didn't know Remberto's full name or what room he was in, as he claimed, how was the call made?*

"No," he said impatiently.

George and I examined the list, which had the names and nationalities of everyone staying in the hotel. Neither the name Remberto nor anything similar appeared, nor were there any Bolivians staying on the sixth floor.

"He had the whole right side of the sixth floor," I said, once again deciding against confronting him with the contradiction. "As you exit the elevator, face right, and he had the whole floor."

As the captain and Duncan returned to the Las Vegas, George looked at me, pale and shaken, and said, "This is strange Mike, really strange."

"Tell me about it," I said, remembering the December nightmare trip, when Scuzzo had bellowed, "There are things I'm not telling you." *What were those things?*

Yes, it really was strange.

Duncan and Gómez conferred with the security guard for about ten minutes. When they returned the second time he said, "The guy's name is Remberto Rodríguez. He's a Bolivian. He left the Las Vegas around Christmastime. His wife's supposed to be German . . . no forwarding address." That was *everything* that was known about the man.

Wheeler and I had been there just before Christmas. It had to be Remberto's phone that they tapped.

"What now?" I asked, noticing the security guard, now in the doorway trying to get a look George and me. "Let's just get out of here," I said, before Duncan could answer.

On the way back to our hotel Duncan said that Panamanian Immigration maintained the names of all foreigners registered in hotels in a computer; that all the hotels had to turn in copies of their guest registry cards daily. He said he would get them to check their records to see if Remberto Rodríguez had left the country, or was registered somewhere else. I looked at my watch; it was after midnight, Saturday, January the sixteenth.

At the hotel the international edition of *The Miami Herald* was already on the newsstand. Trifecta was headline news all over South America. The press, as usual, under the complete manipulative control of the Customs and DEA bureaucrats, hailed the case as another drug-war success story. The article, which described the entire operation and included the arrest photos of Méndez and Román, said that Wheeler had seen "175,000 pounds of cocaine" at the Bolivian jungle sites, "ready for delivery."

Publicly, DEA and Customs raised each other's hands in a show of unity, celebrating the "joint" victory. Secretly—as Urquijo and I learned from telephone conversations with agents from our respective agencies—there had been a minor furor over Customs "screwing" DEA in the media war. The San Diego DEA office had been upset over Customs not telling them about the little sneaky bits they were pulling, like bringing a network news crew into the undercover house in the middle of the case, and choreographing the arrests for the media. The screwing up of the case or the safety of the undercover agents was never even mentioned. And the suits in DEA headquarters? They were perfectly happy with the whole case.

The *Herald* article, which listed the names of all the defendants arrested, and those still being sought, included the name of the Panama based money launderer, "Remberto."

At ten-thirty A.M. I received a phone call from Duncan. He said that since it was Saturday he would have to get Panamanian Immigration to "open their offices, to search for Remberto." I thanked him for his help. He said he was going to be busy working on a heroin investigation and would let me know when he heard something.

No sooner did Duncan hang up when I received a call from Scuzzo wanting to know how we were doing. I unloaded on him, detail by detail, everything that had occurred. "In short," I said, "it's like I told you last night. Duncan has done absolutely nothing down here. He didn't even know what room Remberto had stayed in, and George and I had reported that in November."

Scuzzo was silent for a long time. When it didn't seem that he was ever going to speak, I said, "Other than that, we don't know what to do. George and I are just waiting on the plane to get our asses out of here."

"Yeah, they can," droned the voice. "Well, I, uh . . ." *No, dear Lord, no. Not code again!* "I, uh . . . just talked to where they are at—"

"You know the news is out already in South America!" I said, interrupting quickly.

"Yeah, well, let me tell you something. It was like a forest fire here. Between you and me, Customs just totally dumped on us. They even took a cameraman into the attic. You just cannot believe what they did. They photographed the house and everything. . . ."

I was silent. Hoopel had already told me the story in front of him.

"Can you hear me?"

"Wow," I said.

"It was, uh . . . What [Customs] did was, they basically did a snow job on us . . . all the time that they were working with us on a national and managerial level they were stroking us and bullshitting us. . . . They were setting us up for exactly this kind of day.

"But, uh . . . anyway . . . getting back to the thing . . ." *No, Lord. Not again.* "I, uh, just talked to the other country office where our friends are going. . . ."

"Yeah," I said dully.

"I, uh, think that we stand a fair chance—even though the news is out—I still think we stand a fair chance of getting some powder. . . ."

I laughed. "I hope so."

Back on the subject of Duncan again, Scuzzo said, "The more I think about it, I'm almost positive there is a cable asking Duncan to make discreet inquiries. Anyway, that's a problem we'll handle."

"Albert, I don't even want to get involved in this."

"If you do, you'll carry an ulcer out into your retirement."

"Look, I jumped all over Duncan, and then felt bad after I called you."

"Don't feel too bad. There's been a number of things established that document that [Duncan] wasn't tuned in. He at least got the idiot identified."

"It was George and I that got the guy identified last night," I said, musing over Scuzzo calling the money man an idiot. "They hadn't done anything until then. They didn't even know what floor he was registered on." *Or so they said.*

"Well, the thing is," droned Scuzzo, "if the guy did leave around Christmastime, we wouldn't have gotten him anyway. . . ." *You're doing it again, Lord.* "The big thing now is for Duncan and his counterparts to try and find out where this guy's gone." He rambled on for a few more minutes about finding Remberto, along with other people indicted in the case, and extraditing them. I was soon lost and confused in the land of Scuzzo code.

"What basically happened?" I asked, wanting to find out more about the media war. "Did Customs just put it in the news as though it was just their case?"

"Oh, Mike, you can't believe it. I have not even seen the tape myself. But I had people calling me. They didn't really put it on by themselves. . . . What they did was, they had a network camera-man film the house before the bust had gone down."

"Did they use any of our surveillance films?"

"Yeah, they did. They took excerpts out. I haven't seen it, but it was on national network news."

"Jesus." What they had done was incredible. I had cooperated with newspeople before. For them to have used excerpts of the undercover films indicated that Customs was giving them actual evidence before arrests were even made. They had risked agents' lives, ruined follow-up investigations at the source-country level, and helped possibly the biggest link in the South American money-laundering chain to escape.

"I'll tell you one thing," said Fast Albert. "Everyone's calling me and congratulating me and they don't really know how I feel underneath. But if they only knew the truth . . . The problem is, at the national level [DEA headquarters] they are happy with the way it came out. . . . Dave Westrate even called me to congratulate me."

We had managed to "give away" the biggest violators in three countries and DEA headquarters was "happy with the way it came out."

Dumb or not, their primary concern was Snowcap, and their own careers. As Art Egbert had said, DEA's survival depended on its success, and it was going to be successful, *"one way or the other."* It looked like they had chosen *"the other."*

George and I decided to check around ourselves. We taxied over to the Las Vegas Hotel and circled the surrounding streets, waiting for some inspiration to strike us, or for Remberto to appear walking a dog or taking out the garbage.

In retrospect I'm glad he didn't. I have a feeling if we had stumbled on him, George and I might not have made it home for Easter.

As we walked the streets, exposed and vulnerable, the notion of odds and fate struck me, and how many times over the years I had doggedly pursued cases that jeopardized secret interests and privileged, powerful people. The idea of my luck running out had never been a major factor to me, in spite of the many close calls, threats on my life, and warnings I had received from people as unlikely as one of DEA's top suits. For some reason, that day, as we walked, it dawned on me that I had less than two years left to my retirement.

At almost the same moment George noticed that a man in a nondescript *guayabera* shirt, whom he had noticed ten minutes before, was behind us again. We kept walking, as casually as we could, toward a crowded avenue ahead. Just off the corner two men in dark glasses sat peering at us from an unmarked, official-looking vehicle. *A quick vision of Kiki Camarena's broad-daylight arrest in Mexico flashed like a premonition of doom.* As we turned the corner I noticed that the man behind us had been joined by a second man and that they had quickened their pace.

We both knew how easily people "disappeared" in places like Panama, and being an American agent no longer counted for much of anything as protection. It was one thing to be exposing yourself for a purpose, but to wander the streets as exposed as fish in a bowl was ridiculous. We quickly grabbed a cab. I looked back and saw the car swing into traffic behind us in heavy traffic. By the time we arrived at the Marriott, it was gone.

At eleven P.M. Duncan called my room and told me that he had been busy working with DEA agent Rene Delacova all day on the heroin investigation and had not been in contact with the Panamanian authorities.

"Thanks anyway," I said, knowing that he was lying. I had spoken to Delacova earlier. He *had* been working on a heroin investigation, but without Duncan.

There was a moment of silence, then he said, "Don't mention it. Immigration is kind of slow, but I'll let you know as soon as I hear something."

"We are planning on leaving Monday," I said. "Do you think they'll have anything before we go?"

"That's hard to say. . . . I don't know."

I immediately called Scuzzo in San Diego to tell him that Duncan was lying to us, and that I was getting worried and wanted to get out of Panama as soon as possible. Scuzzo said that the Customs jet would be back in Panama by Monday.

George, his face pale with worry, decided he was going to call Customs to make double sure we would be picked up. Something was definitely wrong. We both felt a growing sense of urgency to get our asses out of there.

Over the next twenty hours George and I received and made a dozen calls to DEA and Customs, trying to find out whether or not the execu-jet had completed its mission and if it was going to pick us up on its way home. We were not able to get a clear picture of what was going on, other than that the mission had not been flown yet and appeared unlikely.

The main problem *now* hindering the "attack" on the Corporation's jungle facilities was the war between Customs and DEA. There were ongoing arguments and discussions concerning everything from whether or not Customs agents (designated to protect Wheeler from DEA) would even be allowed on the mission, to whether or not Wheeler would be allowed to carry a weapon.* Two days had gone by since the news release, and they had not even begun looking for the locations; it now appeared certain that the final leg of Trifecta would be a failure. The Corporation had had more than enough time to react to all the press and clean out whatever they could of the facilities visited by Jake and Wheeler.†

By late Sunday evening, January 17, 1988, we still had no idea of the execu-jet's status, nor had we received any word from Duncan. I had no idea what was motivating Duncan, but while I was in "his" country I wasn't going to corner him again.

By the morning of January eighteenth, after a dozen furious phone calls by both George and me, arrangements were made for us to go to the American embassy, where Duncan furnished us with tickets back to the States.

As we were getting ready to leave, I could not resist asking: "Anything new on Remberto?"

"No," Duncan said simply.

---

* Later, during the trial, a DEA agent assigned to the operation in Bolivia would tell me that DEA's South American offices had not been apprised of the operation, and had no idea what was going on until shortly before Wheeler and Jake's arrival, and had made no preparations for the mission.

† Eventually, with Jake guiding them (according to DEA cables), DEA pilots did find Román's abandoned cocaine lab, reported to be the largest cocaine lab ever seized in the Beni area of Bolivia, with a four-hundred-kilo-a-day output capacity. Wheeler would claim that it was he who guided the aircraft.

It was not until we were halfway to Miami that my anger cooled enough for me to think clearly. Through all my years of undercover and the thousands of dealers I had put away, my image of the enemy in this drug war had been clearly defined. If you sold drugs—I didn't care if it was grams, ounces, or pounds—you were the enemy. I would do all I could to screw you. Operation Trifecta had blurred that image forever.

A possible answer to the riddle of Remberto Rodríguez might be found in two press articles about the indictment of Panamanian strongman General Manuel Noriega for cocaine trafficking, shortly thereafter. The first, a *New York Times* article, "Doubts on Panama," said, "As late as three weeks ago some senior Justice Department and Drug Enforcement Administration officials were arguing that Panama should be praised for agreeing to cooperate in a recent international cocaine smuggling case in San Diego [Trifecta]. . . ."*

The second, also appearing in *The New York Times*—"Drug Unit Said to Have Neglected Evidence of Noriega Trafficking"—accredits an anonymous "Justice Department official" as having remarked, "I hate to say it, but the hunger for publicity may have played an important part in this [DEA's overlooking Noriega's ties to the drug trade]. . . . The DEA is an agency without enough friends, and if it could get a big case with assistance from Panama, maybe it wouldn't pay too much attention to what was happening with Noriega."†

Months later, in New York, I received a cable from Panama with the cryptic message that "No evidence can be found of Remberto Rodríguez having left Panama. It is therefore assumed that he used a false passport."

I, once again in my career, angrily threw caution to the wind and fired off a cable stating, *That leaves open the possibility that he is still there, doesn't it?*

I have still not received a reply.

The case suddenly, and as mysteriously as everything else that had happened, vanished from the media. A source of mine indicated

---

* Elaine Sciolino, *New York Times* (February 5, 1988).
† Philip Shenon, *New York Times* (February 12, 1988).

that the attorney general himself had ordered the heads of both Customs and DEA to stop making any statements. It did not surprise me. Any inquiry at all would have revealed that the "drug war" was a fraud and as rotten as an apple infested to its core with the worms of bureaucratic and political interests and corruption. And above all, like its predecessor the Vietnam war, it was not being fought to win.

■

Meanwhile in Bolivia, after more days of bickering between Customs and DEA, it was finally decided that Wheeler's Customs-agent protector would be allowed to fly the mission but would not be allowed to leave the helicopter while it was on the ground. The two CIs were finally allowed to lead a small army of Bolivians and DEA agents in helicopters to three of the Corporation's cocaine laboratories. Román's lab, just as he had told me, had a production capacity of two hundred to four hundred kilograms a day.*

Months later DEA would proclaim fiscal year 1988 as "a year of success," for Operation Snowcap. They had spent a hundred million dollars to seize a combined total of fifteen thousand kilos of cocaine products† in the twelve countries covered by the operation —less than eleven weeks' production for Román's lab; an amount that I could have bought for half the price. In Bolivia, where it was estimated that Snowcap cost about sixty million dollars a year, the total seizure of refined cocaine for 1988 was an astounding 546 pounds (one day's production for Jorge Román), and not a single one of the "top people" (in the words of the suits) had been arrested.

---

* Experts later testified at the trial in San Diego that the lab had a four-hundred-kilo-a-day capacity.
† The figure included cocaine base and other less than fully processed forms of cocaine.

NINE

THE MEMO BOMB

My first night back in New York from Panama, and I couldn't sleep a wink. I didn't think I'd ever sleep again unless I did something. "Headquarters is happy with the way it turned out" were Scuzzo's words. They had gotten a lot of press mileage and that was it. Everyone was happy, fucking happy. I could see all the suits tucked away in their nice, safe homes in the Washington suburbs sleeping . . . fucking sleeping. I found a bottle of codeine my dentist had prescribed after root canal surgery, and before dawn had gobbled down three or four pills. I lost count, all they did was make me groggy. The suits slept while I stumbled around my house, bouncing off the walls. Finally I sat down at my computer.

I turned the machine on, slipped the word-processing disc into the slot, and found myself staring at a blank screen. I had enough proof to expose everything that had happened, but what would the end result be? I thought of the lesson I had learned during the Suárez case. I had to find a way of putting everything that had happened down on paper, on some kind of official report, and do it in such a way that the suits would not realize I was forcing them to investigate and *expose* themselves. I had to somehow misdirect them into thinking I was doing something *for* them rather than against them. I had to "do" the suits the same way I'd spent twenty-four years doing dopers. I had to set them up, lull them into complacency, then stick it into them from an angle they never expected. Do them the way they had tried so hard to do me. Only, they deserved it.

I quickly searched through four folders filled to bursting with my detailed notes of almost everything that had happened during the investigation, until I found what I was looking for. I started to type. I headed the report "Allegations of Bribe Taking, Three Unidentified Special Agents, Miami Field Division." An hour later I had completed a two-page memorandum addressed to OPR* detailing everything Wheeler had said about paying off DEA agents in Miami. I read it over carefully—the suits hated errors in spelling and grammar. It was perfect. It was the righteous memorandum of a DEA agent doing his duty and reporting allegations of corruption. The only thing it lacked was the "bait." I added one more paragraph:

> *It bears repeating, however, that during the length of this investigation the informant, openly and often, made comments about DEA corruption in the presence of numerous Customs supervisory personnel. The real danger in his accusations, unless thoroughly investigated, is the fact that the instant case has received much media attention and that, by profession, the informant is a screenwriter. Thus the potential for damage to DEA's image is considerable.*

That final sentence would get their attention. It was a memo that would be passed through more in-boxes in DEA headquarters than the Super Bowl betting pool. I lay down and pictured the hurried little meetings that would be called, trying to decide what the next step should be. I already knew what they were going to do before they did. It was a feeling of power. I was finally fighting back on my own turf—I was doing an undercover job on the suits. This

---

* Office of Professional Responsibility. The dreaded internal-investigations unit of DEA.

was my turf and it felt good. I fell asleep as soon as my head hit the pillow.

On January 20, 1988, I mailed the memorandum to OPR and waited.

On January 22, 1988, I received a copy of an edict by Administrator Lawn warning all DEA agents against talking other agents out of volunteering for Operation Snowcap. Even the wackiest of agents was no longer anxious to volunteer. Lawn's edict threatened swift disciplinary action for any violators.

On January twenty-sixth I received a phone call from Jorge Urquijo. He had been called into his SAC's* office and told that Attorney General Meese had telephoned the attorney general of Mexico, Sergio García-Ramírez, and warned him about the case, the night before the arrests, and that after the case made front-page headlines Meese ordered Commissioner of Customs von Raab and DEA Administrator John Lawn to make no further comments to the press. That explained why Trifecta had completely vanished from the news after one day of international headlines and news coverage.

The Meese incident, which later became public, infuriated many DEA and Customs street agents, especially those familiar with the Camarena murder, who already despised Meese for what was perceived as his "wimpishness" and "unnatural" closeness to the Mexican government in general, and Mexican Attorney General García-Ramírez in particular. In the aftermath of Kiki's murder the Mexican government had stonewalled all efforts—first in finding Camarena's body, second in stopping his killers from escaping, and finally in investigating the event. Many of the Justice Department, DEA, and State Department suits and politicians—with an interest in projecting an image (no matter how false) of a progressive and honest Mexican government that was cooperating in our antidrug efforts—wanted to downplay and put the Camarena incident out of the front pages as quickly as possible. It had been up to Kiki's street brothers, the DEA street agents, who fought tooth and nail to keep the investigation alive and a hot flame under the ass of the Mexican

* Special agent in charge of the San Diego Customs office.

government. To many of my brother street agents this latest atrocity was just more proof of how little an agent's life meant alongside political interests.

It seemed to me that the Customs suits' informing Urquijo of Meese's phone call (while it was still secret), and emphasizing the attorney general's "order of silence," was an indication that they were afraid of him. It was their way of letting him know that if he opened his mouth about anything, he would be bucking the attorney general himself.

On January twenty-seventh the suits took my bait—hook, line, and sinker. I received a call from an OPR inspector in Washington, D.C., wanting to know what it was all about. I told him in vague terms that a lot of ugly and potentially embarrassing incidents had happened during the long undercover case and that Wheeler was either present or had been made aware of everything, and that DEA was not going to look very good if any of it was made public. There was a long silence. Then he said, "I want a complete report of everything that happened." He wanted all the details of the investigation, everything Wheeler had said, done, and above all, everything he was privy to. My heart pounding in my chest, I assured him I would give the report the highest priority.

I slowly replaced the phone on its cradle. My hands trembled from the rush of adrenaline. I fought the urge to scream out in victory. I was being given the opportunity to make an official record of one of the most sinister examples of the fraud that the war on drugs has become. And an official report in a Kafkaesque bureaucracy like the Drug Enforcement Administration is something that does not simply go away. Very carefully prescribed action *must* be taken on all official reports, particularly those that hint of corruption. Or it has to be "disposed" of secretly. Either way it would be a cause of great concern to the eunuch suits who daily bullshitted the media. And I would be watching them closely.

It would be my opportunity to name names, cite deeds, and point my finger at those who were to blame for the intentional destruction of what should have been the biggest, most far-reaching case in drug-enforcement history; to expose those to whom the lives of agents meant nothing alongside their own political interests. And even more important, I was sure the report would lead to the world's finally being shown that Operation Trifecta was no fluke, it was typical of how all drug enforcement was being handled.

I was also struck by the irony of the situation. There is something nauseating to me about informants—men and women who, for the promise of money or lenient treatment, will sell out a family member or the trust of a friend—and yet here I was being given my long-awaited opportunity because of DEA's paranoia concerning one slime-ball informant.

There was no time for daydreaming or flights of fancy. I had to move forward very cautiously. The Suárez case had taught me what happens when the suits think you're a threat. The next step was to further disguise my attack by making it appear as though it were coming from three different directions. I called Gene Blahato and Luis Pizarro into my office and closed the door. I told them of the phone call from OPR and ordered them to prepare memorandums of everything they had seen and heard, from Wheeler's allegations of DEA corruption to the drinking binges in Panama and the press ambush in San Diego—everything.

When they left I sat down at my typewriter and began to type. I addressed the document to the OPR inspector and began with the statement "The following narrative is furnished you as per your telephone request of today's date." I titled the document "Chronology of Events and Statements Involving U.S. Customs Informant David Wheeler." It seemed innocuous enough. I looked at my watch; it was twelve noon. I grabbed a sheet off a stack of typing paper, slipped it into the machine, and let my fingers fly. By eight P.M. I had a thick stack of roughly typed pages and a headache. The office was empty. I decided to do the final draft on my computer at home.

Twelve hours later, as the milky light of a cold winter morning filled the room, I watched groggily as my computer printed out forty-two pages of a narrative detailing, in short, torpedolike statements, everything that had happened during the investigation that Wheeler—by any stretch of the imagination—*might* have been privy to. It included: Customs's offer to supply the five-million-dollar buy money and DEA's vacillation and refusal; DEA's mysterious insistence that the operation be carried out in the one place the traffickers would suspect—the Panama Marriott; all Wheeler's lies and inconsistent statements, along with his numerous accusations of having "bought and paid off" DEA; the inexplicable behavior of DEA's agent-in-charge in Panama, Alfredo Duncan; the strange disappearance of Remberto the Panama money launderer; the life-threatening, secrecy-blowing press conference called by the heads of Customs and DEA; Wheeler's success at preventing me from recording the voice of the Mexican general Poblano Silva; the drinking binges during the aborted buy-bust operation in Panama; Customs's secretly bringing an NBC camera crew into the undercover house during the operation; my denouncing Ross's "whitewashed" version of the Panama debacle as "bullshit." I had even gone so far as to include a mention of Colonel Carranza's involvement with the CIA and the Nicaraguan Contras. I hoped that the last was not too transparent. Hell, why should it be? The colonel had not only said it in Wheeler's and my presence, he had said it on camera.

I slipped the forty-two-page memorandum into my attaché case and hefted it. The case seemed heavier than ever, but not heavy enough. I had left out some of the most important items—the possible CIA connections to everything that had happened (Bill Brown's Panama statement "The CIA is in it now"),* a statement about Remberto's probable connection to Panamanian military strongman Manuel Noriega, and, most important, Operation Snowcap and how the suits' fears for its public image "might" have affected their strange actions in Trifecta.

The inclusion of those items would have been stretching my Wheeler alibi too far. They'd see right through it, and as happened in the Suárez case, I would become the target. I was already taking a hell of a chance. No, I decided, I would have to save that for another, safer opportunity. I would have to have patience. It was January 28, 1988; I was due to retire on December 20, 1989. I just might

---

* Later, during the trial, Wheeler, too, on many occasions and in front of many witnesses, spoke of being privy to information indicating CIA involvement in Trifecta.

have to wait that long. I hoped that my silence wouldn't cost any lives.

Still and all, the memo included enough facts—if investigated and made public—to cause, within the "la-la land" of the war on drugs, the bureaucratic equivalent of a nuclear explosion—it was my *"memo bomb."*

When I arrived at the office that morning there was a message waiting for me to call OPR. I telephoned the inspector, who told me that he wanted corroborating memorandums from Luis Pizarro and Gene Blahato, but, he cautioned, the memorandums should *only* concentrate on what Wheeler had said and done about DEA corruption. For a moment I was terrified that he would tell me to do the same, but he didn't. After I hung up I looked at my calendar and realized that I had to be in Washington on the following Monday, February first, to take part in a field inspection of the D.C. enforcement office. One of my collateral duties in DEA was as an inspector in residence, which meant that from time to time I was called on to aid in the inspection of the various enforcement offices to insure that they were functioning according to the myriad DEA enforcement, administrative, and personnel requirements. I called the inspector back and told him I would hand-deliver the memorandum. He told me that he would not be there, but that OPR inspector S. Raphael Halperin, who was going to work on the investigation with him, would be, and that I should give it to him.

On February first, at nine-thirty A.M., I sat across a gray metal desk in DEA headquarters, Washington, D.C., watching Ray Halperin read my memo, trying hard not to show my anxiety or the exultation I felt about his having been assigned to the investigation. I could not have chosen a better man for the job myself. Now I was certain that everything would be brought out into the open.

Ray Halperin, a large graying man, over six feet three and 220 pounds, in his mid-forties, was neither a typical inspector nor a suit. He had the reputation of being a hard-nosed investigator who could not be swayed by either politics or ambition. I had worked in the same offices with him during various times in our careers, but only on one occasion did I work *with* him. A year earlier I had been assigned to accompany him to the Bahamas to inspect our office there. He was the senior man and assigned me to inspect the effectiveness of another highly vaunted, expensive DEA international operation dubbed "Operation Bat." It turned out to be another bunch of statistical bullshit, much like then Vice President Bush's South Florida Task Force—all statistics and no substance. The Bahamian police were seizing boatloads of drugs en route to the U.S. and making their own deals with the drug traffickers. They allowed DEA agents along for the ride so that the agency could claim the statistics, but I could not find a single case with any follow-up leads or investigations whatsoever. No ringleaders or sources were ever indicted or even identified. The seized boats' crews would rarely spend more than a couple of weeks or months in jail. And sometimes money would arrive from somewhere and the seized boat, crew, and cargo would, by some magic, disappear.

I wrote the operation up as a violation of DEA's foreign-operations guidelines. Halperin did not hesitate in approving the report and adding his own signature to it in spite of the fact that it was undoubtedly some suit or politician's "baby." Our report, as usual, had no effect on anything, but I was impressed with Ray. I had confidence in him. I was sure he would live up to the other stories I had heard of his dogged investigative talents.

Ray read about fifteen pages before looking up at me. He shook his head and whistled. "Hot stuff." I tried to read some reaction in his eyes. He had *inscrutable* down to a fine art. And he wasn't saying much either. "I'll call you if I need you," he said, leading me to the door. Well, I thought, as I headed toward the Metro stop on the corner, feeling a sense of relief, everything was out of my hands. The bomb was dropped. It was official. They couldn't duck it anymore. The only thing that still bothered me was Operation Snowcap. It was a deadly fraud and my "bomb" wouldn't reach it.

The subway roared off toward southeast D.C., and the district office, where I had two glorious weeks of inspection ahead of me. It was the tedious kind of work that would help take my mind off everything, at least until I heard from the suits. That shouldn't be long in coming. I'd probably get a call from Lawn himself, or maybe Kelly, his assistant. Maybe they would offer me a promotion to shut me up, or a transfer to anywhere I wanted to go, the way Customs was doing with Urquijo. How would I handle it then? Only time would tell.

On February sixth I sat in my motel room across the highway from Washington National Airport, staring at my phone. I hadn't heard a word. During the week both Pizarro and Blahato had spoken to inspectors, who had again ordered them to restrict their written memos "only" to Wheeler's statements and actions. I considered calling Halperin and then realized it was Sunday, the office was closed.

A news bulletin suddenly flashed on the television screen. Two DEA agents had been killed in a shootout in Los Angeles. The announcer identified them as George Montoya and Paul Seema. My heart sank. Paul was this beautiful little guy, built like a block of steel, who had worked for me in New York in 1976. I had been his first "street" supervisor in DEA. He had been a Thai-national CIA employee during the Vietnam War years. He later married a DEA secretary assigned to the American embassy in Bangkok, where he became an American citizen and a DEA agent. He was then transferred to DEA headquarters, Washington, D.C., where it was discovered that he could barely speak English. An unusual state of affairs for an American law-enforcement officer. So what do the suits do? They transfer him to New York.

English or no English, Paul fit right into Group 33, "The Alimony Boys." Some of his exploits as a non–English-speaking narc in the streets of New York were comic legend.* But only we could laugh at him. He was one of us. He shared the streets and our lives with us. He was our brother. How could these suits who knew nothing of this brotherhood feel the loss that we felt? They would use his death, as they've used all the deaths and injuries of my brothers, to bullshit the world about the justness of their cause; as flags to hide behind to defend themselves against anyone who would question their motives and integrity; when all they really care about is their

---

* Some of Paul's escapades were captured beautifully by Donald Goddard in *Undercover* (New York: Times Books, 1988). Dell paperback, 1990.

bureaucracy, their media images, and their own careers. What scoundrels they are, what awful scoundrels.

On February ninth I had finished my work in D.C. Before taking the shuttle back to New York I called Halperin to see if I was needed. "We'll let you know if we need you," he said simply.

On February tenth Barbara Barclay, a group supervisor in my division in New York, informed me that OPR was investigating my shooting of the dog that had almost removed Luis Pizarro's groin during the Bronx drug raid.

█

By February twenty-second, I could stand the silence no longer. I called Ray Halperin and asked if anything was new. There was a long, thoughtful silence at his end of the line. Then he said, "Wheeler denied ever making an allegation."

"But he said it in front of Pizarro, Blahato, all the Customs people, Hoopel . . ."

"Yeah, but he refuses to talk to us."

I could push Halperin no farther. If my memo had really been written out of concern for DEA's image, pushing him farther *would* be going too far. Once again he told me he would call me if he needed me and hung up. It did not take much imagination to see the bottom line. A high-level conference between the DEA and Customs suits must have occurred. Customs must have assured DEA that Wheeler still had a sentencing date with a judge in Oklahoma and was completely under control. The best route for the suits of both agencies was to treat my memo as an uncorroborated corruption allegation, period.

I placed another *X* on my calendar. Only twenty months to go for my retirement.

On February twenty-sixth, twenty-two-year-old rookie New York City patrolman Edward Byrne was murdered as he sat in his patrol car guarding the house of a witness in a drug trial. He was killed on the orders of a local cocaine and crack dealer. The murder, aside from it being another life wasted in a drug war, struck me particularly hard. My own son, Keith, also a New York City patrolman, had just turned twenty-three.

The presidential race was getting into gear and all the politicians were acting as though they had just discovered that we were in a drug war, and the popular cry by both parties had become "demand reduction." So it was that on the morning of the Byrne murder, the clowns whose salaries we are paying fought each other for a spot in front of microphones and cameras, and moaned, yowled, lamented, or bellowed the latest battle cry, that the user was as guilty as the seller, and we must stop using and promoting the use of drugs. "Demand reduction is the answer," they cried, one and all. *Demand reduction, demand reduction, demand reduction,* the phrase was everywhere, on the lips of every suit and politician, on every television channel and in every newspaper. *Demand reduction, demand reduction, demand reduction.*

On Monday, February twenty-ninth, the day of young Edward Byrne's funeral, I was awakened at six A.M. by my radio alarm. It was tuned to the Howard Stern show, the highest-rated talk show in New York. The papers said the guy's show grossed more than fifteen million a year in advertising revenues. He had enormous selling power. Stern was saying:

> *I was, like, all for it. . . . Unlike Nancy Reagan, I was, like: "Yes, please let me go see if I can dig something up for you." . . . Because I think [cocaine] makes for better television, when the guests are all drugged out. So you didn't see me for a good hour before the show began, because I was busy hunting down drugs.*

I flipped out, I couldn't believe it. The guy was not only saying drugs were an okay, great, fun thing, he was bragging about getting cocaine for guests on one of his shows. All that same morning, and for the rest of the week, you could tune to any television news program at any time of day, and see some suit or politician wailing about "demand reduction" being "the only answer," and how there will always be a drug problem as long as there is a demand.

What effect, I wondered, did a radio personality with over a million listeners in seven states, *bragging about violating the drug laws,* have on demand? Didn't anyone see how tough it already was for a kid to grow up resisting peer pressure to try drugs, *without* that kind of message from so popular a personality? If the suits and politicians were really sincere, they should have considered a guy *plugging* the use of cocaine over a fifty-thousand-watt radio station more a criminal than the biggest of drug dealers. He was part of the reason the Corporation and the Medellín cartel had the monstrous economic power they did.

I kept listening. Instead of it all sounding like some sort of a joke, one of his employees got on the air and said that he had, in fact, obtained the drugs *and* supplied it to the people Stern had wanted supplied. I had never heard anything like it in my life; the two had admitted to thirty years' worth of federal felonies. I had put dozens of guys in jail for saying less than that on wiretap investigations—people with a hell of a lot less power over influencing others to use drugs, or capability of doing anywhere near the damage that this man did. In a drug conspiracy case all you need is proof of the conspiracy—the *agreement* to violate the law (which they had provided over the air)—and proof of some overt act in furtherance of the conspiracy. All I needed to prove the case was a credible witness that either Stern or his employee had made an *attempt* to get drugs; and it would be sufficient to convict.

Don't forget, in all of Operation Trifecta there were no actual drugs involved. And at one point during the December trip to Panama, all the defendants were about to be arrested and charged with conspiracy, without drugs ever having been seen.

Another week went by, during which Stern continued talking openly, during his four-hour-a-day broadcast (heard also, via radio relay, in Washington, D.C., and Philadelphia), about what he had done. During that same week the suits and politicians kept bemoaning the evils of the casual users, accusing them—and those promoting casual use—of being the major cause of our drug problems.

By the end of the week not a suit or politician had said a word about the broadcasts. A woman, the mother of a teenaged daughter, wrote Stern a letter and said pretty much what the politicians and suits should have said—that he was as much the cause of Patrolman

Byrne's murder as any of the drug dealers. Stern found the woman's number in the phone book, called her up, and told her, among other things, that she wasn't fit to bring up children. That was the day that I finally called the United States attorney's office in Manhattan and told them that I wanted to write a letter to the editor of one of the daily newspapers, appealing for witnesses to what Stern had bragged he had done.

"If a credible witness comes forward," I asked, "will you present the case to a grand jury?"

"Absolutely!" I was told.

And so I wrote a letter to the editor of the New York *Daily News* and instead of them printing it in the "Voice of the People" section, as I had requested, they made a news story out of it. What followed was a national media furor over the incident. The whole idea of the investigation was lost in the tempest. The DEA suits, terrified of the media, immediately backed down. The SAC of New York, Robert Stutman, "affectionately" called "Captain Video" by the New York street guys for his eagerness to appear on the little screen, called me into his office. "Are you sure this guy wasn't joking?" he asked.

A year later, when undercover Special Agent Everett Hatcher was murdered during negotiations in a cocaine deal, Stutman appeared on dozens of nationally broadcast news shows, Hatcher's body still slumped over in his OGV in the background, and said, *"If there's anyone who thinks doing a line of coke is funny, just take a look at this young man and see how funny it is."* And then he and all the other suits and politicians screamed, *Demand reduction! Demand reduction! Demand reduction!* for a couple of more weeks.

Captain Video ordered me to make no statements to the press and informed me that I would have nothing to do with the Stern investigation. That morning at least one person had contacted the office with information. The whole investigation was turned over to an agent who had just graduated the DEA academy two weeks before. Sometime later the agent would inform me, "I was told, 'Do nothing [with the Stern investigation]. Just sit on it.' "

The latest word from Hoopel in San Diego was that the defense attorneys for both the Bolivians and the Mexicans had asked for delays in the trial. It didn't make sense. It would seem that it would be more advantageous to the defense to get to trial as soon as possible, before DEA and Customs could broaden their investigations in both countries. Only time would tell. In the meantime there was a drug-enforcement experiment that I had always wanted to try, and a unique opportunity to do it had just presented itself.

I had always been intrigued by the methodology used by China and Japan in eliminating massive drug problems in a short time. Both countries had focused all their efforts on removing the user from society, either for a long enough period of time for the market to dry up, or permanently. The user was the enemy; the one guilty of the spread of the disease; the one feeding it with money. The user was also the part of the disease most vulnerable to attack. Easy money was enough of an incentive for a never-ending supply of sellers—no matter what the penalty. But change the image of the user from "victim" to "worthless leech" and *guarantee* him a long stay in a jail for *using* drugs, and you will quickly eliminate most of the market.

The "Oriental solution" seemed simple and logical, yet none of our suits or politicians ever adopted it as a plan of action. On the contrary, if you arrested someone with user quantities of drugs, you not only could not get a district attorney to prosecute, you stood a good chance of being reprimanded by the DEA suits for not working "quality" cases. To the suits *quality* and *newsworthy* were synonymous. In recent years I had begun to suspect that it was a case of bureaucratic survival. These bastards simply didn't want to enforce themselves out of a job. I had an idea that would illustrate—if it worked—how effective the Oriental plan could be.

An article had appeared in *The New York Times* about the Dominican cocaine and crack gangs controlling West 109th Street in Manhattan.* Drug dealing was so profitable in the neighborhood that as fast as the police arrested a seller, another would immedi-

---

* Selwyn Raab, "Brutal Gangs Wage War of Terror in Upper Manhattan," *New York Times* (March 15, 1989).

ately replace him. Thousands of arrests had been made on the street, yet the crack cocaine business had never been more profitable. I had a friend who lived above two basement apartments on 109th Street, in one of the most raided buildings on the street. My friend said that cars would line up all night to buy drugs regardless of almost weekly raids and arrests. I was invited to witness it with my own eyes.

I spent about a week sitting in the darkened window watching car after car arrive, about half of them with out-of-state license plates, most of them carrying middle- to upper-class, well-dressed people, out to buy some "recreational drugs." The transactions were done so openly that I had to remind myself that I was observing an act that carried a thirty-year penalty with it. The buyer would casually cross the sidewalk from his car, skip down the basement steps below my window, and knock on the window. Sometimes I could hear them say what they wanted—an eighth, an ounce, a gram, some love drug.

Even the police raids were sort of casual. One night, in the midst of thriving dope business, a half-dozen unmarked cars screeched to a halt out front, followed by some marked cars. Plainclothes officers raced into the basement while uniformed officers stopped people on the street. Within minutes the whole thing was over. Four scruffily dressed, illegal-alien Dominican sellers, their necks ringed with heavy gold chains, were brought out in handcuffs. Everyone was all smiles; they had been through the drill a dozen times before. Car doors slammed, engines roared, and they were off to pay their twenty-four-hours-in-jail–pay-bail–jump-bail–change-identities–back-on-the-street-selling-dope-again dues.

The police cars were barely out of sight when four new sellers entered the basement. A line of yuppie, middle-class, out-of-state, out-of-town, uptown, and downtown buyers was already waiting outside. Within minutes it was business as usual. The location was perfect for my experiment. I would close the place down by going after the users. But before I could put the experimental plan into action I had to get authorization from DEA and a prosecutor, and that wasn't going to be easy.

I first approached my division leader, Joe Vanacora, with the story that I needed to work a smaller street operation to give my group—many of whom were brand-new agents—some street experience. I wanted to arrest some buyers, flip them, and get enough probable cause to raid the basement drug market. I used the *Times* article to bolster my case that these were "major" dealers. The idea of arresting buyers was not a comfortable one for a DEA division leader. It not only went against the administration and the U.S. attorney's office philosophy, it was in defiance of the SAC's policy. Stutman liked big numbers. It meant mileage with the media. Another "big" drug-war victory. You lock up users, people will criticize you. And the media-minded SAC did not like to be criticized. Joe, an old street agent himself, suspected that I had something up my sleeve but gave the okay anyway. "Don't overdo it," he warned. "You know what Captain Video thinks of street cases."

The next step was finding a prosecutor who would authorize the arrests. I knew I would have no chance going to the federal court, where it was difficult—unless the case involved a celebrity—to get authorization for less than a kilo, so I contacted Sterling Johnson, New York City's special narcotics prosecutor. I had known Sterling a long time and did not have to bullshit him. He was one of the few people with political clout, sincere about wanting to win a drug war. He was a gambler unafraid of incurring bad press for a principle. He loved the idea and immediately authorized the arrests of buyers. We were in business.

The first night, I had eight agents on the street in four cars. I sat in the window with a portable radio. It was like shooting fish in a barrel. By three A.M. we had grabbed eight yuppies, a couple of grams of coke and crack, and three cars. All of them flipped, crying and blubbering about their careers and their families, made full signed statements describing the sellers, and agreed to testify. All of them, being poor "victimized" users, were released. I already had more than enough to lock up the people who were in the basement, but that would have just been the history of the past three years repeating itself once again. I wanted to see what would happen if we kept locking up the buyers.

Over the next week, from March twenty-fourth to March twenty-ninth, night after night, Group 22 kept locking up buyers. Most of them flipped, signed statements, and blubbered that they would never do it again. The one thing that seemed apparent to me was that most of them never would have been buying drugs in the first place if they'd believed there was a chance they'd be busted. *When will we learn?*

By the end of the week we had arrest and search warrants for the people in the basement, but the flow of buyers had diminished to a trickle. In the meantime the small "insignificant" arrests were causing an uproar among the district attorneys who had to process them. I was put under increasing pressure to end the case. Joe Vanacora mentioned that Stutman had made a point of criticizing me for the volume of "small" arrests. I finally succumbed and planned the raids for March thirtieth, the next night. It would be our last night "terrorizing" the drug buyers of 109th Street.

A strange thing happened the night of the twenty-ninth—there were no more buyers. I had ten agents in five cars hidden within a three-block radius of the basement. All of them were watching street sales going on around them like it was going out of style, but not a customer had arrived at the basement apartments. Around midnight I saw one of the rarest sights ever seen in the streets of New York— coke sellers and no buyers. Two of the sellers came out of the basement and stood on the street looking up and down the block for a few moments. *"¿Qué pasa?"* said one. The other looked around and shrugged his shoulders. *"¿Quién sabe?"*

On the evening of March thirtieth, we raided the basement and found it empty; they had closed down operations. For the first time in three years drugs were not being sold there. Of course, they had probably moved to a location with less "heat" and were still selling. But what would happen if our national policy were changed to attack the user as the enemy, and there were no such thing as a location with less heat? China and Japan did it. Why not America?

I was excited by the possibilities but kept my mouth shut. To the DEA suits it was just another case that turned out badly. I spoke to Sterling Johnson about teaming my group with some city cops to broaden the experiment to one of the worst crack-selling blocks in Washington Heights. He liked the idea. The big problem would be "selling" the idea to Stutman. I figured that I would have to lay low for a while—he was still nervous about the Stern incident—and then present him with a plan that would enable him to appear before the media as a "pioneer" in drug enforcement. Fuck the credit! Let the suits have it. I just wanted to see something change during my career. I had started out twenty-five years before, believing I'd have an effect; now maybe I would.

The plan would never be attempted. Trifecta and Operation Snowcap would continue to plague me and, finally, the street action that had been the life's blood of my career would take me out of action.

The Bastards Are Trying to Kill Me!

During April 1988 DEA was having a hard time recruiting volunteers for Operation Snowcap. I had come to despise the dangerous operation which was still shoveling young bodies into the jungles of Bolivia. They had "sold the operation up and down the Potomac." Those words just rang in my head and kept ringing. What if someone was killed out there? Everyone seemed to agree that it was inevitable. Once again, I did not know enough to keep my mouth shut. I mentioned to a few people—probably the wrong people—what I thought of Snowcap. Word of my feelings about Snowcap circulated quickly. A couple of young agents decided to ask me what I thought before volunteering for the operation. I had no hesitation in talking them out of it.

On April fifth I found a large, sealed, government-issue manila envelope on my desk marked *Personal, for G/S Mike Levine*. There was no return address on it. Inside was a twelve-page memorandum written by Frank White, evaluating Operation Snowcap. White is not a man to mince words or to keep silent for political reasons, and the memo was an example of him at his brash, methodical best. He excoriated the operation as being badly planned, poorly run, and overly hazardous to all the agents assigned. "Unless we immediately revamp our tactical approach to Operation Snowcap," wrote White, "DEA agents are going to agonize alone through an excruciating death on an isolated jungle floor."

White tried to keep his criticisms restricted to the hazardous field conditions, and not to mention any feelings he might have had about the overall fraudulent nature of the mission; he was not entirely successful; he wrote that "It is not my intention to set forth a litany of failure or finger pointing," but that he was recommending sweeping changes to increase the safety and effectiveness of the operation. He mentions agents who are resentful that their lives are being put at risk "because someone is not taking into consideration the realities of the situation."

Translation: This whole idea ain't working—can't work, and never will work—and we don't wanna die on some fool's mission for a bunch of politicians.

"Apparently a favorite saying in DEA," wrote White, "is that 'Operation Snowcap is an irregular war being waged by irregular troops,' a premise that puts us on the path to disaster." The memo went on to describe the total disregard the suits had for the lives of the agents. They were sent to the Bolivian jungles with little or no training, the worst of equipment, poor leadership, virtually no safety precautions taken; no medical support; no motivation or idea of what their mission was; and few could understand or speak the Spanish language.

Finally, White wrote an addendum to his report that seemed to say it all:

> *The day I was submitting this report, I received a phone call from a Snowcap agent asking for help. The agent said that he has been blowing holes on clandestine runways with one-hundred-pound charges of dynamite. These explosives are foreign made, as are the detonators, and are extremely unpredictable and unstable. We should be using American military explosives. The agent told me that he would also be forever grateful if I could get him a functional handgun. I have the knowledge, but not the sanction, to aid this agent, who also happens to be a friend.*

Remember this the next time you see one of the suits posing before television cameras, expressing his "outrage" at some DEA agent's funeral.

White's recommendations to remedy the situation in Bolivia—true to his word—had nothing to do with whether or not the whole idea of the operation that was "sold up and down the Potomac" made sense, or whether or not we belonged there in the first place. To Frank, a Vietnam veteran, the situation was just another war. His first priority was protecting American agents and bringing them home alive. Leave it to the suits to justify the "war." Frank recommended that DEA adopt what amounted to wartime measures; that the agents be equipped and trained like army Special Forces, and that the measures be adopted on an emergency basis, if DEA wanted to reach Snowcap's stated goal [before Congress]: "Reduce by fifty percent the supply of cocaine reaching the United States by the end of 1988."

On April nineteenth John Lawn, the administrator of DEA, sent a cable to all DEA offices claiming that Operation Snowcap—while beset by problems—was "a lot farther than we imagined we would be a year ago." Apparently the street agents were not as enthused as Lawn; his glowing report included a terse warning that seemed almost directed at me:

> *I will not tolerate individuals being discouraged from applying for consideration for participation in [Snowcap]. . . .*

By April nineteenth the suits had had enough of me, and made their move. Joe Vanacora called me into his office to tell me that he had received word from headquarters: "You're being drafted for Operation Snowcap," he said.

"What are they trying to do, fucking kill me?" I said. "Roberto Suárez and Gutiérrez still have contracts offered for my death and I just put two members of *la Corporacíon* in jail in San Diego, who produce more fucking cocaine in a month than Snowcap seized all year. And DEA wants to fucking send me to Bolivia. . . . What, are they kidding? Maybe they want to send me gift wrapped."

Joe shrugged his shoulders. "Go talk to Kevin. Maybe he can do something for you."

I ran the block-long, zigzag corridor to the executive offices. Kevin Gallagher, associate special agent in charge, had his office adjoining Stutman's. There was no sense talking to the little bald man. He'd be the first to put me on the plane. I held my breath and slid by his doorway, hoping he wouldn't see me.

Gallagher was a white-haired, wise, and wizened veteran of too many years of drug war from from the *clongs* of Bangkok to the back alleys of Paris and the streets of New York. Few knew better than Gallagher how poor the percentages were in bucking the system. When I told him what the suits were trying to do to me, he wasn't surprised. "I heard all about it," he said tiredly. "I can't promise you anything, but I'll give Terry Burke a call."

"What's he got to do with it?"

"He's in charge of Snowcap now."

Terry Burke was that boss of the suits who had written me up for playing my radio too loud in the embassy in Buenos Aires. His feelings about me were no secret in DEA. I was in big trouble.

On April twenty-fifth Joe Vanacora called me into his office. From the expression on his face I knew what he had to say before he said it—I was going to Bolivia. Gallagher had called headquarters and—contracts on my life notwithstanding—they wanted my ass in the jungles of Bolivia. At that moment there was no doubt in my mind that if I went, I would never return. The suits had me by the balls. They had been firing guys for refusing to accept transfers, and Snowcap had become—according to Lawn's latest cable—DEA's "highest priority." It was going to be: *Die, or get fired.* I remembered that Bobby Baker, an agent who used to be on the DEA karate team with me, had been assigned to work in the Snowcap section of headquarters. He wasn't a suit; maybe I could talk to him. I got Bobby on the phone and told him my problem.

"You steppin' on yo' dick again, Levine?" He laughed—I didn't. There wasn't anything Baker could do, but he knew who could. He passed the call to one of the agents charged with the administration of Snowcap, Lloyd Clifton.

"I don't know if I ever met you," I said.

"I've certainly heard your name," said Clifton. "Probably with *motherfucker.*" I laughed—he didn't.

My mind raced ahead, plotting the conversation as I would during an undercover meet. You don't get what you want bucking the suits. The way to beat them is to force them into making a decision; an individual decision with one discernible culprit, should things go awry—in this case, if I should die. If I could get them passing the buck, no single suit would have the balls to take the responsibility. Clifton listened as I told of the contracts on my life and my involvement with Operation Trifecta, every so often punctuating my story with a bored "Uh-huh."

"Well"—he laughed, a mean, tight chuckle—"they'll never know you're there, because you're not going to see any civilization. I mean, you're going to be in the jungle." Another tight little chuckle.

I tried to reason with him. Both he and I knew that wherever they sent me it would only be a matter of days before the word that I was there would be all over the country. "It's like putting a red flag in front of a bull's nose," I said.

"What's your schedule otherwise?" asked Clifton, unimpressed. He was sending me to the fucking jungle no matter what I said. He'd probably be one of those interviewed after my death. *Ladies and gentlemen, taxpayers of America, they've killed Levine. This is an outrage. We need more funding to stop those evil drug barons.* I wondered who was really pulling his strings. It was time to hit him with the unexpected.

"I'll be happy to go," I heard myself say. "All I'm asking is that [the suits] get me false credentials. I just don't want to go down there under the name Mike Levine. I'll send you [documentation] of the contracts on my life, in the mail today."

There was a long pause. "That's not necessary," he said finally.

I had him. I was on the right track. I pushed the idea of a fictitious identity, repeating over and over how I would "love to go."

"We may not even need you this tour," he said. "It might be a few months away anyway."

"Tell the powers that be, I'll be happy to go," I heard myself say, just once too often. "The only thing I'm asking is that they send me [to Bolivia] under another name."

There was another pause and then Clifton said, "Okay . . . how are your shots?"

"My vaccinations?" My insides sank. . . . He was sending me anyway.

"Okay," said Clifton, "I'll send you a medical package that will tell you everything that you need."

"Okay," I said lamely. "Maybe they can send me anywhere *but* Bolivia." Snowcap was operational in eleven other countries.

"That's where we need you," said Clifton with finality.

I hung up. There was one final move left. Clifton did not want to see written proof of the threats on my life; well, I wasn't going to give him a choice. One of the first laws of bureaucratic survival is *Put it in writing*. I whirled in my seat to face the typewriter and jammed a sheet of paper into the carriage as if I were throwing a left jab. My fingers stabbed the keys like hard little punches. I referenced my phone call with Clifton and repeated my objections to the assignment in Bolivia and attached copies of cables and investigative reports written in Bolivia, Brazil, and Paraguay, where informants had been offered two hundred thousand dollars to kill *"El agente del DEA, Mike Levine, el Judío trigueño de Argentina"*—DEA agent Mike Levine, the dark Jew from Argentina. I made a half-dozen copies of the packet—one to each of my bosses, one to the suits in headquarters, and one to a lawyer. *Now there was a written document that some suit would have to have the balls to ignore. At least I could leave my family with grounds for a good lawsuit.*

My memo did it. . . . On April twenty-seventh Terry Burke* himself called me. I was astounded at his frankness on the telephone. "Hey, I was not really trying to get back at you for ruining my vacation ten years ago," he said, admitting what I had always known. In the aftermath of the Suárez case, when I had been put under intensive scrutiny by the Internal Security Division, Burke was the supervisor of three inspectors sent to "evaluate" my office in Argentina. These were the men who wrote me up on "charges" of "playing rock music too loud" on my radio in the American embassy, and not knowing the "location of the CIA office," among

---

* Now second-in-command of the Drug Enforcement Agency.

other things. My memo answering the charges, which I thought was pretty funny, got the suits all upset. Burke had to come off of his Christmas vacation to answer it.

"Oooh, man, I don't know," I said, stunned by his admission.

"I didn't know you had a contract on you down there in Bolivia."

I contemplated reminding him that my memo had also criticized the suits under his command for exposing me to an inordinate amount of risk *because* of the contract on my life, but thought better of it. "Oh, you didn't," I said. "I thought everyone knew."

"I didn't. Mike, you know why I thought of you. . . . One of the reasons we're not doing a lot better [in Bolivia] is that nobody has gone down in the Beni* and established an informant network."

"Ohhh," I said, wondering why the Man himself had decided to call me.

"And I was thinking, if there's one guy [who could], first of all, give some leadership to these kids that they're sending down there, number one. And number two, get [something] going, instead of just riding around in choppers and dropping napalm. . . ."

Was he for real? Could the situation be that desperate that they wanted to send the hated, feared Levine to Bolivia? I couldn't believe it. *Dropping napalm? The Man himself telling me that Snowcap wasn't working?* I wondered what bullshit they were telling Congress. For a moment I considered going to Bolivia to see for myself. "If you guys just give me a false identity, [I'd be happy to go]." *Am I fucking nuts, or what?*

"No, I can't take that chance, Mike."

Of course you can't—not with my memo sitting on your desk. "I'd be prepared to do whatever you guys think," I said. "You're right; things should be done [in Bolivia]."

"Well, you know what I'm afraid of; we just keep sending people down there for ninety days. They go in, they kind of flounder around . . ."

He sounded like Jorge Román: The operation was laughable, a

---

* Notorious cocaine-producing zone in Bolivia. Home of Roberto Suárez and other "friends" of mine.

hundred-million-dollar joke. I decided to change the subject to the Roberto Suárez case and Operation Trifecta. "I'll tell you what. When I was in Argentina. It seemed to me that the best thing to do —and I had put in a suggestion that was never followed up on—is a concerted undercover effort into Bolivia, from outside the country. As a matter of fact, that's how we got Roberto Suárez. We sent informers in. The Bolivian traffickers don't want to leave Bolivia.

"For instance, if you look through the case files for the one that's going to trial in San Diego [Trifecta], you'll find that we got great intelligence in Bolivia by suckering the Bolivians out."

"You know," said Burke, "when [Attorney General] Meese went down there with [John] Lawn. The Bolivians had told us, 'Get us a copy of the [Trifecta] indictment . . . and we'll put him on a plane.' We had a girl typing the goddamned indictment for three days so that we could send it down by Teletype. . . . The [Bolivians] were going to do that as a gesture [for Meese]. But it never happened."

"Who?"

"They were going to put Roberto Suárez on a plane."

Of course not. Suárez is a hero to Bolivians, and Meese is just another hypocritical gringo politician. But how would you know that, asshole? "Not Suárez. I'm talking about this latest indictment, out in San Diego."

"Oh, the case with the Mexicans and the Bolivians?"

"Yes."

"Yeah, well, I went down [to Bolivia]. I was the point man going into that lab.* You'll see the pictures in the *DEA World.*"†

"No kidding?" *Point man? The man had been riding a desk for all the years I knew of him. Maybe he meant the point of a pencil.*

"Yeah."

"I'm really curious to see that."

"That was fun. I enjoyed it."

Only a suit would say that.

---

* Cocaine lab belonging to Román and Vargas.
† Quarterly in-house magazine published by DEA.

"Yes. Well, that was a success for Operation Snowcap," I said, choking on the irony.

"Oh, yeah!" said Burke emphatically.

I had to get off the phone. I mouthed a couple of bullshit polite phrases and slammed the receiver down. Trifecta was being touted as a success for Operation Snowcap.

TEN

WAITING FOR TRIAL

I had a dream in which Pedro Rocamora appeared. He was a seven-foot-tall black Amazon warrior god that had been "assigned" to me as my "lifetime protector" by an Argentine *macumbera*.* It was the only time I had ever seen him in a dream. He said nothing. He just stood there towering over me, his spear at the ready, peering around at the darkness. I looked around and realized that I was on a dark, vacant tenement street that I didn't recognize. A vague shadow was moving out of the darkness toward me. I looked at Pedro; he was gone. I awoke frightened. I don't think I am any more superstitious than the next guy, but I had been so lucky for so many years, my luck had to run out sometime. In the weeks that followed I could not shake the feeling that something was going to happen to me. Then an incident happened that was like a warning.

On April sixth Stutman, the ever media-minded New York SAC, asked me to take William Friedkin, the director of *The French Connection,* and Frank Micelotta, a *Time* photographer, on a raid

---

* A priestess in the voodoo-type religion Macumba. I had met one once when I had been cursed by a drug dealer and the Argentine police insisted I undergo a "cure."

with my group. We were going to execute arrest and search warrants in a cocaine and crack den located in a ground-floor apartment at 138th Street and St. Nicholas Avenue. An informant had made several buys and reported that the place was run by members of the infamous Jamaican Posse—a particularly violent group of heavily armed Rastafarians from the island of Jamaica, known for not surrendering without a fight.

I used the parking area at 125th Street and the Hudson River as a staging area. There was a total of sixteen of us, including Friedkin and the *Times* photographer. It was a gray, very cool afternoon. The men seemed more somber than usual and I couldn't help but wonder if they had the same feeling of foreboding that I couldn't shake. I forced thoughts of death from my mind and immersed myself in the planning of the raid. It would be a real tricky affair.

We had no idea how many "bad guys" would be in the apartment. At different times the informant had counted as many as twelve people, and there were always plenty of guns around, including a submachine gun. To make things more complicated, they had a closed-circuit television setup that would warn them of our approach the moment we entered the hallway. We would have to move fast—real fast.

Not much time to think. . . . Good.

The only heavy armament we had was a twelve-gauge shotgun that Willy Gray, my backup supervisor, carried. Willy was a Vietnam combat veteran who never tired of saying, "Man, this shit reminds me of the Nam." It was only weeks before, during a street arrest, that Willy had had to wrestle for his own gun. He had come as close to being killed as he ever had in combat.

In our favor was the fact that the building was built on a steep hill. The rear windows to the apartment were at least a twenty-foot drop, so I assigned only three men to cover them. I didn't think anyone jumping from that height would be able to put up much of a struggle afterward. The rest of us would charge through the front door of the building with a battering ram, run past the surveillance camera, and batter down the door of the apartment at the rear of the hallway.

At about four P.M. our small caravan of cars parked about three blocks south of the location. I sent the informant inside to talk about buying some crack. About ten minutes later he was out. I met him on the street. What he had seen was frightening. There were about a dozen people inside, some of whom were customers. "I seen at least three guns," he reported, watching me for a reaction. I told the informant to get out of the neighborhood, which he did without any additional convincing. Once again I felt the cold stab of fear in my gut. I remembered my dream. Then William Friedkin was beside me with his tape recorder going. His eyes were wide with excitement— not fear, just excitement. I wondered how much real action the man had seen. I told him what I knew. "We'll be going in a few minutes," I said. He said he wanted to go in with us. *The man had to be nuts.* "Be my guest," I said.

Most of my guys assigned to hit the front door were hidden in the back of a van. I repeated the informant's words. A couple of them made the sign of the cross. "Everyone got their flack jackets on?" They all did. There was nothing else to say, so I repeated words I had said a thousand times before: "Okay, remember, this job's not worth your life. Stay safe. Let's do it!" I felt the stab of fear again. This was no time for it. I shoved it deep into a corner of my mind.

The line of cars seemed to take forever to navigate the three blocks to our target. I was in a car behind the van with Friedkin and the *Times* photographer. As we pulled to the curb it seemed that everyone in the neighborhood froze in place to gawk at us. My head was buzzing. I had my portable radio in one hand and my nine-millimeter automatic in the other and was moving quickly in a wave of pounding feet, quick, heavy breathing, and murmured curses. I heard myself scream, "Move! Move! Move!" *It had to be bang! bang! fast. Surprise would keep us alive.*

The men assigned to the back window raced around the corner and out of sight. We swept into the hallway beneath the staring eye of a television camera. *They knew we were there. How would they react, shoot or run?* A huge black man in dreadlocks tried to race up a flight of stairs. I saw him disappear in a pile of pounding fists. Someone screamed, "Police! Police!" I heard the boom of the ram. In the shadows just ahead of me a door exploded inward and the hallway was flooded with light. I ran toward it. Suddenly I found myself in a cluttered apartment, catacombed with little rooms, chasing fleeing shadows. The world exploded in screams. I ran past a huge black woman with her hands over her head in a pose of surrender. Her eyes were wide and white with fear. The place reeked with fear . . . and death. I kicked a gun with my feet and stumbled. A figure disappeared into a back room, I ran toward it. I heard the frightening *kuh-shunk* of metal on metal, as Willy, just behind me, jacked a shell into the chamber of his twelve-gauge.

The back room was jammed with fighting, squirming bodies as seven big, mean-looking Rastafarians were trying to get out one small window. A guy in the window had frozen there, unable to jump. Below him the sight of five of his buddies flattened into bloody pancakes on the hard concrete had given him pause for thought. I had just enough time to drop my portable and leap over the pile with my free hand and grab the back of his shirt. I had a stranglehold on the "cork" in a strange human bottleneck. I turned sideways and saw, to my horror, that Willy and I were alone in that room. The bad guys turned and noticed the same thing. They all started fighting at once. I held on to a fistful of shirt and used my gun as a club. Beside me Willy began stroking heads with the shotgun butt—suddenly we were fighting for our lives and screaming for help. As other agents reached the room the shotgun exploded with a deafening roar.

It was suddenly quiet. Everyone, bad guys and good guys alike, had flattened themselves on the floor. A cloud of smoke wafted lazily in the air. "Everyone all right?" I asked. Thank God, no one had been hurt. The deadly cluster ball of heavy lead pellets had somehow passed between myself and another agent, Jim Kasson. We had both been a hair away from dead.

In the hallway, lying in a pile of frightened humanity, William Friedkin, his arm holding the tape recorder high in the air, peered at me and said, "I love it."

"I know how you feel," I said. "Why else would anyone do this shit?"

On April nineteenth Operation Snowcap announced its biggest cocaine seizure ever, in Bolivia: 1,375 pounds. "It was more than double all the cocaine seized last year," said U.S. Ambassador Robert Gelbard.* *It was less than two days' production in Román's lab.*

■

By May fourth the weather was getting warmer and business was picking up. I had been on another half-dozen raids and had all but forgotten my shaky feelings. We had another raid planned for that day. This time the target scheduled was a Dominican crack- and coke-dealing gang in Washington Heights. The steady flow of action had been good for me; it kept me from thinking of Trifecta and more sleepless nights.

At three P.M. I found myself in a radio car controlling sixteen DEA agents in eight undercover cars in what amounted to a pincer movement aimed at a building on West 154th Street, where we had two search warrants to execute. Undercover agents had made buys and we had arrest warrants for three dealers. I sat, my engine idling softly, just off the corner of 154th and Broadway. I ordered Luis Pizarro, who had made some of the undercover buys, to drive up the block. We had to move soon; the sudden appearance of men in cars on both ends of the block was already attracting too much attention from the street people.

Within a few minutes Luis's voice came over the radio. "They're all out here. There's gotta be twenty or thirty dealers out here. Lotta people on the block."

I grabbed the mike and yelled, "Okay, let's do it! Go! Go! Go!" I slapped the red bubble light on my roof and wheeled the OGV, a brown Camaro, around the corner and raced up the long block. Three cars roared in behind me. Ahead, I could see my guys roaring in from the other direction, closing the trap. People were running in all directions. EVERYONE on that block sells dope.

As I pulled up in front of the old prewar building, I spotted one of the defendants running through the courtyard and into the build-

* Peter McFarren, Associated Press release (April 19, 1989).

ing. I was right behind him. With me were the ever-ready Willy Gray and a half-dozen other agents. Behind us the street echoed with shouts and sirens. *I love it. It's when I feel most alive.*

As we hit the hallway an apartment door slammed in the darkness at the end of the hallway. It was the apartment we had the search warrant for. The battering ram exploded the door inward and I was through it, gun in hand, tearing through another strange apartment, following sounds of movement. I reached a rear bedroom in time to see a man, gun in hand, jump. How high could it be? It was a ground-floor apartment. I went out the window behind him. I remember waiting to hit the ground and all I could feel was my stomach plastered to the top of my rib cage. The other guy had hit, bounced, and run. I could hear his feet pounding the pavement. I was a lot higher up than I had guessed. Maybe God was evening the score for those Rastas the previous month. When I finally hit, I was jarred silly. I sat down on my butt. Pain roared through my ankle and back. *That's the difference between a forty-eight-year-old Jewish narc and a frightened twenty-two-year-old Dominican. He was still able to run.*

I struggled to my feet. Willy was peering down at me from a window a lot higher up than I had imagined. His expression said what I was thinking—I had to be nuts. "You all right?" asked Willy. I wasn't and I knew it. "Just toss me a portable radio. I think my leg's broke." My right ankle was already ballooning out over my shoe and I could barely put any weight on it. Willy dropped a portable radio to me. I drew my pistol and limped toward the end of the alley. It seemed that the whole rear courtyard was fenced in; there was a chance the guy was trapped back there with me.

At the rear of the yard I found myself peering up a seven-foot embankment on top of which stood a group of Pakistani construction laborers staring at me, their faces pale with fear. One of them, in broken English, said, "He go there." He pointed behind him. The fleeing drug dealer had not only survived the jump, he had also managed to scale a seven-foot embankment. Incredible. *We've got to come up with an Olympic event for these guys.* There was nothing I could do.

I raised the portable radio to call for help. Out of the corner of my eye I caught a sudden movement. I turned just in time to see a huge Doberman coming at me. He did not make a sound; he was all business, fangs and furious red eyes. I just got my gun up in time to fire. The bullet hit him in the neck above the shoulder. The wound only stopped the huge dog momentarily. It was good thing it did— my gun was jammed. I was able to get a round in the chamber just in time for his second charge. I fired again, this time hitting him in the head. He went down.

"Hey, that was great," said a voice behind me. I turned. Wally Cerniak, a brand-new agent on his first raid, was behind me. "It was just like a jungle movie. I mean, he was charging," said Wally. He and another agent, Junius Simmons, heard the first shot and jumped from the same window I did, to come to my aid. They had both survived the jump uninjured. *That was the moment I knew for sure that I was too old for this job.*

As it turned out, the dog had been loosed at me by one of the other drug dealers hiding in the basement. He was charged with (among his drug charges) assault on a federal officer. If I were in Vietnam my wounds would have been called "million-dollar wounds" because they had finally taken me out of action, permanently. Both my leg and back would keep me in braces, hospitals, and doctor's offices for the rest of the year. I would not return to duty until the Trifecta trial, which would be postponed until January 1989. The injuries will keep me in some discomfort and pain for the rest of my life, but in a strange way I am thankful for the event. I have a feeling Pedro Rocamora was behind it, saving my life, and a fate worse than death—a funeral presided over by the suits.

On May twentieth the first DEA agent was killed on Operation Snowcap. Special Agent Rick Finley died, along with eight other non–DEA people, when a plane ferrying him from one of the Snowcap jungle base camps in Peru crashed.

Death Contracts and Other Lies

On June twenty-second an FBI informant provided DEA with information that "a 'hit' list had been compiled by persons associated with the Medellín [cocaine] cartel" and that I was marked for death. Also on the list were Sterling Johnson, New York City special narcotics prosecutor, and four other DEA agents, all of whom had taken active frontline roles as undercover or case agents in significant Colombian cocaine cases. The Colombians, according to the informant, also had targeted the wife of one of the agents for death.

It has always astonished me how impressed the public is with this kind of bullshit. I guess it sells newspapers. Anyone who has worked the streets as a narcotics agent for any length of time is threatened with contracts on his life about as often as his wife threatens him with divorce. It happens so often that it almost takes on comical overtones. One guy in my group, Willy Gray, had contracts on his life in half the drug-dealing neighborhoods in New York. After each arrest, just to stick it in the face of these dopers, we would go down to the neighborhood of the alleged contract and lock up a few more of the assholes. The bottom line is, if you are easily frightened by threats you had better turn your narc badge in. It's just not a line of work for you. Especially if you work undercover, where you screw people in a very personal way.

In my twenty-five years as an agent, virtually all of it working undercover, out of the hundreds of reported contracts on my life, there were only four that I was—and am—concerned enough about to take special precautions, which don't amount to much more than my reminding myself to be a little more on the alert. The first was when I had worked three months undercover living with motorcycle gangs. They are some sick bastards to whom killing is a kind of proof of their brand of machismo.* I didn't doubt for a second that they would do it. But the idiots were so dumb and so stoned all the

---

* The story was written about in *Undercover*.

time that I doubted that they could (as the expression goes) find a Jew in Miami.

The second was the Roberto Suárez contract. It was—and is—very real. The informants reporting the information were paid killers in different countries in South America, who had been offered the money to kill me. They had been furnished the information about what I looked like and where I could be found—information that they would have had no way of knowing unless the offer was bona fide.

The third case was for my undercover work in Operation Hun, an investigation that ended with the indictment of Luis Arce-Gómez, ex–Bolivian minister of the interior, and Octavio "Papo" Mejía, one of the most prolific Colombian murderers in that country's bloody history.*

The final price on my head—that I take seriously—was put there as a result of Operation Trifecta. There is no doubt in my mind that David Wheeler, George Urquijo, and I will have to be on our guard for the rest of our lives. There won't be any vacation trips to Panama, Mexico, or Bolivia.

When I received the latest information I telephoned Sterling Johnson as a courtesy. We had a laugh about it. If the Medellín cartel was going to kill DEA agents, there were a whole bunch of them stationed right there in Colombia who were a real threat, and *thank God!* we had not lost an agent in Colombia in more than ten years. The other thing about contracts, that all narcotics agents are well aware of, is that informants use them to suck money out of a government eager to pay for information. It's an easy way for a streetwise stool to get a quick couple of hundred bucks. The more frightened and inexperienced the agent, the more likely he is to fall for this.

There was another sad fact that both Sterling and I were aware of, which made the notion of Colombians coming to the U.S. to kill *any* U.S. official extremely unlikely, if not ridiculous. Our law-en-

---

* The U.S. has never been able to extradite Luis Arce-Gómez, so the indictment still stands but he has never been convicted. Mejía was convicted and is serving a thirty-year sentence. One of the defendants, Ana Tomayo, was among the Colombians extradited to the U.S. on October 12, 1989, during the Colombian drug wars.

forcement efforts to stop them had been laughably ineffective. In New York the total cocaine seizure for the entire year was less than two months' production in Román's laboratory. Why would Colombian cocaine dealers want to kill Americans when we weren't even effective enough to cause the slightest rise in cocaine prices? It made no sense. If the Medellín cartel had proven themselves to be anything in the past decade it was consummate businessmen, and a contract on an American official was not only illogical, it was bad business.

So it was with a mixture of amusement and wonder that I read a July second *Daily News* editorial reporting the threats on our lives. Someone must have leaked the information.

> *According to federal authorities, the drug lords have marked for assassination New York City Special Narcotics Prosecutor Sterling Johnson. His reaction to the threat? "I'm gonna keep on keepin' on . . . doing my job. I'm gonna keep kickin' them in the ass until their noses bleed."*
>
> *On the new "hit list" are the names of Johnson and a Miami prosecutor and four DEA agents. And the wife of a DEA agent. Which tells you something about the malevolence and ruthlessness of the cartel.*

I was not surprised, some time later, when the informant who had originated the information was put on a polygraph machine and flunked.

A week later another informant reported a similar threat against the lives of DEA, New York SAC Robert Stutman, Mayor Edward I. Koch, and Governor Mario Cuomo. Mayor Koch said he was "flattered" by the attention. Governor Cuomo seemed surprised and mildly amused. It was, after all, good politics to be on a Colombian "hit" list. Neither man took any special precautions. Stutman's reaction, however, was quite different—but not unexpected.

An "emergency" meeting was called in DEA's New York headquarters. Agents were drafted from every group to form a "Stutman protective detail" that was worked around the clock. Only the most streetwise agents were selected. Numerous drug investigations were put on hold as some of the best narcotics investigators in the world formed flying wedges around the frightened DEA executive on his way to lunch, dinner, or some speech or television appearance. A private security firm was contracted to provide armed guards in the hallway outside our elevators. The New York Police Department was requested to make the DEA's New York City headquarters a permanent, two-man, fixed post.

Early in my career I had been assigned, often, to augment the Secret Service in the protection of Presidents Nixon, Johnson, Vice President Humphrey, and various diplomats and candidates for the presidency. The Stutman protective detail rivaled any of them. One of the most depressing experiences in my life was seeing my own son, then a patrolman assigned to the Midtown North precinct, standing in the rain, "guarding" this pathetic, frightened man ensconced in a building full of armed-to-the-teeth DEA agents, electric doors, bulletproof glass, and surrounded by private security guards.

Captain Video held press conference after press conference explaining that his death had been ordered because "the Medellín cartel was furious at DEA's seizing two huge cocaine caches, disrupting their efforts at entering the New York market." He made personal appearances on any show that would have him. On the nationally televised *Nightline* the caption TARGETED FOR DEATH BY COLOMBIAN COCAINE CARTEL appeared on the screen beneath his image throughout his interview. The "contract" on his life rocketed him to national celebrity status. *No one seemed to remember that he had done exactly the same thing several years earlier when, as the SAC of Boston DEA office, he had also been targeted for death by Medellín cartel for his work in interrupting the flow of cocaine to the New England area.*

At first it was amusing to the real narcs, who were used to seeing incredible bullshit being fed to the public, but as time dragged on and the detail, along with the appearances, continued, it became embarrassing to all of us. It was rumored that even the suits were questioning the veracity of this latest contract. Jokes began to circulate the hallways of the New York office. A map of the world was posted on a bulletin board with arrows and lines drawn as if by a madman, tracing wild, sweeping routes across both poles and in every direction with no rhyme or reason. *Stutman security routes* was inscribed below it.

Finally, an OPR inspector was detailed to polygraph the informant guilty of originating the information. He flunked, and no one was surprised.

This information was not on *Nightline* or any of the network news programs, or in any newspaper that I know of. In fact, the news was not even widely known among DEA agents. The protective detail was quietly ended with no comment. The security guards stayed in the hallway for a couple of months because Stutman had committed the agency to a lengthy and expensive contract. What I found depressingly dangerous about the whole episode was captured in an Associated Press wire story some months later. The story quoted a *Houston Chronicle* story about phony drug raids staged by DEA to "help [undercover] agents gain the confidence of drug lords."*

" 'It's an investigative procedure that is used,' said DEA spokesman Maurice Hill, in Washington, D.C. 'But I can't begin to tell you with what frequency.' " The story detailed how DEA enlisted local police to lie to the press; it said, "Newspaper clippings on the fake seizures help convince the traffickers that the seizures are for real."

" 'If the DEA is willing to lie to the media and public about this issue, what else might they be willing to lie about?" asked *Chronicle* managing editor Tony Pederson.

" 'There seems to have been no accountability in the entire process,' Pederson added. 'At least some type of judicial review has always been necessary for other elements of law enforcement deception, the key example being wiretaps. But who, if anyone, has reviewed this process?'

"Paul LaRocque, an assistant journalism professor at Southern Methodist University in Dallas, asked, 'How can the public trust what they read in the paper, if the paper has been converted to an arm of government?' " *Answer: The public cannot trust a thing the*

---

* Associated Press wire report 1530 (November 27, 1988).

government tells you about the drug war. The suits and politicians have been allowed to lie for so long, and with such impunity, that— as they did in Vietnam—they're lying our way into another shooting war.

During the next seven months my street war became a war with the Office of Workers' Compensation, trying to get them to pay my rapidly mounting medical bills. At the same time a book about my earlier undercover exploits, *Undercover,* by Donald Goddard, was nearing its publication date and DEA's public relations staff finally got around to reading the manuscript. They hated it. The book told of my street-gang days in the South Bronx, my brother's heroin addiction and suicide; it also painted the bureaucracy in an unflattering light.

"You're a legend in DEA," said Cornelius Dougherty of DEA's headquarters staff. "We can't let people know we hire people like you."

I waited a moment to see if he was joking—he wasn't. DEA officially ordered me not to make any public appearances to promote the book. Later they refused to allow me to make any public appearances whatsoever. An "informant" of mine in headquarters advised me that it was my views on the drug war in general and Operation Snowcap in particular that had them more worried than anything else.

Over the years I had made numerous appearances on behalf of DEA, representing the derring-do life of an undercover agent. These public presentations were always tightly controlled, almost scripted. On one 1986 radio interview* the suits were so paranoid about what I *might* say that they would only allow me to be interviewed on a speaker phone with a "chaperon" sitting beside me. He was to control the direction of the interview, insuring that it was *only* about undercover work.

This fear soon translated itself—as it did during the Roberto Suárez case—to another OPR investigation. This time they were investigating whether or not I had received "official" permission to

---

* The *Stevie Jay* show. Station DWSA, Chicago, Illinois (August 26, 1986).

collaborate on a book in the first place. If they determined that I had not, I could be fired and the pension I had earned after twenty-five years of undercover work would be lost. More effort and time would be spent on this investigation than on my forty-two pages of allegations about the running of Trifecta. In the end—in spite of several suits wanting to push the issue—the findings of OPR that the case against me would be "a loser" prevailed. I would be "permitted" to retire.

Trifecta Trial

In the meantime, in San Diego, Washington, and Mexico City, a Trifecta controversy was beginning to heat up. The trial and events surrounding it—revealed here for the first time—would epitomize every ugly and fraudulent facet of the drug war and why it can never be won while we fight it as a house divided.

One of the implications of Operation Trifecta was that the Mexican government could be bought if the price were right. Colonel Carranza had brought his graduation yearbook from the Mexican military academy with him to meet "Luis" in San Diego. On camera he had pointed out all the officers that I, as a drug dealer, could "work with"—which was most of them. He had even indicated that General Juan Arévalo Gardoqui, the Mexican secretary of defense, "could be used." Not since the torture death of my brother DEA agent Enrique "Kiki" Camarena, at the hands of Mexican police and drug traffickers, and the subsequent cover-up action by the government of Mexico, had there been any allegations more serious. The Mexican government had a lot to lose if the charges were proven credible.

Our State Department made a yearly grant to narcotics-source countries that were deemed "cooperating" in our antidrug efforts. A clause in the 1986 omnibus drug bill required that the President certify that recipients of any aid were "fully cooperative." Incredibly, in spite of the Camarena murder, the cover-up, and their failure to bring many of those responsible to justice, Mexico was still receiving more than fifty million a year of our taxpayer dollars, as a "cooperating country." In addition, if they were "decertified," all U.S. representatives to multinational development banks would be required to vote against them for any loans.

The Mexicans had always been able to count on our State Department to cast a blind eye on almost anything they did, short of invading Texas or California, before they would be considered less than cooperating. During the furor after the Camarena murder Mexico also learned that they could count on various members of the Justice Department, like Attorney General Edwin Meese, to side with them. Mexico was least concerned with DEA, whose new FBI "leadership" during the Camarena affair had proven themselves to be totally ineffective in getting any cooperation whatsoever; they would bend with the strongest wind, or in whatever direction the State Department told them to. However, the Trifecta arrests, coming so close on the heels of Camarena's death, might be one scandal too many. Mexico stood a good chance of losing "cooperating country" status—unless they could discredit the case. Thanks to Attorney General Meese's phone call to the Mexican attorney general, warning him about the ongoing Trifecta operation, when the arrests were made, a public defense had already been formulated.

An unnamed Customs official, outraged at what Meese had done, was quoted as saying, "One phone call is all it takes."* I wondered if he was one of those who had slipped the NBC camera crew into the undercover house that night in December.

The official Mexican government claim was that Colonel Carranza had been discharged from the army eighteen years before and had no current affiliation with the military; that Pablo Girón was not a federal policeman and that Hector Álvarez had no affiliation whatsoever with the president or Mexico's ruling political party. They concluded that the men were imposters who were trying to "sting" the undercover agents for their money.

The Mexicans got an immediate ally in U.S. Ambassador Charles Pilliod, who, after checking with a few government officials (including General Juan Arévalo Gardoqui), agreed with the "sting"

---

* Elaine Shannon, *Desperados: Latin Drug Lords, U.S. Lawmen, and the War America Can't Win* (New York: Viking Penguin Inc., 1988).

assessment. In a February twenty-second *San Diego Union* news release, under the headline U.S. EXPERTS TO EXAMINE TAPE IN MEXICO DRUG CASE, the ambassador was quoted:

> *So we stung a sting. Now in the process, they [the suspects] also involved a general, Poblano de Silva. . . . Well, as everyone else was false, we still had to find out whether Poblano de Silva was valid or not, and we are attempting to do that now.*

The rest of the article seemed particularly sinister to me. It was my guess that the newspaper had been the victim of intentionally false information:

> *The United States is sending a team of audio experts to Mexico in an effort to determine whether a voice on an incriminating tape is really that of a fugitive Mexican army general indicted last month in San Diego on cocaine-smuggling charges.*
>
> *If the voice on the tape is that of the general, the Mexican government has agreed to prosecute him in Mexico, U.S. Ambassador to Mexico, Charles Pilliod, said.*
>
> *Pilliod said the United States was dispatching the experts to Mexico because other major figures indicted in the case have lied about their affiliations, and the voice identified as that of the general could be that of someone else.*

There was no voice tape of General Silva—Wheeler and Ross had successfully prevented me from getting it during the final two days of the undercover operation—Wheeler took Carranza to Sea World instead—and by February twenty-second the ambassador had to know that. A defense was being constructed *for* the Mexican government.

When it should finally be revealed to the press that the voice on the tape *was* someone else's, the Mexican position—and that of Ambassador Pilliod—would be strengthened. The tape-recorded voice of "Pablo" (who Carranza had said was General Silva's brother) would be not only be useless as evidence, it would be used *against* us. In the world press—the only battleground that mattered to the suits and politicians—it would appear that we had been "fooled" into thinking we were dealing with a Mexican general; that Operation Trifecta was just as the ambassador and the Mexican government were claiming: American undercover agents trying to pull a sting on Mexican con men, while the con men were trying to do the same to us—stingers getting stung. Or, in the words of Ambassador Pilliod, "We stung a sting."

Of course, an investigation by DEA's Mexico City office, linking the telephone number, address, or voice of "Pablo" to the Mexican military, in any way, would shoot the "stung-a-sting" theory to hell. But, as Hoopel had said, "It's strange." DEA, Mexico, was not responding to any requests for support in the investigation.

In my experience working overseas and at DEA headquarters, I had never heard of a U.S. ambassador assigned to any country in the world making statements about a DEA investigation, without having first consulted the senior DEA representative in his embassy. Ambassador Pilliod's chief advisor in narcotics matters was the DEA country attaché—in charge of all DEA operations in Mexico —Edward Heath.

Heath had achieved a certain amount of notoriety after Kiki Camarena's murder, when it was revealed that Camarena and his supervisor Jim Kuykendall had sent him numerous cables and memorandums complaining about the deadly conditions in Guadalajara, none of which were ever passed on to DEA headquarters. Guadalajara was—and still is—one of the most dangerous cities in the world for DEA agents. At the time of the Camarena murder DEA had employed extraordinary safety precautions for its agents in Colombia—who were given hazardous-duty pay—while nothing was done for the agents in Guadalajara.

"Does somebody have to die [before something is done]?" were Kiki's sadly prophetic words, shortly before his death.

Kuykendall and the other DEA agents stationed in Guadalajara were certain that "bad news" stayed bottled up with Ed Heath in the American embassy, where the State Department officials, as well as some of the DEA personnel assigned there, would let the

Mexican government get away with just about anything to preserve the "special relationship" between the U.S. and Mexico.

U.S. Ambassador Charles "Stung-a-Sting" Pilliod was one of those who had pressured the U.S. to certify Mexico as "fully cooperative" after the Camarena murder. The retired chairman of the Goodyear Tire and Rubber Company was against the idea of linking commerce to drug controls. He had urged his staff at the American embassy to write more "objective" cables about Mexico in order to create a more positive attitude about the country than had his predecessor, John Gavin. Could his "stung-a-sting" comment about Trifecta have been an example of his objectivity?

It came as no surprise to anyone, after Kiki's death—when few DEA agents were renewing their tours in Mexico, and Ed Heath seemed to want to stay—that Pilliod praised Heath to Administrator John Lawn as a "team player."*

Pilliod and the government of Mexico had now provided the Trifecta defense lawyers with a strategy. Their claim would be that the defendants really were confidence men who had never intended to deliver what they promised, and were not really in a position to do so even if they wanted to. They advised government prosecutors that they intended to subpoena both ambassador Pilliod and Ed Heath as witnesses for the defense.

Colonel Carranza (grandson of ex–Mexican President Venustiano Carranza) was key to the defense. His claim—mimicking the Mexican government's—was that he had been discharged in 1971 and had neither contact nor influence with the Mexican military, and that everything that David Wheeler had said about his undercover trip to Mexico was lies. Proving Wheeler to be a consummate liar might be the easiest part of the strategy—depending on how thorough an investigation the defense could carry out.

The tape-recorded phone call to "Pablo" had now not only become important in the world press arena, it had become crucial in the trial, if we were to prove that the Mexicans were more than con men.

* Elaine Shannon, *Desperados: Latin Drug Lords, U.S. Lawmen, and the War America Can't Win* (New York: Viking Penguin, Inc., 1988).

As to Pablo Girón and Hector Álvarez: If they were not who they said they were, who were they? I was never one-hundred-percent sure from my undercover meetings that Girón was really a Mexican federal cop. He was, after all, the only contact Wheeler knew before the Trifecta saga began, and came across as more or less a Mexican version of the the informant—a bit of a con man and bullshitter. Brummel was still a mystery. All that was necessary was that DEA's Mexico City office carry out an investigation of Pablo, the phone number, and into the backgrounds of Girón and Álvarez.

It was easier said than done.

On July third the Trifecta controversy made national news. A *Washington Post* article reported that "U.S. prosecutors and Mexico were at odds" over the San Diego case.* The Mexican government was angry at the charges brought against General Poblano Silva and Colonel Salvador de la Vega and would not investigate the charges against the two currently active officers unless "more concrete evidence" was forthcoming than just the word of an informer. The article quoted "a well-informed foreign narcotics expert" who suggested that "Carranza, Girón, and Álvarez were essentially 'flimflam men' who 'threw names around to try to impress people.' " The "expert" was unidentified.

By August twenty-fourth I was still on "traumatic injury leave," recuperating from my raid injuries, and had heard nothing about my memo or the trial, so I telephoned Hoopel. He told me that the defense had nine attorneys working and that he had no idea when the trial would be scheduled. There was absolutely nothing new on Remberto Rodríguez. It seemed that one of the biggest money launderers in Panama had vanished into the woodwork and no one seemed to care. As if that weren't enough, all requests to Ed Heath's office in Mexico City for backup investigation had still gone unanswered. Eight months had passed since the arrests, and the government could *still* not disprove the claim that they were nothing more than flimflam men.

By September twentieth I had spent too much time at home

* William Branigin, "U.S. Prosecutors, Mexico at Odds over Drug Case," *Washington Post* (July 3, 1988).

mulling over everything that had happened. I woke up that morning with a start. I had the sudden realization that I hadn't heard anything about my memo. It was clear that if I allowed it to, it would vanish into the woodwork along with Remberto Rodríguez, José Roberto Gasser, the whole Roberto Suárez case, and God knows how many other skeletons. I had the perfect legal right to question what had been done with my memo. I would have to testify to *all* reports I had written, under oath. It was my *duty* to call the existence of my memorandum to the attention of the San Diego prosecutor.

In the morning I first called OPR and was told that the memorandum was "not 3500 material," and therefore unnecessary to reveal to the defense. Before I could speak, the OPR agent said, "Let me check on it. I'll call you back." Within minutes he called and advised me to call the prosecuting attorney, Steve Nelson, in San Diego and ask him "if he wants to see it. If he does," said the agent, "he'll have to request it in writing from OPR."

When I dialed Steve Nelson's San Diego office, I had no idea what to expect. He was a well-known prosecutor with a reputation for winning the big, complicated conspiracy cases. I was calling him with a big problem.

ELEVEN

THE TRIAL

Cover-up in Mexico

The only thing I knew about Steve Nelson prior to the phone call was that he was a dedicated career prosecutor with a reputation as an aggressive courtroom battler and the winner of some of the biggest and most celebrated drug cases in history. Some of his investigative and courtroom exploits had been written about in James Mills's *The Underground Empire*. I was a little nervous as his secretary paged him. My memo represented big problems for a prosecutor. The revelations would not make our government's drug war look too good and would definitely affect the jury—and the rest of America, I hoped—but I did not believe it would affect the outcome of the trial; the seven should be found guilty regardless of the memo. But still, it did not make for an easy prosecution.

Steve Nelson came across on the phone as warm and friendly. We discussed all the trial preparations for a while, and I was relieved to learn he was not the AUSA who had made the decision *not* to put the Title 3 wiretap on the undercover house. Steve had been assigned the case after the arrests. Finally, when it seemed that he wasn't even going to mention the memo, I did.

"No problem," said Nelson, "it's already been taken care of." *I felt my heart squeezed.* Nelson cheerfully explained that he had presented the memorandum to the judge—before furnishing it to the defense attorneys—requesting that all my personal comments, value judgments, allegations of government misconduct, be deleted as "irrelevant to the trial issues," and the judge (William Enright) had agreed.

"That's great," I said, feeling a rush of anger. How much could they have cut out? He sounded cheerful as hell about it—why? Couldn't he see that these bastards deserved to be exposed?

I hung up after a long, cordial conversation. I had agreed to come to San Diego during the first week of January to begin trial preparations. When my anger passed, I realized that I could not fault either Nelson or the judge. It was the system. They had played by the rules, and they were one-hundred-percent correct. My memo should have been investigated by OPR, Congress, and the Senate—*not* made part of a drug trial. And OPR had shoved it under a rug.

I arrived in San Diego late in the evening of January 4, 1989, almost a full year since the arrests. A year had gone by and there were still no answers. As I moved along the seemingly endless sameness of airport corridors, with the endless sameness of the flow of passengers, my back and leg aching from the combination of the long, cramped flight and my crack-house raid injuries, it suddenly dawned on me that I had fucked up—somewhere at the end of the corridor Hoopel would be waiting for me.

I had nothing to say to him.

By now everyone in San Diego had probably heard about my memo, and I certainly hadn't spared him in it. I had already been told by a friend in San Diego—whose name I won't mention because he is still on the job there—that the SAC (the head suit), did not even want to see me in the DEA office. I was persona non grata in San Diego: I had told the truth. Maybe Hoopel would have the balls to simply not show up.

But when I reached the main terminal, I saw Hoopel backed up against the wall, craning his neck, before he noticed me. One unguarded look at his tense, unhappy face told me everything.

"Hiya doing, Hubert?" I said.

"Mikey," he said, forcing a smile. We did not shake hands. Twenty minutes and not much conversation later we were stuck in a tangle of cars inching our way toward the airport exit. Somehow it figured that the only traffic jam I was ever in in San Diego would be at the airport at eleven o'clock at night with Hoopel at the wheel. He sat there grinning his grin, as everyone in the parking lot edged in front of him. I had heard rumors that his wife had left him and that he was all broken up about it.

"Do I have a car?" I asked when we were finally moving.

He seemed embarrassed. "Uh, we're workin' on it. I spoke to my supervisor."

"Great!" I kept my mouth shut. They were putting me in a hotel that was out in the middle of the bay without a car. For a moment the thought occurred to me that I was being set up. I looked at Hoopel's face and dismissed the thought. He just wasn't capable.

Twenty minutes later we were northbound on I-5 when he broke the silence again. "You know, Wheeler's already sold the movie rights to this case."

"You're shitting me!" Here was a lowlife stool pigeon arrested for dealing a lousy eight hundred grams of coke in Oklahoma and selling out his Mexican friend to save his own ass, selling the movie rights to the government's case before he had either testified in it, or been sentenced in his own case. I was not even sure if it was legal. I *was* sure that if *I* had done it, DEA would be indicting me.

"No," said Hoopel, laughing nervously. I wondered what the hell he thought was funny. "Dennis Hopper bought the rights. It's no bullshit, 'cause the other day I picked up [Wheeler's] phone and it was him on the line, asking for Dave. Can you fuckin' believe it?"

We were just passing a Sea World sign and I remembered our lost opportunity at getting the Mexican general on tape. "No, I fucking can't."

January fifth, at seven-thirty A.M., my hotel phone rang for the first time. I picked it up thinking it would be Hoopel with my car, or maybe Steve Nelson. It was Wheeler. "You recognize my voice?"

"Do I recognize that fucking voice," I said, hoping he couldn't hear the anger. I wanted to keep him talking freely. With all his bullshit he was still the best source of information I had about the case. How ironic it was that after twenty-five years of undercover work, I was in the biggest case of my career—in history—and the stool knew more about it than I did. I had to hand it to Wheeler, he had managed to "flip" the government.

"Just wanted to see how you were doing," he said. He told me that Jake the pilot was there taking a shower, and that they had an "escort" of armed Customs agents protecting them. The sudden closeness of the two seemed somehow suspicious, but I just couldn't put my finger on it. Hell, everything about Wheeler seemed suspicious. He confirmed that he and Dennis Hopper were doing a movie about the case. He mentioned that Touchstone Productions had picked up the option. He had a lot of questions about *Undercover* and whether I had sold the movie rights. I soon realized that he was pumping me for information almost as hard as I was him.

"I want to put you on the big screen," he said, laughing. Christ! Now I had heard everything. I wondered whether he had even *considered* the possibility of his going to jail for the cocaine he had been caught with.

"A lot of people want to do that," I said. *Never try to con a con man.* I had to cut the conversation short before he sensed it. After I hung up I realized we hadn't even said a word about the trial. I had to hand it to him, he had managed to draw me into playing his game.

At about twelve noon my phone rang again. Wheeler was in the lobby with his team of bodyguards, inviting me to lunch. I had to be wary. There was no love lost between us. A guy like Wheeler doesn't "just" show up casually. He was after something. But then, so was I. It was an offer I just couldn't refuse.

Ten minutes later we were seated around a table in the Hotel Bahia restaurant. Wheeler's bodyguards were a nice young all-American-looking couple named Curtis and Carol, who seemed as enamored with the informant as Ross and the others had been the year before. The son of a bitch had not lost his touch. He might have had a great career as an undercover.

It wasn't long before I got a general idea of what he was after. He wanted the behind-the-scenes story of what had happened in DEA headquarters during the all-day Operation Trifecta planning session, for which he would "trade" me the "inside" story of DEA's "sorry" performance in the Bolivian jungle.

"No," I said. "I don't think I need it." It didn't seem to matter. He was so proud of his performance that he started to tell me about it anyway.

"Do you know, I was the only gringo with the *Leopardos**
when they went through that jungle to find [Román's] lab."

"You're shitting me." I laughed. "This guy from headquarters, Terry Burke, told me he was on point when they found the labs."

Wheeler laughed. He said he had met Terry Burke. "I was the *only* gringo with them when we found the lab sites," he insisted. "The DEA agents were fucking useless. They were huddled together in a small bunch, back in the jungle, afraid to move." Enjoying himself, he went into great detail about the jungle adventure. He told of a DEA agent drinking himself into a stupor and refusing to get off the helicopter, of a DEA supervisor fainting from heat exhaustion, and of others so terrified by the many poisonous snakes that they were reduced to clumping together and inching their way through the jungle in a terrified human knot. He said that a *Leopardo* commander, in disgust at the DEA agents' inability to maintain a skirmish line, gave an automatic weapon to Wheeler and put him on point. "And *that,*" insisted Wheeler with finality, "was how we found the main lab site."

I brought up the subject of the Panama money launderer. I was curious as to whether he had heard anything about that. No one in the government seemed to know or care about him. He did not disappoint me. His eyes bugged wide with excitement.

"Let me tell you something. The CIA whisked him right to Contadora Island, and placed him under twenty-four-hour guard until the whole thing blew over. If you and George [Urquijo] would have lucked onto him, you would have been fucking dead."

My blood chilled with a flash of memory: strangers following

---

* Specially trained Bolivian police unit used to combat the cocaine traffickers.

George and me through the Panama City streets. "How do you know that?"

He looked at Curtis and Carol significantly. "Are you kidding? [Remberto] was hooked into the Iberoamerican Bank. There were two other hidden accounts hooked to his—Noriega's, and a CIA account for transferring money to the Contras. Do you think they were going to let him get busted?"

I again didn't know what to think. The Iberoamerican part of the story was accurate, but Wheeler had been there with me when Román had told me about it. It also seemed certain that anyone laundering the amounts of cash that the Corporation handled would have to be tied to Noriega. And thanks to Iranscam the CIA's use of Panama to shuttle funds to the Contras was no secret. Try as I might, I could not get him to be specific about his source.

"Do you know," said Wheeler, as if it explained everything, "that while we were in Panama, [Alfredo] Duncan kept defending Noriega, telling me that he was cooperating [with DEA] one hundred percent. He then made a specific allegation of corruption that has never been confirmed.

"Did you tell this to anyone?"

Wheeler looked at me as if I were crazy. Neither of us had mentioned his earlier accusations against DEA and, of course, my memo. I wasn't going to bring it up if he didn't. In spite of it he did not seem intimidated about talking to me in front of the two Customs agents. Maybe he was confident that they would back him later if he decided to deny *this* conversation too. Besides, he had gotten away so easily with recanting his other statements, what reason did he have to worry? The government was giving him a license to lie.

"You said you were thinking of going to a senator," I said, reminding him of what he had said in Panama. For the first time he looked a little uncomfortable. Something was up.

"We've been talking to Senator Nunn's people," he said cagily, "but they don't want us to say anything until the trial is over."

I wondered who the "we" was, and how the "we" was going to explain some of Wheeler's and Customs's actions—the press ambush, the NBC visit to the undercover house, the Mexican trip to Sea World, and the press conference that put all our lives in jeopardy

—but decided not to push any farther. I hoped he did go to the senator. If he didn't, maybe I would.

The conversation ebbed for a few minutes; then, out of the blue, Wheeler was talking about the Cayman Islands again, mentioning my friend's name. I wondered whether Ross had told him about the lies I had caught him in. "I helped the guy build a restaurant in the Caymans," he explained to Curtis and Carol. *Well, at least he was no longer a partner.*

We talked for a few more minutes about the difficulties of testifying and being cross-examined. Wheeler was nervous about it. "Just tell the truth," I said, "and you won't have any problems. Just tell the truth."

On January sixth I met with George Urquijo for breakfast. In the year since we had seen each other last, every one of the Customs agents assigned to the case—except for George—had been promoted. I didn't say anything, but I had a feeling that his being friends with me had had a lot to do with his being held back.

I had been looking forward to seeing George again. Aside from the fact that I liked and respected him for the highly principled man that he is, and just plain enjoyed his company, he had also been a first-hand witness to some of the more outrageous events in the case. A lot of agents had heard about Customs bringing NBC news- and cameramen into the undercover house, but George was the man who was there when it happened, and I needed him to confirm the story.

"It happened in November," he said.

I was stunned. "You mean we worked *two months* undercover with the press knowing about the house and everything?" *I had believed that they had done it during the nearly disastrous Marriott Hotel operation in December.*

George shrugged his shoulders, "They probably thought the case was going to end sooner—not that that was any excuse." He described the way it had happened. He was alone in the undercover house in La Jolla, fielding telephone calls from Bolivia and Mexico. The door to the house suddenly opened. "I almost went for my gun," said George. "I mean, all the bad guys knew where the house was. We were doing a twenty, thirty-million-dollar deal. What would it take for them to have a couple of guys watch our house? They could have hired a private detective. I know I would have. So you can imagine my surprise when two top Customs officials walked through the door at the head of a group of people with television cameras and equipment.

" 'Just press,' said Schruhan. 'Don't worry, kid, they won't tell anybody.' "

Once again the thought of a bunch of press people walking around for all that time with knowledge that could have gotten us killed, overwhelmed me for a moment. They did it *before* we went to Panama; just an idle comment at a cocktail party would have been all it took. *"Just one phone call is all it takes,"* the Customs suit had said about Meese's warning to the Mexicans. Then I got angry.

"Who the fuck are these people to play with our lives?"

"Look, I was a new agent," said George apologetically. "They told me not to tell anyone."

"I'm not blaming you, man," I said, wondering what young Mike Levine, as a new agent, would have done in the same circumstances. Probably just what George did, but who knows? In any case, it was George who had gone back to Panama with me after Remberto. And just telling me now took a lot of courage. "So what did they film?"

George laughed a bitter laugh. "Man, they filmed everything. They brought their cameras up into the attic and filmed all our equipment, the video monitors, everything. They even filmed the lamps with the hidden cameras. I mean everything, everything."

We were silent for a long moment. Later, George said this about Attorney General Edwin Meese's calling the Mexican attorney general to warn them about Trifecta:

"Ross told me that Meese made the call twenty-four hours before the case went down," said George. "It's pretty wild, considering that [Pablo] Girón was working out of the [Mexican] attorney general's office."

We were both quiet for a long time. It is a terrible and frightening lesson to learn that there are people to whom, alongside their own selfish interests, your life is worth nothing. Even more frightening when those people are in control of your life. At that moment the hurt and anger I saw in George's eyes told me it was a lesson he would never forget. No words were necessary.

On Saturday, January seventh, I went to Steve Nelson's office for my first pretrial conference.

The streets of downtown San Diego, around the federal building, were empty and bright with sunlight that morning. As I parked my car I could see Jim Ross walking toward me. The icy look told me that he had read my memo. As he led me through the deserted government office building, he did his best to be cordial. I think the strain might have been a little too much. By the time we reached Steve Nelson's office, in a partitioned-off section of the building designated for the use of the OCDETF* we were both silent.

Steve Nelson is not a man accustomed to losing. He is an athletic, graying man in his late forties, whose blue eyes spark with competitiveness. As he came around the desk to shake my hand I took mental note of an office inundated with Operation Trifecta files, evidence, maps, and charts and immediately saw that we had at least one thing in common—the case had taken over our lives. I had worked with many federal prosecutors in my life. Most were too intelligent not to realize that the drug war, for the most part, was a political sham, and focused all their efforts and objectivity on one goal—winning in court. Philosophical questions of right and wrong meant nothing. I did not know Nelson well enough yet to judge whether he fit that picture, but I was sure of one thing: If he was like most prosecutors, Trifecta was going to be more of a test of his sense of justice than any case he'd ever prosecuted before.

"I'm getting absolutely no cooperation from DEA, or State," said Nelson. "I wondered whether you had any ideas." He complained that in the full year that had passed since the arrests he had been unable to get any information from the State Department or any investigative support from DEA, to contradict the Mexican government claim that Álvarez, Girón, and Carranza were imposters who were trying to steal a drug dealer's money with a promise of Mexican military protection that they could in no way fulfill. The

* Organized Crime Drug Enforcement Task Force

only thing the Mexican government would say officially was that Pablo Girón was not a federal police official, that Colonel Carranza had retired from the military in 1971, that Álvarez was in no way connected to the PRI,* and that General Poblano Silva was not the commander of Puebla.† They would make no comment about our recording of Carranza's final conversation with Pablo, the general's alleged brother. They refused to investigate any claims against the general unless more concrete evidence, such as tape recordings or videotapes of the general himself, were produced.

Once again I fought anger surging up in my gut. I looked at Ross, who had been silently floating in and out of the office and now sat staring at some papers in his lap, and remembered the Mexicans' trip to Sea World—our last opportunity to tape the general's voice. "I'll take the responsibility for that decision," Ross had said that night.

What's more, said Nelson, the defense was going to subpoena Charles Pilliod, the American ambassador to Mexico, and Ed Heath, the SAC of DEA's Mexico City office, as witnesses. Pilliod had come out strongly in the press in support of the Mexican government's claim that we had been stung. He had assured the Mexican government that the United States had no evidence against Carranza, General Silva, or Colonel de la Vega and that Carranza would not even be prosecuted. As the ambassador to Mexico he had to be getting all his advice and counsel from the senior DEA man on his staff, Ed Heath, who, in the year since the arrests, had not responded to any of Nelson's requests for aid in investigating the Mexican defendants. A key part of that investigation was the identity of the man who had answered Carranza's final phone call to Mexico before his arrest—"Pablo, the general's brother."

Nelson pointed out a serious problem he had with Heath's less than cooperative attitude. Moments after Carranza's arrest he claimed to be "a friend of Ed Heath's." He also had a medal on his uniform that represented his participation in Operation Condor—a DEA crop-eradication program run by Heath's office in 1985 (long

* Current ruling political party in Mexico.
† The district in Mexico where we had contracted to land our cocaine-laden plane.

after the Mexican government said he had retired), and Heath's home address and phone in his address book. Edward Heath—a man so mistrusted by the street agents working for him in Mexico, that they conducted enforcement operations without informing him —had some explaining to do.

Nelson also informed me that he was in the process of trying to contact as many of the old Customs and DEA border rats as he could. He was going to conduct his own investigation—without DEA, if he had to. There was a good possibility that one of the agents who had worked in Mexico, or on the border, particularly on Operation Condor, might have met either Colonel Carranza or Pablo Girón. Nelson correctly judged that no street agent was going to cover for a suit. I immediately understood his openness with me. Nelson was getting no help from the DEA; on the contrary, they seemed to have plenty to hide. He knew that if push came to shove and he wound up at war with DEA over this case, he could count on me, an "insider" who also happened to be very much in the public eye, to side with him. Steve Nelson was getting ready to win the war in this one, even if he lost the battle in court.

I had plenty of ideas. "If Colonel Carranza said that Ed Heath was a friend of his, make DEA investigate it for you," I said. "Call OPR and tell them that an arrested fucking dope dealer said Ed Heath is a friend of his, let *him* explain it to them." *I doubted that the suits would ever investigate one of their own for any allegation less than mass murder.*

Nelson listened noncommittally. Calling OPR would really be going for the throat. It would be accusing Heath of having violated the law or some ethical code of conduct. From the look Nelson gave me, I didn't think he was pissed enough to go that far . . . yet.

I brought up contacting the CIA to see if they had files on any of the Mexicans. We both agreed that in view of Carranza's mention of having worked with the Contras in both Nicaragua and Mexico, it might not be a good idea. I also suggested that he contact Military Intelligence, who often worked independently of the CIA, and possibly some trusted newsmen who might be used to research some Mexican newspaper morgues for mention of any of our people. Nelson liked the ideas. He was cautious, but I could sense a growing impatience. I started to think of him as a possible ally.

We spent a couple of hours talking about the case and the ambivalence of our government's position in the war on drugs. Nelson surprised me by saying that somewhere down the line the public ought to be made aware of what had happened in this case and others like it. His statement encouraged me. Once again I heard my mouth speaking two or three beats ahead of my brain. "I hope you can see why I wrote that memo," I began, glad that Ross was still sitting there. "I wanted to make some official record of some of the atrocities that were committed in this case."

Nelson stared at me for a long moment and said, "Mike, the more I see of this case the more I understand your memo." It was a statement he would make several times over the coming weeks.

Before I left his office that day, he gave me my copy of what was left of the memo after all my observations and allegations had been deleted. There was hardly anything intelligible left. It would take one hell of a defense attorney to make head or tail out of it. Henceforth I would call it "the eunuch papers."

David Wheeler began his testimony on January sixth and immediately began attracting international press coverage. During his earlier years of dope trafficking in Mexico, he claimed to have worked with Nazar Haro, the onetime head of the Mexican DFS* who had recently been appointed the head of the Mexico City Police Intelligence unit. In 1974 the San Diego U.S. attorney, William Kennedy, had tried to prosecute Nazar Haro for his participation in an international car-theft ring but found the prosecution blocked by the CIA and the Justice Department, which did not want to lose Haro as a prized intelligence source. When Kennedy, now a San Diego superior court judge, made this public, he was fired from his post.

I could see that Steve Nelson, only an assistant United States attorney, was treading on some thin ice. It was also obvious that

---

* The DFS (Federal Security Directorate) was the Mexican equivalent to the CIA during the 1970s. It was later disbanded and its work turned over to the military.

there were a lot of people in our own government, including some within the DEA, who would love to see the jury believe that the case was, as Ambassador Pilliod had described it, "a sting of a sting."

On January ninth I returned to Nelson's office to see what progress he had made with DEA. Things were really starting to move. Ed Heath, after having been advised that he was going to be subpoenaed by the defense, had called Nelson and informed him that there *was* a file on Pablo Girón. Steve thought this "interesting" considering that the prior, cabled response from DEA Mexico had indicated that there was "no information" on Girón. "Maybe he's getting his act together," said Steve hopefully.

"I doubt it," I said. "He's got all the time in the world to answer you. What's to stop him from stonewalling you until the trial's over, and just not answering your requests? He managed to do it for a year already."

Nelson just looked at me.

Wheeler showed up with his bodyguards. He was giddy with the press coverage and his "performance" before the jury. "God, I've got 'em right on the edge of their seats," he said. The tall, angular dope dealer/screenwriter turned informant curled up in a seat, beaming. He was on a roll.

"I just spoke to my agent," he bragged. "Every script I ever wrote is hot now." He said that his "friend" Dennis Hopper had gotten him one of the top agents in Hollywood, Michael Ovitz, and that he had already signed a $365,000 deal for a screenplay based on the case.

"They've already written checks," he said smugly.

On the afternoon of January twelfth I was back in Steve Nelson's office to go over testimony. Wheeler had held up well under cross-examination and was reaching new highs of self-importance. He had a hell of an act, and I could see that he was playing it, at least partially, for my benefit. I smiled with an expression in my eyes that said, *I know you are full of shit.* Much to Ross's chagrin Wheeler then began talking to him, in front of me, about the supersecret money-laundering case. The son of a bitch was easier to manipulate than he knew.

I later found out that I was not the only one Wheeler had made aware of this "top secret" investigation. Months before the trial, using a pseudonym, he had bragged to the author of a recently published book on the drug wars that he had been "recently asked to place"—invest—about one hundred million dollars for some top Mexican DFS officials, and that on the basis of his statement Customs officials had launched a money-laundering investigation. *Some secret.*

Wheeler was really on a roll, so I thought the moment a good one to bring up the second undercover trip to Panama. I wanted him to repeat in front of Steve Nelson some of the things he had told me. Without much prompting he was describing the "mountains of beer cans" he had seen in Scuzzo's room. Then he obliged me by repeating his conversations with Duncan about Noriega, complete with a description of the photo of the "four-hundred-thousand-dollar yacht" he said Duncan had shown him.

You can never have too many witnesses in this business.

Apparently things were not going too well with Ed Heath's cooperation. Nelson was still having a hard time fathoming Heath's initial insistence that he had nothing on any of the defendants. I reminded him again that it was common practice for DEA suits to stonewall a problem until it withered and died. "What are you going to do," I asked, "if Heath simply does not answer you until the trial is over?" Nelson said nothing. But I could see a definite stir in his Irish.

Late in the afternoon of January thirteenth, Wheeler finished testifying as to the chronology of events leading up to the September twenty-first undercover meetings in La Jolla. I was somewhat surprised that the defense had not worked him over about having sold the movie rights to the case. I had heard they had employed a topnotch private detective agency, yet Wheeler had survived the cross-examination of seven defense attorneys without a scratch—so well that he was beginning to give pointers to Ross and some of the other agents about the finer points of testifying. At one point he even offered advice to Steve Nelson on his prosecutorial strategy. Nelson bristled and looked away. Wheeler never noticed a thing. It was easy to imagine him telling strangers how he'd single-handedly had to take charge of the government's case in court. He made me wonder about a legal system that could put someone in jail on just the word of an informant.

Wheeler caught me watching him and asked me what I was going to do for the long weekend we had ahead of us. There would be no court until January eighteenth. "You want to go to Albuquerque? I'm going to be with Dennis [Hopper]. I thought maybe you'd like to hang out with us."

On the morning of January eighteenth, I finally took the witness seat. Minutes later the seven prisoners were paraded across the courtroom before me to their seats at the defense table. Méndez, with a white full beard and mop of white hair, looking like Moses down from Mt. Sinai, smiled at me, and so did Mario Vargas. The others stared glumly off into space. They were seven lost souls, the tragedy of whose lives really concerned nobody. I watched them all put on sets of headphones that were connected to the microphone of a pretty but very proper-looking interpreter, without whose words they wouldn't have the slightest idea of the poker game that was being played with their lives. *They have no one to blame but themselves,* I had to remind myself. The old man was watching me and still smiling.

I spent most of the morning testifying about my first trip to San Diego as "Luis García," and the fantasy criminal organization I had created in the minds of Girón, Méndez, and Alvarez. I wondered whether the Bolivians, who watched me with dark, intent eyes, and Colonel Carranza, who sat looking lost and in another world, realized that it was this fantasy, carefully placed and cultivated in the minds of others, that had brought them to this place. As if in answer Román shot me a dark, murderous look and then looked away.

By the end of the day, one by one, the seven defense attorneys had tried to pick apart the story of the first meeting. The direction of their questioning was obvious; they were trying to prove that I had no way of knowing who the defendants really were, other than Wheeler's words. Colonel Carranza's defense attorney Cindy Aarons went a little bit too far when she said, "So, Officer Levine, you were aware that no efforts had been made to identify these defendants." I quickly answered, "I am aware of the Mexican government thwarting all our efforts to find out who they are." Ms. Aarons objected to my answer, to which Judge William Enright stated, "You asked the question, counselor."

Later that afternoon Nelson told me that he had called OPR about Ed Heath. He was really pissed; DEA and Heath had been ducking him. I could have said, "I told you so," but I didn't.

On January nineteenth it was Urquijo's turn on the witness stand testifying about his and Wheeler's contact with the defendants leading up to our first meeting with the Bolivians in Panama. I got to Steve Nelson's office during the noon break, where a huge bear of a man, his long graying hair tied in a knot behind his head, seemed to be holding court. Beside him was a pretty, smiling woman in a peasant's dress. A beaming Wheeler introduced them to me as Djordje Milicevic and his wife, Beth. According to Wheeler he and Milicevic were working on the movie script together. Later Wheeler would tell me that Milicevic "wrote and directed the movie *Runaway Train*."* It was lunchtime and they invited me to accompany them to a restaurant. There was something about the whole setup that was really bothering me, but I went along.

As we crossed the busy street from the courthouse to the Horton Plaza mall, Wheeler, flanked by Ross and two bodyguards, spoke busily to Milicevic, who was quite noticeably and understandably "eating" the scene up. At that moment it seemed to me that it was a scene that had been carefully choreographed by Wheeler. He had converted Operation Trifecta to his own living theater, and me into one of the players. By the time we reached the restaurant I was no longer hungry. I excused myself and headed back to Nelson's office.

The office was empty. On Nelson's desk was a telephone message for Ross and Wheeler to return the call of two Senate investiga-

---

* Milicevic is the first listed among three screenwriters for *Runaway Train*. The movie was directed by Andrei Konchalovsky. The screenplay itself was based on an initial screenplay by Akira Kurosawa.

tors in Washington, D.C. . It seemed that Mr. Wheeler was already choreographing the end of his movie—a Senate investigation of the whole drug-war effort. I sat back and wondered about the man's mental image of himself, and if it had even occurred to him that such a move might be hastening his own demise. Whatever the case, on his own, Dave Wheeler had discovered and was following the route I wanted him to take.

Later that evening Steve Nelson, Ross, Urquijo, Wheeler, and I met at an empty Mexican restaurant near my hotel in Mission Bay, to discuss the testimony about our first meeting with the Bolivians in Panama. Wheeler was on a verbal roll again. As we ordered dinner he was once again on the topic of how "screwed up" DEA is; once again reliving his trek through the jungles with the terrified agents in tow. To my surprise—he and I had still not discussed his recanting his earlier accusations—he was again talking of how he "used to buy information from corrupt DEA agents." I looked at Steve Nelson to see if he was listening. From the look on his face he had heard everything but wished he hadn't.

Everything was relaxed and casual and Wheeler's tongue as loose as I had ever heard it. It was time to check out another Wheeler story in front of witnesses. He had claimed that he was doing a favor for Nilo Batista by delivering a "kilo" (which was actually only eight hundred grams) of cocaine to his son Eric Batista in Oklahoma—the reason for his arrest in the first place. The idea that a man like Nilo Batista—known for dealing cocaine in hundred-kilo (220-pound) lots—would have anything to do with a sale of eight hundred grams (less than two pounds) seemed preposterous, especially if, as Wheeler had reported, he was "on the outs" with his son. Yet no one, to my knowledge, had ever tried to verify it. Recently, I had heard from Urquijo, Hoopel, and others that Wheeler claimed that Nilo Batista was "the son of Fulgencio Batista," one-time Cuban dictator. I wanted to hear Wheeler say it himself. I brought up the subject of his old arrest.

"Was he really the son of Batista, the Cuban dictator?" I asked with as much awe as I could muster.

"Yes," said Wheeler, swelling like a puff adder.

I later checked Nilo Batista's record and found that his place of birth was listed as "Uruguay." Somehow, I was not surprised. I telephoned one of the Oklahoma Bureau of Narcotics agents who had originally arrested Wheeler and asked him about the claim. The cop said he remembered hearing the same thing, but since it was "international stuff"—like all Wheeler's other stories—they had not checked it out. They had left it to DEA. I wondered just how much of anything the man claimed had *ever* been checked out.

The next morning I was back in Nelson's office, again going over my Panama testimony. At lunch in the cafeteria of the Federal Building, George introduced me to a pretty blond woman who had been attending the trial every day and taking notes. She was the owner of the undercover house in La Jolla. She told of first learning about the true identity of her tenants when the arrests were shown on national television. She, of course, was suing the government.

The afternoon turned out to be a startling and informative one for me. I thought I had already heard everything about the case that would surprise or anger me. The whole cast was assembled in Steve Nelson's office—Nelson, Wheeler, Ross, Hoopel, Urquijo and myself —discussing the case. I forget what the issue was, but I heard Wheeler suddenly say, "I'll bet the thirty-five-thousand-dollar lump-sum payment the government paid me on it." I turned and he was looking at me, grinning.

If he was trying to impress me, he certainly had. The idea of Customs paying this convicted felon, this out-on-bail, two-bit drug dealer, a nickel for his services was outrageous. A drug dealer arrested by DEA—"working off a beef," as we say—would have to make two or three cases for us without receiving anything (not even expenses), before he would get any consideration at sentencing—not to mention being paid. You can imagine what I felt later, when I learned that Customs had paid him *an additional $250,000.* Wheeler was later quoted as saying, "I got twenty-seven thousand dollars a week for my jail time." I guess he had it figured down to the day.

"Do you know," he continued, "every agent in this case has used me as a father confessor. They tell me everything."

"Have I?" I asked, feeling the hair stand up on the back of my neck.

"No," he said, "You're the only one that hasn't."

"Thank God for that," I said, wondering what it was that drove Wheeler to try and impress me. It seemed that part of his mental scenario was to gain my acceptance as some sort of an equal. I supposed I should have been grateful for it, kept him talking, telling me things I was not supposed to know, yet at the same time it was unnerving. He was telling me with almost blunt directness that by any measure—money, acceptance as an equal, and confidence—he had seduced the others. I was the last remaining plum on an already plucked tree.

The topic shifted to our second nightmarish trip to Panama, when it seemed that the whole government was conspiring to destroy the case. It was a part of the mind game that Wheeler and I played regularly, using the others as our audience. It was now my turn to recount how I had "saved" the case with my idea of bringing the Mexicans and the Bolivians back to San Diego for their arrest. I loved telling it to watch him squirm uncomfortably with facts that did not fit well into his screenplay. This "move" on my part would usually put Wheeler into a silent shell for a while. This time he surprised me.

"Yeah," he said, his eyes darting from me to Nelson, "while you were sitting out at that hotel, I had to march back into the Las Vegas Hotel with Lydia clumping along with me." He watched me, grinning devilishly at the implications of what he had said. Lydia Soto was supposed to play the undercover role of my girlfriend. Aside from the fact that after we got to Panama it was agreed that Román was far too suspicious and Lydia far too inexperienced in undercover work to meet him, and that the bringing of one's woman into an illegal dealing in South America was too serious an event to play with, no one had ever told me about the meeting. A day later, on December twenty-third, I had been allowed to meet Efrén Méndez at the airport hotel. If the old man had realized, in that incredibly volatile situation, that I did not know that my "girlfriend" had been to Román's room, he would have known immediately that something was wrong. The consequences might have ranged from the blowing of the case to our being killed.

"I cannot believe I was not fucking told!" I snapped. "It just doesn't make sense." I was furious, but my mind was working clearly. There were other rumors I had heard and only lacked the proper opportunity to verify. "And Román also said he wanted to kill me, and you didn't tell me about that either."

Wheeler suddenly flushed red and said, "That's not all! You don't know the half of it. Scuzzo told me not to tell you anything—" Wheeler looked at Hoopel and stopped himself in midsentence.

"And in San Diego," I continued angrily, "Girón also spoke to you about killing me, didn't he?" The room was silent. "And no one told me about that either." I turned to Steve Nelson. "Two defendants in an undercover case talk about killing the undercover agent and no one tells him. You understand a little better, Steve?"

The next morning, January twenty-fourth, on the witness stand, I told the story of our first meetings with Román and Mario Vargas in Panama. By the end of the day Nelson was happy with the way the trial was going but not too happy with the surrounding events. Wheeler had been caught giving an interview to *The Washington Post* (for which he was allegedly chewed out) and DEA and Ed Heath were still stonewalling him.

Nelson told me that he had had Hoopel send a cable to Mexico demanding that Heath explain his association with Carranza, as well as what investigative steps he had taken to identify the defendants and "Pablo," the person who answered the phone and who was believed to be a relative of one of the defendants. I could not imagine Hoopel demanding anything.

"Like I said, Steve. I think your only shot is to demand that OPR investigate the whole thing."

Nelson didn't say anything, but I could tell he was getting close to the limit of what he would take from DEA, Heath, or anyone else. The trouble was that the trial was also getting closer to finished.

"What about when the defense calls them as witnesses?"

"I'll shred them," he said quickly. But then he explained that in all likelihood the ambassador would never testify. The Department of State had already requested that Nelson move to quash the subpoena, and Heath had not been subpoenaed yet.

On January twenty-sixth I found a very pissed-off Steve Nelson in his office. He was through waiting. He showed me a letter he had addressed to Charles Hill, the DEA's San Diego SAC. "I'm going to give you a copy. If they don't answer it, you put it in your book and let the people know."

I read the five-page letter. It was direct and to the point, reviewing the whole case, then the defense's claim that there were no drugs or protection involved—"they wanted to rob the American drug dealers." Nelson attributed the defense's "ludicrous" claim to "gratuitous statements made last January by our American ambassador to Mexico."

The memorandum then listed some three and a half pages of items that Nelson had requested be investigated during the prior year, that Heath's office had failed to do. While the wording of Nelson's memo did not directly accuse DEA and Ed Heath of covering up, it certainly put the ball in their court to prove that they didn't:

> *In order to rebut these defense claims and to demonstrate that DEA did a thorough, comprehensive, first-class investigation into the background and status of the [Mexican] defendants, it is imperative that the following be done as quickly as possible:*
>
> *1. At one point [Heath's office] advised that Pablo Girón was once a State officer. If this was the case, please verify [Girón's] dates of employment and rank within the Puebla State Judicial Police.*
>
> *2. In addition to Pablo Girón's own admissions during taped undercover negotiations with government agents, DEA [Dan Diego] has independent C/I information that Pablo Girón has been a member of Mexico's DFS during the late 1970s and early 1980s.* It is requested that any information, if possible, concerning Girón's position within the DFS be verified in Mexico. In this regard it should be noted that two unimpeachable sources have confirmed that Girón was a DFS co-mandante under both Esteban Guzmán and Arnulfo "Negro" Ríos.†*

---

* Nelson had DEA San Diego working against Ed Heath. DEA agents assigned to the loyal office had come up with informants who could positively identify Girón.
† Esteban Guzmán was indicted with Nazar Haro, in the case that caused U.S. Attorney William Kennedy to be fired. He has never been apprehended or convicted.

3. Per info received from Mexico City, it was learned that Girón was arrested for fraud in 1978. It is requested that any official arrest/court records reflecting the arrest and/or prosecution of Girón in Mexico during 1978 be obtained to determine circumstances surrounding the arrest.

4. It is requested that Mexico City [Heath's office] verify Jorge Carranza-Peniche's background in the Mexican army, which should include service records, rank, and assignments. It was related during the course of the investigation that Carranza was a Mexican colonel. His defense is now claiming he never rose above the rank of major.

5. The defense has produced an ambiguous Mexican Army archive report that Carranza obtained a "leave of absence" from the Mexican Army in 1970. However, there are no entries after 1970, which, according to a reliable informant who is himself an officer in the Mexican Army, is highly unusual, since a Mexican Army officer is always subject to recall and is never "separated" from the Army. It is requested that information as to Carranza's leave of absence, his rank at the time of his leave, and reasons for his leave be obtained. If, in fact, he has been "separated" from the military since 1970 was he still in an active status working for the military in another capacity? What has Carranza been doing for the last eighteen years? During taped undercover negotiations with Jorge Carranza he provided information about his participation in "Operation Condor" (Mexico's drug eradication program), which took place in the late 1970s and early 1980s. Additionally, Carranza talked about the fact that he had worked with DEA in Mexico and fought with the anti-Sandinistas in Central America. It is requested that any information as to Carranza's participation in Operation Condor or liaison with DEA or the CIA be verified.

Up to this point in the memorandum I was sure that Heath and DEA would easily avoid answering every request that Nelson had made, by a simple stall tactic. Once the trial was over and the press was no longer interested, who would care? A San Diego prosecutor and an aging and battered DEA agent were no bother. They had managed to cover up the Roberto Suárez abortion for all these years; Trifecta would be a piece of cake. But then I read item number six and felt a glimmer of hope:

> *6. On January 14, 1988, Jorge Carranza was arrested by DEA and Customs agents in La Jolla, California. Subsequent to his arrest Carranza had in his possession a personal telephone book which listed "Embassy U.S.A. Narcoticos" under "Ed Heath's" name. During a postarrest statement made by Carranza he stated that he was a friend of "Ed Heath." Any information as to Carranza's relationship to DEA and/or personnel in Mexico should also be verified. In particular a detailed statement from SAC Ed Heath is requested regarding his knowledge of one Jorge Carranza-Peniche—for example, if he knows Carranza, how long has he known him? When did they meet and under what circumstances? How many times has SAC Heath seen or been with Carranza and under what circumstances? When was the last time SAC Heath met or spoke with Carranza and what were the underlying circumstances? [etc., etc].*

The memorandum went on to list all the names and phone numbers in Carranza's and Alvarez's address books, which read like a Who's Who of the Mexican military, requesting that their "identities, service records, ranks, and assignments be verified." Nelson's memo went on:

> *As to General Juan Poblano Silva, it is requested that Mexico City [DEA] provide information as to his present duty station and posts of duty for 1986, 1987, and 1988, military background, a current photograph, and his current rank or position in relation to the minister of defense and/or general staff. Also requested are any and all addresses of General Poblano Silva's personal and/or family residences and all telephone numbers subscribed*

*to by General Silva or any member of his immediate
family.*

As to Mexico City telephone number ————,
please ascertain subscriber, physical location of telephone, how long phone has been at that address, and who
pays the bill. As to the house or apartment where this
telephone is located, who owns it and who has lived there
for the last three years?*

*It is also requested that Mexico determine who owns
a house or apartment located at [address] and who lives
at the location and for how long. Photographs of this
location should be taken and forwarded to San Diego.*

*It is also requested that one "Pablo,"† living at the
above address, be completely identified, e.g., age, job,
background, physical condition (i.e., is he disabled in any
way or confined to a wheelchair?), and, in particular, his
familial relationship to General Poblano Silva.*

Nelson ended the memo with a blockbuster paragraph that was
all-inclusive, laying it on DEA and Ed Heath to prove they had done
anything at all to support the prosecution case:

*Lastly, since the defense in this case is going to do
everything in its power to embarrass DEA and claim that
no effort was ever made to verify the status and backgrounds of Girón, Alvarez, and Carranza, the Mexico
City DEA office should provide a detailed memorandum
documenting the scope of their search or investigation as
to the above, the individuals who performed or participated in the investigation, the approximate time spent,
and the individuals and sources accessed or contacted. In
this regard, please be advised that Mexico officials, who
are themselves or their agencies or organizations the subjects of this continuing grand jury investigation, are not*

---

* The investigation (circumventing DEA Mexico), had revealed that not only had Carranza
telephoned the general at this number at my request on the day of his arrest, but had telephoned the same number several times in Las Vegas and in San Diego to "talk to the general."
† The "Pablo" who answered Carranza's phone call to General Silva on January fourteenth.
Described by Carranza as "the general's crippled brother."

considered reliable, independent sources and should not be contacted. *

I put the memo down and asked Nelson if he had already sent it. He said he had. For the first time in ten years I did not feel I was fighting the suits alone. Steve Nelson—albeit for reasons quite different from mine—had written the second memo "bomb" in Operation Trifecta. They had ducked mine easily. Now, I wondered, how they would handle his?

---

* This last was in reference to Ed Heath's allegedly having gone to Juan Arévalo Gardoqui, Mexican defense minister—named by Colonel Carranza (on camera), as being involved in Mexican drug trafficking—for verification of Carranza's military status.

TWELVE

THE
VERDICT

Winning the Battle, Losing the War

On the afternoon of Monday, February sixth, after a week's recess, I was back in Steve Nelson's office. The next morning would be the defense's final opportunity to cross-examine me about the November 1987 Panama undercover meetings. As usual, Wheeler and Ross were already there. Nelson motioned for me to join him in another room. Within minutes a nervous-looking Ross followed us. For some reason Nelson and I speaking alone was obviously threatening to him.

Nelson's letter had worked a lot faster than he had anticipated. Heath had called him from Mexico, wondering what kind of questions the defense might ask him. Nelson said he had played "devil's advocate" and asked Heath the kinds of questions he anticipated the defense would. Questions that all had to do with what efforts Heath, "as DEA's head of operations for all of Mexico," had made in identifying and investigating Carranza, Alvarez, and Girón.

On February seventh the trial was once again recessed due to the illness of one of the jurors. Efrén Méndez's attorney, Louis Katz, made a motion for all of Wheeler's tax returns, contracts, movie scripts, and the statements he had made after his arrest in Oklahoma. Katz said he thought Wheeler had lied on every application he had ever signed, and that he suspected him of "double-dealing" the government.

That afternoon Nelson received Heath's written reply only to questions about his relationship with Carranza.

Heath wrote that he had met Carranza in the spring of 1981, when he (Carranza) "was assigned to the [Mexican] military at Mazatlán"; that a non-Mexican acquaintance of Heath's had needed a Mexican national with whom to go into a restaurant business,* and he had used Carranza; that Carranza knew he (Heath) was in charge of DEA in Mexico and spoke to him of his own activities in the Mexican eradication campaign (Operation Condor) and that Carranza had boasted about his being the grandson of Mexico's ex-president Venustiano Carranza; and finally, that he had not seen Carranza again between the years 1981 and 1983, during which time he was stationed back in the United States.

Heath's memo stated that on his (Heath's) return to Mexico in August 1983, he made contacts with various Mexican bureaucrats. One of them, Pepe Tort, director of security for Mexico's social security system, brought—"without prior advice"—Carranza to a restaurant meeting with Heath. Part of Tort's duties, according to Heath, was the oversight and control of prescription drugs in Mexico, which was the basic theme of their meeting. Heath wrote that throughout the meeting Carranza interjected that "Mexico should have better controls of prescription drugs."

Months later Carranza contacted Heath claiming to have some information, and asked to meet in a restaurant. Heath met him at a coffee shop close to the embassy, where he discovered that "Carranza had no information." His real motive, said Heath, was an attempt to sell items that belonged to his grandfather the former president, "particularly his sword, which [Carranza] described as a museum piece," and some property he owned about sixty miles out-

---

* Mexican law requires that a Mexican national must own the controlling interest of all businesses in that country.

side of Mexico City. Carranza wanted Heath to recommend buyers in the American embassy. He said that he had left the military under "bad circumstances" and needed the money. Carranza called again at "a later date," at which time Heath said that he "politely advised him, that [he] could not find anyone who was interested in buying the items he was offering."

On a subsequent date, in May 1987, according to Heath, Tort called him requesting a meeting, advising Heath that he (Tort) had been reassigned as the deputy director of operations for the Federal District Police. Tort showed up at the meeting—"again without notice"—accompanied by Carranza and Colonel Mario Acosta-Chaparro.* The purpose of the meeting was extremely sensitive—the establishment of a "discreet method of communication between [Heath] and Mexican Military Intelligence." During the meeting Chaparro urged Heath to "brief the Army's chief of staff on the seriousness of drug trafficking in Mexico, with the aim of getting the Mexican military more involved in the fight against drugs." The meeting with the Army chief of staff never took place because, as Heath stated, he did not pursue the situation, as it was "not politically convenient for DEA," and the issue was dropped.

Heath's next contact with Carranza came in July 1987—just two months before my first meeting with Girón, Méndez, and Alvarez—when Carranza called him at the American embassy to request his aid in getting a "lady friend" a visa to the United States. Heath complied. Carranza called days later to thank Heath and inform him that he was about to get married. "I congratulated him," wrote Heath, "and we concluded our conversation without any further commitment. That was the last time I spoke to Carranza."

Heath said that he did not hear about Carranza again until January 14, 1988, when he received a San Diego cable announcing the arrests. "Given the name and description," wrote Heath, "I was sure it was the Jorge Carranza I had met in Mexico City and I so advised Ambassador Pilliod, members of my office, and DEA headquarters."

Heath's statement raised many questions: If he *had* advised the

---

* Since promoted to general.

ambassador on January 14, 1988, about who Carranza was, then why was the ambassador quoted in *The San Diego Union** and the *Los Angeles Times*,† backing the Mexican government's claim that Carranza had been discharged from the military in 1970? Heath had reported in his memo that he had met Carranza in the spring of 1981, when he (Carranza) "was assigned to the [Mexican] military at Mazatlán"; and that Carranza had told Heath that he had left the Mexican military under "bad circumstances" in 1983. Even more sinister was the fact that Heath had reported Carranza being present at at least two highly sensitive meetings with Mexican military and police officials, one as late as 1987, just months before Carranza's arrest.

"How the hell does Heath explain his silence for thirteen months, while the Mexicans and Ambassador Pilliod were telling the press that Carranza had retired from the military in 1970?" I asked.

Nelson shrugged his shoulders.

On February eighth the defense finished cross-examining me about the first trip to Panama. Wheeler was back on the stand testifying about events leading up to his trip with Jake to Bolivia to check the cocaine labs. Urquijo was back from L.A. to testify about his participation. That afternoon, in Nelson's office, a supremely confident Wheeler counseled Urquijo on some of the finer points of dealing with defense attorneys: "If you don't understand the question, George, feel free to tell them."

Another behind-the-scenes mystery was developing. Jake the pilot had gone back to his home in the Midwest to await his turn to testify and was now missing. Wheeler, who had developed a close friendship with him—or so he said—had taken it on himself to try and find him. He had been in constant contact with Jake's family who reported that he had gone to Colombia on "DEA business." Wheeler was acting strangely about the whole thing, almost manic.

---

* "U.S. Experts to Examine Tape in Mexico Drug Case," *San Diego Union* (February 22, 1988).
† "Stingers May Have Been Stung in U.S. Drug Bust of Mexicans," *Los Angeles Times*, San Diego edition (February 4, 1989).

He kept running to the phone, making mysterious calls for news of Jake, his mood ranging from worried to jubilant.

"He's been missing in Colombia for forty-eight hours," Wheeler reported. "They think he's either dead or they're holding him as hostage for the Bolivians. He's working for [Mike] Powers," he added. Nelson seemed troubled by the whole affair. I sensed there was something he was not saying. I was tempted to call Mike Powers but decided to wait.

The next morning the mystery deepened. The moment I arrived at Nelson's office I knew something was up. Wheeler was upset and barely talking—a condition I had never seen him in. I learned he had been ordered to stop trying to contact Jake.

"We've located Jake," said Nelson, himself looking disturbed. "But I don't think I'm going to need him to testify. He doesn't speak Spanish; Wheeler did all the talking, so what could he testify to anyway?"

This was really strange. Jake was the only witness to corroborate Wheeler's Bolivian trip. His *not* testifying was a drastic change in Nelson's strategy. Hoopel was there looking flustered, a good sign that he was straining against the yoke of carrying a secret. The topic of Jake the pilot was suddenly one no one wanted to talk about.

That night I telephoned my old friend and fellow veteran of New York narcotics enforcement Mike Powers, in Tampa. The mystery was solved immediately. Jake had been arrested with another CI/pilot after dumping a load of cocaine off the Bahamas. They had been caught trying to smuggle the drugs in from Colombia for some U.S.-based drug-dealing operation. The cocaine had not been recovered but Jake had admitted to the whole plot.*

I suddenly understood the informer's strange behavior. I asked Mike if he had ever met Wheeler. His answer didn't surprise me. Wheeler had come to Tampa several months before with Jake and Fred, trying to sell Powers on getting DEA backing and financing for the three of them to go on an "undercover" excursion to Colombia. *This was a man free on bail in the custody of U.S. Customs for selling drugs, who did not trust DEA.* The only thing that seemed

* All charges against "Jake the pilot" were later dropped.

certain was that Mr. Wheeler had other things on his mind than making a drug case. And Mike Powers had instinctively recognized that something phony was afoot.

"They looked like the unholy trio," said Mike. "I just didn't trust them."

Later that evening Steve Nelson, Hoopel, and I went to dinner and began going over my testimony about the December 1987 trip to Panama under the command of Fast Albert Scuzzo. We spoke about Alfredo Duncan's strange behavior and Hoopel once again reaffirmed that Duncan had told him that there were wiretaps on Remberto's phone in the Las Vegas Hotel

The topic of Wheeler having a contract for a screenplay came up. If the defense found out about it, they would have good grounds to question his credibility. He had a definite monetary reason to exaggerate his role and the importance of everyone he was testifying against. Once again I repeated my opinion that we had enough to convict the seven defendants on trial, with or without Wheeler, but wherever it was only his uncorroborated testimony as proof, there would be a problem.

Nelson said that he was not sure how much of Wheeler's film-contract talk was real. I let the subject drop. He had learned from DEA, Bolivia, that the most powerful dealer in the Corporation was Rocha Suárez.* If Mendez or one of the Bolivians decided to flip and cooperate with the government, and his testimony corroborated Wheeler's, Nelson could indict Rocha Suárez, Winston Rodríguez, and the other members of the Corporation Wheeler claimed he had met. He was not very much disposed to talking about his informant's film career. And I wasn't sure I could blame him.

The next morning George and I stood outside the courtroom as Wheeler testified about his trip to Bolivia. Bill Ott, a reporter for *The San Diego Union,* stepped out in the hallway. "Say, that guy Wheeler really tells a great story," he said.

---

* A nephew of Roberto Suárez and a defendant in my original Roberto Suárez case of 1980.

George and I looked at each other. "Yeah," he's good," I said. "You can sure tell he's a screenwriter," added Ott.

George and I returned to Nelson's office in the evening to find a pale and shaky Wheeler. His world was tottering. The defense had asked him if he had signed a contract for a screenplay based on the case, and he had answered no.

"You said no?" I asked. Either he had been lying to all of us all along or he had lied on the witness stand.

"My contract has nothing to do with this case, it's about drugs and the CIA. I never said anything about this case."

"Look, Dave," I said, wondering how dumb he thought we were. "You're talking to me. The defense has private detectives. What they'll probably do is subpoena Dennis Hopper and Djordje Milicevic and whatever scripts they're working on, and compare them, line by line, with this case." Wheeler looked like he was having a dizzy spell. George, on the verge of laughter, had to turn his face.

For the second time in the fifteen months I had known him, Wheeler was silent. He had outsmarted himself. From the chalk-white color of his skin and his bugged-out eyes, I knew it wouldn't be necessary to educate him on the perjury laws.

Nelson came into the office, followed by Ross. Steve was happy with the way the trial was going, except for one item. "It's unfortunate," he said, "they got on Dave about that script business."

Later that night George confided that he had suspected Wheeler of being a fraud "all the way back at the beginning." Among the informant's many claims was that it was he who had brought *sinsemilla** to Mexico. I remembered Wheeler telling me about it when we first met. I had joked, "You're sort of the Johnny Appleseed of pot." Wheeler had laughed; he liked the comparison. He said that his knowledge of the potent form of marijuana was so extensive that he had been asked to speak on the subject by college professors and world experts. *Sinsemilla* was a subject George had

---

* The very potent seedless form of marijuana.

some knowledge of and Wheeler's explanation of how it was grown, according to George, "seemed more like something learned from a book." But George was in no position to be critical. His Customs supervisors had put him in a position subservient to the informant. He had, in fact, been told that his main purpose was "to protect the informant."

On Friday, February twenty-fourth, I finally had my turn to testify about the January tenth undercover meeting. As court did not convene until nine-fifteen, we had some time to review my testimony and discuss the case. I discussed Carranza's knowledge of Snowcap and my feeling that he had to have learned it from Heath.

"He's disappeared," complained Nelson. He had been trying to contact DEA's chief of Mexican operations by telephone. No one knew where either Heath or his second-in-command, Dick Cañas—who had also been present during the May 1987 (Carranza-Tort-Chaparro) meeting—was, and they were not returning Nelson's phone calls. Nelson said he was going to call Heath's boss, Steve Green, chief of foreign operations in Washington. He handed me a copy of the March 31, 1969, edition of *Sports Illustrated* and said, "There's an article in there about Carranza." As I leafed through the magazine Nelson dialed.

The article was a story about sport fishing in Mexico* that featured "a twenty-eight-year-old major in the Mexican army, Jorge Carranza," whom the author called the "James Bond of Mexico." It told of some of Carranza's nonfishing exploits like the "capturing [of] huge amounts of drugs" and parachuting onto an island to capture escaped prisoners.

The only "official" information we had received from the government of Mexico about the little colonel was that he had been granted "unlimited leave" from the Mexican army in 1971. There was no updated information available. A logical explanation would be that he had been assigned to the kind of sensitive duties that would require him to disassociate himself from the army "officially." Carranza had made reference several times to his training of the

---

* Robert Jones, "Sport Fishing in Mexico," *Sports Illustrated,* (March 31, 1969).

Contras in Honduras; he had done so during the January tenth meeting. His secret association with our government would go a long way toward explaining a lot of what was happening.

Later, on the witness stand, I testified about my first meeting with Carranza. I told of his knowledge of DEA's most classified operation and, under Nelson's questioning repeated Carranza's words, "I trained the Contras in Honduras." Nelson paused a moment and asked me what the Contras were. I said, "The Nicaraguan anti-Sandinistas." There was a long pause. I looked around the court. There were only a few spectators and not a member of the press. The trial was old news, and with the election over and the new "drug czar," William Bennett, just appointed, so was the drug war.

On Monday, February twenty-seventh, things really started to get interesting. It was not a court day, so I stopped by Nelson's office to see if anything was new. Steve still had not heard from Heath, but he had received photos of Pablo's house taken by operatives connected with George's private-investigator friend. Steve stepped out of the office and a phone call came in from Hoopel. The intelligence analyst had also been hard at work, contacting very sensitive sources within the Mexican military and telephone company. What they had learned was astounding.

Hoopel said he had, in his possession, telephone-toll slips for Pablo López's telephone indicating that calls had been made to the residence of Colonel de la Vega, and to the military academy at Puebla, during the time-period of the conspiracy, and that, at that time, General Poblano Silva was the commanding officer at the academy. The sources also said that right after the arrests in January 1988, the general had been "quietly transferred." And, also that General Silva was married to the sister of Mexican Secretary of Defense Arévalo Gardoqui.

Everything now seemed to fall into place. Some of the Mexico experts had felt that even General Silva could not have carried off what Carranza had promised—military protection for the landing and refueling of drug planes—without the knowledge and approval of Mexican government officials at a higher level than a mere general. You wouldn't have to go any higher than secretary of defense.

By early evening, after a couple of missed communications,

Steve finally spoke to Heath. He acknowledged that he was now aware of Arévalo Gardoqui's relationship with General Silva and that in light of all the information he was "now" aware of, he agreed that Colonel Carranza was capable of doing what he had promised. "You can see," Nelson had told him, "that with Carranza testifying, your meetings with him are going to be very important." Heath said that he would not be able to testify in March, though, because, he had to accompany the Mexican attorney general to Washington for a meeting with the U.S. attorney general.

"Anyone can accompany him," I said. "Cañas (Heath's deputy) can do it."

Nelson said he would be just as happy if he could get Ambassador Pilliod—who was, reportedly, "very upset" about the latest developments, and trying to reach him—to testify for the prosecution.

On February twenty-eighth I spent most of the day in the witness chair, testifying about the final meeting with the Mexicans— their last hours of freedom. When I finished telling how I had set Colonel Carranza up for that final attempt at getting the general on tape, I was praying that at least one of the seven defense attorneys would question why no attempt had been made earlier. I wanted them to know what I knew. I wanted them to ask the hard questions that I had been unable to. . . . They did not.

On March first some of the most startling information of the entire case was uncovered. General Mario Acosta-Chaparro, the man who had introduced Heath to Colonel Carranza, was listed in NADDIS as a man who "associates with and provides protection for narcotics traffickers." There was also a report that Chaparro had met with Miguel Félix-Gallardo (the top-level Mexican drug dealer believed to have ordered the death of Kiki Camarena) during May 1988. I thought that these facts, combined with Heath's own written statement, were more than enough to warrant that Heath be brought to San Diego to explain. Once again Steve was noncommittal.

That evening, on the six P.M. NBC news, Washington correspondent Lisa Meyers reported that our State Department had praised Mexico for its antidrug efforts and certified it to receive a grant of antinarcotics funds.

Later that night I heard that New York DEA agent Everett Hatcher had been killed during an undercover meet. His backup team found the forty-six-year-old father of two slumped over his steering wheel, four bullets in his head. The news showed a pale and shaken Robert Stutman, who said, "If there's anyone who's ever done a line of coke and thought it was funny, just take a look at this young man and see how funny it is."

On the morning of March second George and I arrived at Nelson's office to find Angel Pérez, an agent assigned to Operation Snowcap in Bolivia, who had participated in the Bolivian operation and had been brought to San Diego to testify, running a half-hour videotape of the raids at the jungle lab sites. I watched with great curiosity. I would finally get to the bottom of the who-was-on-point question. The film, as it turned out, was a heavily edited, combined version of the three raids. Burke was nowhere to be seen. Near the end of the film the four helicopters returning to their jungle base were seen from the ground as they each peeled off into a "victory roll" signifying success.

"There were all kinds of congressman and press on the ground," reported Wheeler proudly. "The operation really drew a lot of big attention."

Undaunted, I commented to Pérez, "I didn't see Terry Burke in the film."

"No," agreed Perez nervously.

"Was he on point or wasn't he?"

Pérez grinned and said, "Well, the *Umopars** had already secured the place and [Burke] led the press in."

When a suit says that he was "on point" in a DEA jungle operation, it means he was leading the press.

On Tuesday, March seventh, George and I reported to Nelson's office at about eight forty-five A.M. I was due to testify about the final meeting with the Bolivians and their arrests—my final under-

---

* Bolivian military troops.

cover act in Operation Trifecta. Wheeler was to follow me with his final testimony.

"I guess this will be their last shot at me," said a nervous Wheeler. As usual, an equally nervous Ross hovered nearby.

"For this trial," I said.

"You mean there'll be an appeal?"

"Appeal, maybe. But you can bet this case is going to be heard in a lot of courts before it's over," I said as enigmatically as I could. *Sweat, stool pigeon, sweat.*

My testimony lasted until the noon lunch-break. There was very little cross-examination. It was clear that the Mexicans' defense was solidly anchored in proving that Carranza was a phony and could not do what he had promised if he wanted to; and that Wheeler had lied about his meetings with General Silva and Colonel de la Vega. The Bolivians' defense—if they had any—was still a mystery.

In spite of the fact that Ed Heath was the strongest witness against the Carranza claim, Nelson had decided not to call him as a prosecution witness. He was going to rely on the defense to call him, at which time he would rip into him in his cross-examination. What, I wondered, would happen if the defense didn't call him?

The next morning Ron Gospadarik arrived from headquarters to testify as an "expert" witness that the photos taken of Román's lab could not be anything but a cocaine lab. I found it hard to talk to the tall, pale desk-jockey without remembering that hot day in Miami when he had acted as the suits' emissary in the attempted destruction of Trifecta. In answer to a question put to him by George, he explained that his "expertise" on cocaine labs was based on his daily examination of photos, combined with his academic training as a chemist. This was the man the suits had sent to Miami to judge whether or not a five-million-dollar buy was to be made. A fucking chemist who spent his days looking at pictures at his desk in Washington.

Steve Nelson surprised me by telling me that the defense had requested that both Wheeler and I stay in town. They were going to call us as defense witnesses. I couldn't tell if Nelson was upset or not, but Wheeler was, and that was good enough for me.

George and I took a ride to a university library to try and find Carranza's name in some obscure Mexican military reference books. By the time we returned, late in the afternoon, the trial was still going and Gospadarik was alone in Nelson's office, talking on the telephone. I couldn't help but hear that he was talking anxiously about his plane reservations back to Washington. *Does anything ever change?* George, being the nice guy that he is, invited him to coffee with us. I swallowed bile and tried to make conversation. When Gospadarik said that the latest word in headquarters was that William Bennett, the new drug czar, was going to draft Dave Westrate and Robert Stutman as his aides, I could only laugh.

About four P.M. Wheeler joined us in Nelson's office. He had finished testifying earlier and was anxious to tell me about more government "secrets" he had been made privy to. "You know the big secret meetings Customs is having right now?" he asked, eyeing me triumphantly.

"No," I said, glancing at George, who gave me a quick, mischievous smile. I was aware that Customs had called in many of their California supervisors for a meeting, but unaware that it was a secret.

"They've called in everyone for a top-level meeting," he said excitedly, watching me for a reaction. "They've discovered the biggest Mexican heroin pipeline in history. . . . And that's what it's all about."

My mind drifted to the days in narcotics enforcement when DEA fired you for bringing an informer into an office where he *might* see other agents. What was Ross going to do if Wheeler received the jail sentence he deserved?

On March fourteenth I learned that the defense attorneys had decided against calling me as a witness. My official role in Operation Trifecta had come to an end. I stopped by Nelson's office to say good-bye and learned that the defense had finally subpoenaed Ed Heath and Ambassador Pilliod as witnesses. Nelson had prepared another very strong letter to Heath, once again repeating all the requests he had made and affirming Heath's resultant inaction. Nelson told me he was having the letter "hand-delivered" to Heath, who was in Washington, D.C., accompanying the Mexican attorney general on his visit to Attorney General Meese.

"Tear em' up," I told Steve. We shook hands. I really like him. I think he's a good man. It's tough to be the only guy playing straight in a crooked card-game.

Dave Wheeler was there with his Customs bodyguards, complaining to Nelson that some studio executive named Tom Stern had been pressuring him for the screenplay. It was still in the hands of the defense lawyers and there was nothing Nelson could do to get it back.

On March 15, 1989, at nine-thirty A.M., I was on a flight back to New York, already trying to organize the mass of notes I had compiled over the two-month trial. I had twenty months left toward my retirement. I was forty-eight years old, with twenty-five of those years in our so-called war on drugs; and they had taken more than their toll. And Operation Trifecta, as they say in Spanish, was *el colmo*—"the topper." I was feeling worn out, old, and beaten. But I was sure of one thing: whatever energies I did have left were going into my final campaign in the drug war—one of exposure.

On April 6, 1989, Ed Heath finally testified. He claimed that he had been trying, all along, to get from the Mexican government all the information that Nelson had requested, but that they had been "stonewalling" him and not responding. Nelson never asked Heath any of the hard questions about his full year of not responding—particularly about his meeting with Carranza and General Acosta-Chaparro in May of 1987, just seven months before Carranza's arrest.

On April 12, 1989, Mexican police arrested Miguel Félix-Gallardo, believed to be the man who ordered Kiki Camarena's murder. Gallardo, coincidentally, had been seen with General Chaparro, on May 13, 1987, the same month of his (Chaparro's) meeting with Heath and Carranza. Coinciding with Chaparro's arrest were the arrests of six "senior law-enforcement personnel accused of providing him with protection and intelligence."* Ed Heath was subse-

* William Branigin, "Bodyguard's Eating Habits Eased Capture of Drug Kingpin," *Washington Post* (April 13, 1989).

quently quoted in the press, lauding the Mexican government for its "cooperation" in the drug war.*

On April 17, 1989, I got a telephone call in New York from Jim Ross. He needed some information to help Steve Nelson prepare his closing arguments. The trial was at an end. Ross told me that both Heath and the ambassador had testified for the defense and that Steve had to take it easy on them in his cross-examination. "We couldn't make him look too bad," said Ross. "It would have hurt the case."

"Steve let him skate," I said.

"Yes," said Ross. "He had to."

■

On May 15, 1989, after almost a month of deliberations, the jury found all seven defendants guilty of all charges. They subsequently received the following sentences:

> Efrén Méndez-Dueñas (the old man): thirty years in prison.
> Hector Álvarez (the man who loved me): thirty years in prison.
> Jorge Carranza (the little colonel): twenty-four years, five months in prison.
> Rolando Ayala (the pilot): twenty-four years, five months in prison.
> Mario Vargas-Bruun: thirty years, five months in prison.
> Pablo Girón (Wheeler's buddy): twenty-seven years, three months in prison.
> Jorge Román: thirty years, five months in prison.

At the sentencing on August 4, 1989, Assistant United States Attorney Steve Nelson said:

> *This was the first time we actually penetrated the cartel and came face-to-face with the members of the*

---

* Later, in a *Los Angeles Times* article, 8/19/89, "Cover-up Alleged in Drug Agent's Death" by Kim Murphy, the U.S. government would be accused of covering up evidence that Félix-Gallardo had participated in the torture-murder of DEA agent Enrique Camarena to "avoid the embarrassment of disclosing compelling evidence that the freedom fight of the Contras was funded by illicit drug revenues with the tacit approval of branches of the United States government."

*board. It is unfortunate that someone in the U.S. Depart-
ment of Justice decided not to provide five million dollars
to set up the rest of the drug buys, so that more members
of the cartel, including politicians and military officers,
could be arrested.*

EPILOGUE

The rest of 1989 was a year that saw Operation Snowcap escalate, with more DEA agents than ever before being sent to dangerous jungle outposts, where some will almost certainly be killed.* Rumors flooded the agency that among the equipment purchased for the operation was a quantity of body bags. A DEA agent who had been in Vietnam remarked, "It reminds me of how the Nam began, back in the sixties."

It was a year that saw the resignation of Attorney General Edwin Meese, who recounted what he considered were his most important contributions for the television news cameras—one of them was Operation Snowcap. "It will cut the amount of cocaine being imported into the U.S. by fifty percent," said Meese.

On July 14, 1989, in the Western Judicial District federal court, Oklahoma City, Oklahoma, Judge Ralph Thompson sentenced David Wheeler to five years probation and $125 in court costs for his part in the sale of the eight hundred grams of cocaine. By that time Wheeler had already received a total "reward" payment, for his role in Operation Trifecta, of $285,000, not counting the monies paid him for expenses. The amount of money he actually received for his screenplay and other monies he made from the case is unknown, but is believed to be quite substantial. For David Wheeler, crime certainly *did* pay.

Since the trial and sentencing Steve Nelson has been trying to get DEA and Bolivian cooperation to indict some of the other top

---

* The suits make sure that the number of agents sent on the operation, like the amount of money spent, is classified.

Corporation members, whose names surfaced during Operation Trifecta. Taped evidence that Steve has forwarded to the Bolivian government through DEA has mysteriously disappeared on two occasions, and as late as September 1989 he has gotten no cooperation from the State Department, DEA, or the Bolivian nation, on any of his requests for investigative support or information. Yet the State Department and DEA suits are still publicly lauding Bolivia for its efforts in the drug war, and insuring its continued status as a "cooperating nation" and recipient of hundreds of millions of dollars in antidrug funding.

On August 1, 1989, William von Raab angrily resigned his post as commissioner of Customs, blasting the government's war on drugs. He said that there are too many people within the Department of State and other agencies to whom there are "other interests more important than winning a war on drugs." He said that unnamed State Department bureaucrats would "rather make the world safe for cocktail parties" than win a drug war.

On September 12, 1989, the United States Senate Permanent Subcommittee on Investigations held a hearing in the Senate Office Building on "Structure and Operation of International Drug Cartels." Two of the key witnesses, advising the Senate were David L. Westrate, assistant administrator for operations, Drug Enforcement Administration, the "father" of Operation Snowcap; and David Wheeler.

Wheeler outdid himself. He began by recounting to the silently attentive senators how he had lived among the Indians of Mexico for twenty years, learning to cultivate seedless marijuana. "The Indians taught me and assisted me in keeping the *federales* at bay and in return I brought them food and medicine," said Dave Wheeler.* He was really "wowing" them this time.

---

* United States Senate, Committee on Governmental Affairs, transcript of Permanent Subcommittee on Investigations Hearing, "Structure of International Drug Cartels," September 12, 1989, 106 Dirksen Senate Office Building.

Late in 1989, I was in California and visited Jorge "George" Urquijo. He is one of the most honest and principled men I have ever known and—for me—Customs assigning him to work Operation Trifecta was a godsend. George told me of sitting alongside President Bush at a recent special luncheon for the President and some Customs undercover agents. At one point the President leaned over and asked George, "Just what does an undercover agent do?"

"Well, Mr. President," George replied, "He's like the kid they use down in Louisiana as alligator bait. They tie him to the end of a rope and he walks out into the swamp. All the kid can do is hope they jerk the rope back in time."

Glossary of Terms and Acronyms Used in Narcotics Enforcement and Undercover Work

Agency, the—The CIA.

ASAC—Assistant special agent in charge.

Asshole—Anyone who is not a DEA agent.

AUSA—Assistant United States attorney.

Base—Cocaine base, the intermediate stage in the crystallization of cocaine. Similar to crack. Also called bazooka, *pichicata.*

Body pack—Smuggling method of concealing drugs beneath clothing.

Border rats—Customs and DEA agents who work the Mexican border.

Bug—A hidden electronic listening device.

Burn—To be recognized, or revealed, as an undercover law-enforcement officer, usually as the result of some treasonous action on the part of an informant.

Buy—An undercover operation where a buy of drugs is made and no arrests made. Usually done so that an undercover agent may penetrate more deeply into an illegal organization.

Buy-bust operation—The undercover agent fakes making a drug buy, to entice the drug dealer to deliver drugs to a location, where he is arrested.

CA—Country attaché. DEA's chief officer at foreign posts of duty.

Contract—An assassination order, or an offer of money for the death of a person.

Contractor—Any person who, for a fee, performs special services for DEA.

Contractor/Pilot—A contractor whose special services are primarily the flying of undercover missions, both within and outside the United States.

Crook—Drug dealer, or any criminal defendant.

CI—Cooperating individual, or confidential informant.

Cold hit—A lucky guess, or a random selection, of a person or place to be searched.

Company, the—The CIA.

DEA—The Drug Enforcement Administration.

Deal—An enforcement operation; usually pertaining to undercover.

DFS—Mexican equivalent of the CIA, disbanded in the early 1980s.

Desk—A DEA headquarters section overseeing investigations concerning a particular drug, i.e., cocaine desk, heroin desk, et cetera.

Desk officer—An agent assigned to a particular desk; usually for administrative duties.

Dirty—Corrupt; with something to hide; concealing contraband.

Flash—To show money during an undercover meet.

Flash roll—Money, usually a large amount, used to fool drug dealers into believing an undercover agent is going to make a buy.

Flip—Turn an arrested defendant into an informant.

Game, to run a—To fool, to con, to perform any deceitful action.

G/S—Group supervisor. Usually in charge of ten to fifteen men in a street enforcement group.

IMNS—Immigration and Naturalization Service.

Jewish bankroll—a thick wad of single dollar bills, with a large denomination bill—usually a hundred-dollar bill—showing.

Knock-off—A raid or an arrest.

Make—To recognize someone as an undercover agent.

Mule—Drug or money courier used for smuggling. In South America prostitutes are commonly used.

NADDIS—Narcotics and Dangerous Drugs Information System.

NYDETF—New York Drug Enforcement Task Force. An operational unit comprised of DEA agents, New York City and state police.

OCDETF—Organized Crime Drug Enforcement Task Force. A multiagency task force dedicated to the prosecution of large organized criminal organizations involved in drug trafficking.

OGV—Official government vehicle.

Operation Condor—DEA's drug-crop eradication program in Mexico between 1976 to 1983, centered in the Mexican states of Chihuahua, Sinaloa, and Durango.

Operation Snowcap—DEA's twelve-country paramilitary effort in South and Central America to attack drug production at its source.

Operation Leyenda—The international effort to bring all who had anything to do with the torture death of DEA agent Enrique "Kiki" Camarena to justice.

PC—Probable cause. Legal grounds to believe a crime is being committed, used to obtain arrest warrants, search warrants, and Title 3 intercept orders.

PEPI—Special funding account used by DEA agents for the "purchase of evidence, or purchase of information."

SAC—Special agent in charge. DEA's chief officer in a particular geographical area.

Scam—Any ruse used to deceive.

Skate—Get away with something.

Snitch—Informer.

Spooks, the—CIA.

Stool pigeon, stool, stoolie—Informer.

Suit—Upper management of DEA.

Title 3 or Title 3 intercept—A court-ordered wiretap.

U/C—Undercover, undercover agent.

U/C phone—An unregistered, untraceable undercover phone, usually in a DEA office.

Wire—A wiretap.